Birdscaping Your Garden

Birdscaping
Your Garden

*A Practical Guide to Backyard Birds
and the Plants That Attract Them*

GEORGE ADAMS

Rodale Press, Emmaus, Pennsylvania

Published 1994 by Rodale Press, Inc.
By arrangement with Lansdowne Publishing Pty Limited,
Level 5, 70 George Street, Sydney, 2000, Australia

Lansdowne Publishing staff:
 Managing Director: Jane Curry
 Production Manager: Sally Stokes
 Publishing Manager: Deborah Nixon
 Editor: Bronwyn Hilton

Rodale Press Staff:
 Executive Editor: Margaret Lydic Balitas
 Managing Editor: Barbara W. Ellis
 Editor: Ellen Phillips

Technical Editors: Sally Roth, Nancy Ondra
Copy Editor: Sarah Dunn

Design concept: Kathie Baxter Smith
Page Layouts: Veronica Hilton

If you have any questions or comments concerning this book,
please write to:
 Rodale Press, Inc.
 Book Readers' Service
 33 East Minor Street
 Emmaus, PA 18098

Library of Congress Cataloging-in-Publication Data

Adams, George Martin
Birdscaping your garden : a practical guide to backyard birds
and the plants that attract them / George Adams.
                    p. cm.
Includes bibliographical references and index.
ISBN 0–87596–635–7
1. Bird attracting—United States. 2. Bird attracting—Canada.
3. Gardening to attract birds—United States. 4. Gardening to
attract birds—Canada. 5. Native plant gardening—United
States. 6. Native plant gardening—Canada. I. Title
QL676.55.A33 1994
598.2973—dc20   93–43391
                    CIP

Printed in Singapore by Tien Wah Press (Pte) Ltd

Distributed in the book trade by St. Martin's Press

2 4 6 8 10 9 7 5 3 1 hardcover

Note: For information about pictures on the cover, endpapers, title pages and
chapter openers of this book, see page 208.
For a key to the map color regions in the Bird Directory, see page 208.

CONTENTS

How to Use
This Book

*B*irdscaping Your Garden will help you turn an
ordinary landscape into an extraordinary
birdscape — a backyard filled with lively,
colorful birds. It's easy to do if you follow the advice
in the following sections. Start with "From Landscape
to Birdscape" on page 7. You'll find the five basic
things all birds need — cover, shelter, nesting sites,
food and water — and plenty of practical suggestions
for providing them in your yard. You'll also find
some basic facts about birds that you can use when
you turn to the next section, the "Bird Directory."

In *Birdscaping Your Garden*, you'll find 64 delightful
birds that you may want to attract to your backyard
garden. In the "Bird Directory" on page 15, I have
featured the most beloved birds from coast to coast,
from the eastern bluebird to the Anna's
hummingbird. Each entry has a photo of the bird and
one of my original drawings of the bird in a favorite
native plant. You'll find a description of the bird and
its habits, what its song sounds like, plus its preferred
habitat, breeding behavior, nesting style and feeding
habits. A range map is provided for each bird, along
with its migration and winter range and its breeding
range, so you can see if it lives or spends time in your
area. The yellow area on the range map is the bird's
breeding range, the blue area is its winter range, and
the green is where it lives year-round. A list of plants
for food and shelter tells you good choices to plant
to attract each bird. You can find more about these
plants in the "Plant Directory."

To help you get your birdscape up and growing, I
have included a section called "Growing Native
Plants" on page 145, which includes how-to-grow
techniques. It covers all the growing basics — soil
care, planting, care and feeding, even propagation.
And to make this section even more useful, I've
added tips on how to choose and use plants in your
birdscape to attract the most diverse range of birds.

In the "Plant Directory" on page 153, I have
described important North American plants that

provide food, shelter and nesting sites for native
birds. Birdscaping with native plants provides natural
food and shelter that is very attractive to certain
species. The trees, shrubs, vines, perennials, annuals,
groundcovers and grasses I have described are all
suitable for cultivation. They are beautiful landscape
plants that will appeal to the gardener as much as to
the birds. Many of them may already occur naturally
in your area. Each genus is described and many are
illustrated with a color photograph. You'll find a list
of birds attracted to the plants. Then I give the best
species for birdscaping, with descriptions,
distribution, cultivation information and hardiness
zones for each. You'll find both growing and
landscaping information in the cultivation section.
You'll also find a copy of the USDA Plant Hardiness
Zone Map on page 196, so you can determine which
hardiness zone you live in.

The page references will help you to find the
plants for your area in the "Plant Directory."

If you want to learn more about birding and
birdscaping, I have also included a section called
"Resources for Birdscapers" on page 197, which
provides addresses for bird-related associations,
societies and publications. Joining some of these
organizations is not only a great way to learn more
about birds — it's a wonderful way to meet fellow
bird-lovers! Finally, I've provided a list of recommended reading on page 198, divided into sections of
books on birdscaping, birds and plants, so it's easy to
find just what you're looking for.

Birdscaping Your Garden provides information
that I hope will provide you and your family with
countless hours of pleasure from the birds, native
plants and natural environment around you. As
you watch the colorful birds flitting through your
yard, your own backyard birdscape will become a
restful escape from the pressures outside. You'll find
it a source of entertainment and comfort. And you'll
be doing your part to give birds a good home.

FROM LANDSCAPE TO BIRDSCAPE

How do you turn your yard into an inviting sanctuary where birds will come to nest, raise their families and seek shelter for the winter? The way to start is to look at your yard from a bird's-eye view. Find a vantage point where you can see the whole front yard or backyard at once (try the back steps or an upstairs window). Then ask yourself these questions:

• **Are there places for birds to hide?** Songbirds need protective cover from potential enemies like cats, snakes and hawks.

• **Are there places for birds to nest?** Birds will be drawn to your yard during the breeding season if you have inviting places for them to nest, such as trees, shrubs, hedges, brambles and even vines.

• **Are there sheltered areas where birds can protect themselves from the elements?** Evergreens, shrubs planted against walls and other sheltered areas will give birds a place out of the cold, wind and rain.

• **Is there food and water?** Bird feeders and birdbaths are great helps to overwintering birds (in fact, a heated birdbath is often critical to winter survival). But during the rest of the year, it's important to provide natural food sources — flower nectar, grass seedheads, fruits, berries and a diversity of plants to attract insects, since many songbirds are insectivores. You can landscape for winter by choosing plants that keep their berries or seeds well into the coldest months. You'll find that the extra color and texture these plants provide really perk up your landscape, too! A small pond, pool or puddle will attract thirsty birds and an interesting assortment of wildlife, including frogs, toads and dragonflies.

In the following pages, I'll discuss each of these necessities — cover and shelter, nest sites, food and water — and give you plenty of tips on how you can provide them in your backyard birdscape. But first, let's review some general landscape considerations.

PLANNING YOUR BIRDSCAPE

Before you go any farther, take an inventory of your home and yard. Make a rough plan of your yard on graph paper. Draw in existing trees and shrubs you wish to keep, and outline the house, garage, windows, paths and so on. Mark any pleasant views you wish to preserve or views you wish to screen out. Note changes in elevation, soil differences and shade patterns which may affect the planting. Consider wind protection requirements. A slope facing south will be warmer than one facing north, and a hillside will have better drainage than a level lot.

Once you know what's already on your property, familiarize yourself with what grows well in your area. Visit local botanical gardens, arboreta, private gardens and natural areas to see what's growing. If pine trees grow naturally in your neighborhood, native plants that love shade and an acid soil should thrive in your birdscape. Beech trees indicate that plants that thrive in semi-shade and a less acid soil would be more appropriate. Maple trees indicate a more neutral soil. If you're a beginning birdscaper, you'll get best results if you stick to plants found growing naturally and in similar conditions within a radius of 100 miles of your garden.

In fact, I recommend using native plants in your birdscape whether you're a beginning, intermediate or advanced birdscaper. The most effective birdscapes seem to have grown out of the local woods or other vegetation, and native plants look both attractive and suitable in naturalistic landscapes. They also blend best with your area's natural vegetation. And you know they'll be hardy where you live. I derive extra satisfaction from growing native plants that evolved with most of the birds in my area. I believe that the birds will feel comfortable with these familiar species, many of which are favorite food plants. I have recommended a wide range of native plants in the "Plant Directory" on page 153, all excellent plants for birdscaping.

A good way to find out about plants that are suited to your area is to contact a local wildflower society. For example, on the East Coast, you could contact the North Carolina Wildflower Preservation Society, the New England Wildflower Society and the Western Pennsylvania Conservancy. Other extremely helpful organizations in the West include the National Wildflower Research Center and the California Native Plant Society. You can always contact these organizations for guidance or, better still, join up and help to preserve wild plants. They can also recommend reputable nurseries that sell a wide selection of nursery-propagated native plants. Other helpful contacts are your local extension agent, state college of agriculture and state foresters.

Once you've found out which plants will grow well in your area, it's time to narrow the list. But don't make your choices too narrow — a diversity of plants will encourage a diversity of insects, fruits and flowers, so the most bird species will be attracted.

Select plants that will provide alternate layers of foliage. For example, grow tall trees with shorter trees, shrubs, wildflowers and groundcovers to create continuous layers of foliage from ground level to the tallest foliage. Layering plants provides cover for birds. If you choose plants that display a variety of shapes and foliage textures, you'll also attract more birds.

Group shrubs in natural-looking drifts, mixing early-fruiting shrubs with shrubs that hold their fruits throughout the winter, to create a garden that's attractive to look at and useful to birds in all seasons. Shrub borders are an excellent way to mark your property boundaries and provide for the birds. To give birds protective cover and a suitable nesting

environment, the narrowest part of a shrub border between the property line and the lawn should be at least 8 feet wide. For a more naturalistic planting, allow room for a dense thicket of tangled vines and shrubs in an out-of-the-way corner.

Consider reclaiming the front yard for your private use by screening it with an evergreen hedge that's also useful to birds. Hedge plants like hemlocks, native roses and hollies provide food and offer protection from predators. A group of evergreens, such as red cedars, spruces or pines, provides essential shelter for birds. Site them in a "grove" in the backyard.

Plan your lawn area with informal curved borders, and break it up with gardens, shrubs, trees and groundcovers to create an "edge effect." Large lawns are useless to most birds except for robins, flickers and starlings. Instead, allow annuals to reseed and make a place for a "wild garden," or unmown lawn area. Cardinals, juncos, buntings and rose-breasted grosbeaks are among the seed-eaters attracted to such an area.

You'll get the most pleasure from your birdscape if you plan pathways through the garden so you can enjoy it up close. But don't forget to leave undisturbed areas for nesting.

Before you proceed with your plan, test it by marking the different garden areas using lengths of hose or rope. Use plastic leaf bags or filled garbage bags to represent shrubs, and poles or stakes to indicate the positions of trees. Check the position of your "plants" from several angles before you start planting. You'll find more tips for using plants in your birdscape in "Growing Native Plants" on page 145.

PROVIDING COVER AND SHELTER

Concealing, protective cover is vital to the survival of songbirds. Not only does it provide protection from predators, it also serves as shelter at night or during inclement weather. In areas where winters are often severely cold, many birds depend on evergreen shelter for their survival. The birds seek warmth and protection within the foliage.

In a deciduous forest, birds and other wildlife can count on evergreen trees and shrubs for protective cover from predators and shelter in winter. Pines, hemlocks and red cedars provide wildlife with protection from wind, snow and rain. In your birdscape, you can provide effective protective cover for birds in cold northern regions by planting a hemlock hedge or thick stand of evergreen conifers such as white pine, spruces and junipers.

An overgrown thicket in a "wild" corner of the garden will provide protective cover for birds. A thickly planted grouping of honeysuckle, native blackberry or raspberry and native rose will attract many birds, including field and song sparrows, juncos, bobolinks, brown thrashers and veerys.

Broadleaved evergreen shrubs or vines may also be used to provide year-round shelter. Shrubs should be allowed to form dense clumps or masses in some parts of the garden. Excellent broadleaved choices include evergreen hollies, rhododendrons and bayberries.

You can also make an old tree stump into a great cover for birds by planting ivy plants around the base and training them over the trunk. Smaller birds, such as wrens and chickadees, will roost and find shelter in the foliage, and birds will nest in the network of thick ivy branches. It's a wonderful way to turn an eyesore into an attraction!

By leaving nest boxes up all year, you allow birds to use them for roosting as well as for nesting. These boxes can be supplemented with specially designed roosting boxes. Roosting boxes may be used by screech owls, flickers, woodpeckers, nuthatches, chickadees, wrens and bluebirds.

PLANTS FOR SHADE AND SHELTER

These native trees and shrubs have dense foliage, providing shade and shelter for birds. Some also provide food and nesting sites. To find more about these plants, look them up in the "Plant Directory" on page 153. It provides descriptions, growing information and lists of birds attracted to each species.

Firs (*Abies* spp.)
The evergreen foliage of firs is valuable to a wide variety of birds for shelter and roosting.

Alders (*Alnus* spp.)
Alders are good shelter trees for many birds, including blue jays.

Hollies (*Ilex* spp.)
The dense, prickly foliage of hollies provides good protective shelter.

Junipers (*Juniperus* spp.)
Important food trees, junipers also provide valuable shelter. Juncos, sparrows and yellow-rumped warblers are among the birds that frequently roost in the foliage.

Mulberries (*Morus* spp.)
Mulberries are useful for shelter and cover, as well as being outstanding food trees and providing secure nesting sites.

Bayberries (*Myrica* spp.)
These evergreen shrubs provide valuable shelter for many birds.

Spruces (*Picea* spp.)
Spruces provide excellent year-round nesting and roosting sites, as well as shelter for birds.

Pines (*Pinus* spp.)
Excellent shelter for many birds, larger pines are favored roosting sites for migrating robins and warblers.

Oaks (*Quercus* spp.)
Oaks provide food, shelter and nesting sites for many birds.

Rhododendrons and Azaleas (*Rhododendron* spp.)
Rhododendrons and azaleas provide valuable shelter when planted in thickets.

Sumacs (*Rhus* spp.)
Sumacs provide good summer shelter.

Roses (*Rosa* spp.)
Thorny native rose thickets provide excellent shelter and protective cover for many birds.

Blackberries and Raspberries (*Rubus* spp.)
Prickly bramble shrubs provide shelter for towhees, native sparrows, warblers, thrushes and buntings.

Hemlocks (*Tsuga* spp.)
Outstanding nesting plants, hemlocks also provide excellent shelter. Chickadees, titmice, juncos and cardinals are among the birds that shelter in the evergreen hemlock foliage.

PROVIDING NEST SITES

Birds choose their nesting sites carefully. A breeding pair usually selects an area large enough to provide food, nest-building materials and a good place to nest. The pair then defends their site against intruders of the same species. The territory is initially defended by the male, who is able to warn off members of his own species with his song. By keeping their nest site and breeding territory "off limits" to members of the same species that are competing for the same food, the birds ensure more food for their own family while the young are being fed.

The individual breeding territory for each species varies in size. In the case of swallows, which nest communally, the breeding "territory" is limited to the nest itself. A pair of golden eagles, at the other extreme, commands many square miles of territory.

Nesting sites must have some protective cover. The eggs and nestlings are most vulnerable to predators, and the degree of exposure often determines the nesting location. Songbirds usually seek protective shelter in dense foliage or prickly shrubs.

By providing a variety of places to build their nests, you'll attract more bird species to nest in your birdscape. Besides trees, shrubs, vines and tall grasses, don't overlook the value of a dead tree (called a "snag") or dead limbs on an old tree. Many North American birds, from chickadees to woodpeckers, nest in tree hollows. As long as dead limbs or snags can't fall on a walk, road, building or power line, consider leaving them in place for the birds.

If you have a dead tree or tree limbs, you can create nesting holes in it using a brace and bit. Existing holes can be enlarged, and others started for woodpeckers to finish. The holes should face away from hot sun and direct cold winds. Cavity-nesting birds frequently also use nest boxes. The building of nest boxes is a good family project, even for inexperienced woodworkers, and plans are readily available at your local library or bird supply store.

Many birds, including catbirds, mockingbirds, cardinals, thrashers and towhees, choose to make their nests in tangled thickets and shrubbery. You can create a "wild" corner of the garden by planting native roses, blackberries, raspberries and honeysuckle together to make an ideal nesting environment for these birds. An effective nesting thicket should be at least 8 feet wide and 3 to 15 feet tall. Other birds that may nest in garden thickets or hedge plants include white-eyed vireo, yellow warbler, common yellowthroat, yellow-breasted chat, American goldfinch, chipping and song sparrows and purple finch.

If you plant a dense evergreen hedge of conifers, such as hemlocks, spruces or pines, you may attract many birds for nesting, including the mourning dove, blue jay, house finch, purple finch and chipping sparrow. Many more birds will gratefully use your evergreen hedge for shelter during the winter.

Tree-nesting birds build their nests in a crotch or fork of the tree or "saddled" on a limb, at heights from 3 feet to 50 feet or more above the ground. Crotch-nesters apparently prefer wide angles (about 70°), as this angle provides plenty of room and support for the nest. To increase the number of nest sites in the garden, try a little judicious pruning of plants in early spring or autumn to create wider crotch angles at various heights in a hedge or tree.

PROVIDING FOOD

Each species of bird has its own food preferences, based on the bird's behavior and physical characteristics, so different species can live in the same territory without competing for food. A bird's beak is its most important implement in gathering food, and the size and shape of a bird's beak is a good indication of the type of food eaten by a species. For example, hummingbirds have slender, pointed bills especially adapted to probing flowers for nectar. Sparrows have short, heavy, conical bills that are well adapted for cracking seeds. Woodpeckers have strong, sharp-pointed bills for digging into tree trunks for wood-boring insects. Insectivorous birds generally tend to have small, weak beaks that open wide to enable them to catch insects while in flight.

You can lure a wide variety of birds to your birdscape with a careful selection of garden plants that will provide a succession of flowering, fruiting and seed set. The plants listed in this book, with their long flowering time and abundant supply of fruit, nectar and seeds, are ideal for birdscaping. By choosing plants that provide food during every season, your garden will attract birds throughout the year, even in winter. For example, many trees and shrubs will hold their fruits well into winter, and many ornamental grasses also keep their seedheads over winter.

If you design your birdscape following the suggestions in this book, you can attract many species of birds to areas where they have not been seen for many years. Within the space of your yard, you may find hummingbirds sipping nectar from flowers, chickadees gleaning insects from foliage, woodpeckers extracting insects from tree trunks, cedar waxwings eating fruits, sparrows munching on grass seeds, wrens searching the understory for insects, and swallows flying overhead, mouths agape to take flying insects on the wing.

Bird feeders are an important source of food for birds — as well as providing hours of enjoyment for birdscapers — over the winter. Use them to supplement

NATIVE PLANTS FOR NESTING

You can attract a greater variety of birds to nest on your property if you provide a diversity of nesting situations to suit their specific requirements, such as clumps of shrubbery, tangled thickets and taller trees. The plants listed below are preferred by many birds for nesting. Some of these plants also provide food and shelter for birds. For best nesting success, plant them in masses or clumps, preferably in quieter areas of the yard. Look up these plants in the "Plant Directory" on page 153 for descriptions, growing information, and lists of birds attracted.

Firs (*Abies* spp.)
Tanagers, grosbeaks, robins and jays are among the many birds that nest in firs.

Hackberries (*Celtis* spp.)
Many birds nest in hackberry foliage, including indigo buntings, verdins, hummingbirds and white-winged doves.

Saguaro (*Carnegiea gigantea*)
In the Southwest, this giant cactus is excavated for nesting by flickers and Gila woodpeckers. Their old nest holes provide nest sites for owls, martins, flycatchers, wrens and kestrels.

Dogwoods (*Cornus* spp.)
Bell's vireos and summer tanagers are attracted to nest in dogwoods.

Hawthorns (*Crataegus* spp.)
The thorny branches of hawthorns provide abundant nesting sites for smaller birds, including hummingbirds, cardinals, buntings, verdins and wood thrushes. In the Southwest, roadrunners commonly nest in shrubby hawthorns.

Hollies (*Ilex* spp.)
Dense, prickly holly foliage attracts towhees, thrashers and mockingbirds.

Junipers (*Juniperus* spp.)
Junipers are most valuable nesting plants. Chipping sparrows, robins, song sparrows and mockingbirds are among the many species that nest in these plants.

Opuntias, Prickly Pears (*Opuntia* spp.)
The prickly spines of these cacti provide protective nesting for many birds, including cactus wrens, mourning doves, Inca doves, curve-billed thrashers, roadrunners and house sparrows.

Spruces (*Picea* spp.)
White-crowned sparrows and warblers are among the birds that nest in the evergreen foliage of spruces.

Pines (*Pinus* spp.)
Robins, purple finches, mourning doves, magnolia warblers and white-crowned sparrows are among the many birds that nest in pines.

Oaks (*Quercus* spp.)
Oaks are outstanding trees for nesting. Blue-gray gnatcatchers, orchard orioles, summer tanagers, acorn woodpeckers and blue jays are among the many species that nest in oaks.

Roses (*Rosa* spp.)
The dense, prickly stems of native roses provide excellent nesting sites for smaller birds, including indigo buntings, lazuli buntings, cardinals, yellow warblers, towhees and sparrows.

Blackberries and Raspberries (*Rubus* spp.)
The spiny stems of these brambles provide secure nesting sites for indigo buntings, cardinals, yellow warblers, towhees and sparrows.

Elderberries (*Sambucus* spp.)
Warblers, grosbeaks and goldfinches nest in the foliage.

Hemlocks (*Tsuga* spp.)
Hemlocks are outstanding nesting plants. Many species of warbler, as well as robins, juncos, veerys, American goldfinches and blue jays, are among the birds that nest in hemlocks.

your native plantings. Many excellent models of feeders are on the market, and it's easy to buy a variety of seeds, seed mixes and suet as well. You could check your local nursery or garden center, feed store, or bird supply center for all kinds of feeders and birdfeed. If what you want is unavailable locally, you can also order supplies by mail. Many birds have seed preferences which you should take into consideration. You can lure your favorite songbirds to the backyard birdscape by catering to their preferences. These are listed in the "Feeding Habits" section of the individual bird entries. Don't forget to place the feeders where you can see them, and check them daily to make sure that they are adequately filled.

PROVIDING WATER

A supply of fresh, clean water is an important — and often overlooked — element for attracting birds to your birdscape. Throughout the year, birds will use the water for bathing and drinking. Unless you have a pond or stream on your property, the simplest way to provide water is to set out a birdbath.

Birds bathe and preen in order to keep their feathers in perfect condition for flying and to maintain their waterproofing and insulating properties. The individual feathers are made of the same substance as human fingernails, keratin, and become bent and disarranged with daily activity. The feathers must be repositioned and straightened by preening. The bird usually bathes and then passes the individual feathers through its bill, oiling them and snapping them back into position.

When bathing, birds scoop water up in their bills and splash it over their backs, flapping their wings and ruffling their feathers in a manner that could attract the attention of nearby cats. Wet feathers will hinder the birds' ability to fly and escape a cat, so the position and design of the birdbath is critical for the birds' survival.

Place your birdbath near protective shrubbery, close enough to allow the birds to escape to safety, but not so

A robin enjoying a splash in this pedestal bird bath.

close that a cat can pounce on the unwary birds. A pedestal birdbath is a good protection against cats and is available from garden supply stores. A wide, shallow bowl, preferably made from cast stone and mounted on a pedestal about 40 inches above the ground, is excellent. The birdbath should be shallow, because most birds are terrified by deep water. Ideal dimensions are 1/2 to 1 inch deep at the edges, sloping to a maximum of 2 1/2 to 3 inches in the center. Choose a birdbath with a roughened bottom, allowing the birds to get a firm grip without slipping.

Varying the depth of water in your birdbath will cater to the preferences of a greater variety of birds. Chickadees, goldfinches and song sparrows will bathe in the shallow section, while robins, jays and grackles use the deeper water. You can create different depths in your birdbath by adding stones to form a shallow "shore" on one side, or by placing a large rock just slightly submerged in the center.

Like us, birds need water throughout the year and, in the winter months, it's especially hard for them to find an adequate source. You'll do your birds a big favor if you pay special attention to keeping the water in your birdbath unfrozen. It helps to locate the birdbath where it receives winter sunshine all day. But you'll get guaranteed results if you install a stock tank de-icer or an electrical heating element designed for use in birdbaths, available from bird-supply stores.

BEYOND YOUR BACKYARD

Creating a backyard birdscape is only the first step in creating a more valuable bird habitat. If you're hooked on helping birds, there are a number of ways you can encourage them to find a home in your area. One way is to create a neighborhood birdscape. Think of how much more inviting your neighborhood would be to birds if everyone turned their yards into birdscapes! Approach your neighbors and invite them into your birdscape. Once they've seen how attractive it is and how delightful it would be to have a riot of colorful birds in their own yards, they too may become birdscapers. You could even start a neighborhood birding association!

City parks are another place where birdscaping could open up a whole area for birds. Most parks aren't attractive to birds now because of their formal layout, featuring displays of exotic plants and closely cropped lawns. Sections of these parks could be transformed into more natural and more easily maintained areas of native vegetation that birds would love. If your local park is just begging to be made into a birdscape, approach your city's director of parks and recreation about making the change. Other areas that are ripe for birdscaping include street plantings, freeway borders and school grounds. You might also approach the owners of large industrial parks, and suggest the many benefits of creating a fashionable native landscape and wildlife habitat as a community service.

If you know local areas that shelter wildlife, you can work to have important areas preserved before they are threatened. Many state conservation agencies and national environmental organizations such as the Audubon Society or Nature Conservancy can offer valuable assistance. Reclamation of abandoned sites, such as old mining pits and quarries, could provide valuable wildlife habitat with appropriate plantings. They would also make ideal sanctuaries for water birds.

BIRD HABITATS AND BEHAVIOR

Now that we've covered the basics of birdscaping, I hope you're anxious to start planning your own backyard bird paradise. But before you begin, you'll get more out of your birdscape if you know a few basics about bird behavior. By finding out why birds do certain things, you'll be able to tell what they're up to in your yard. For example, you can recognize courtship behavior, or guess that a bird is migrating through your area. I cover the specific behavior of each bird in the "Bird Directory" on page 15, but here's a brief overview that applies to all birds and supplies some of the whys and wherefores of bird behavior.

All birds have a preferred habitat. Some, including the mourning dove and American robin, are widespread and may be found in very diverse habitats. Other birds, however, have defined habitats and live only where species of particular plants grow. For example, Kirtland's warbler is only found in large tracts of jack-pines.

MATCHING PLANTS TO BIRDS

If you want to attract a favorite bird, the first thing to do is to find out more about it. Turn to the "Bird Directory" beginning on page 15 and look up your bird. Find out if it lives, nests or winters in your area, or if it passes through during migration. (After all, if it never comes near your home, nothing you do will attract it!) If it spends at least some time each year in your area, scan the entry, especially the "Plants for food and shelter include:" section, to see if it has favorite plants. Many birds are closely associated with a particular species of plant. The cedar waxwing, spruce grouse, cactus wren, piñon jay, yellow-rumped warbler and pine warbler are examples of this close association.

Cedar waxwings are fond of the berries of the eastern red cedar, while the needles and buds of spruce trees and other evergreens are a favorite food of the spruce grouse. When the piñon seed crop is poor, flocks of piñon jays may move hundreds of miles in search of a more bountiful supply. The yellow-rumped warbler

was formerly known as the myrtle warbler, a name that reflects its taste for bayberries (also called wax myrtles). During migration, these tiny birds gather

The myrtle warbler (above), now known as the yellow-rumped warbler, was originally named due to its taste for the berries of bayberry or wax myrtle (Myrica pensylvanica) (below).

by the thousands along the Atlantic coast to refuel on waxy gray bayberries. The cactus wren doesn't depend on its namesake plant for food, but it does depend on the thorns of cholla and other spiny plants to discourage predators from reaching its nest in these plants. The pine warbler usually builds its nest in pines, and often binds pine needles and twigs into its cup-shaped nest of spiderweb and plant down.

Many plants with tube-shaped flowers provide nectar for hummingbirds, which pollinate the flowers as they move from one blossom to another. As the diminutive bird sucks up nectar with its long, thin bill, the bird's crown, bill or throat may become dusted with pollen. Then, when the hummingbird visits different plants, it cross-pollinates them.

Birds are attracted to the succulent fruits produced by many North American plants. These fruits are usually green and hidden in the foliage when immature. When the fruits ripen, they turn bright colors that attract birds to the tasty feast. The birds eat the fruits and in the turn spread the seeds, propagating the species and sometimes extending its range. Mistletoe relies totally on birds for colonization. When other food is scarce in winter months, mistletoes provide the birds with apetizing bite-size berries. The berries are a major food for many birds, including bluebirds and cedar waxwings. Jays play a role in reforesting, especially on burned or cut-over lands, by burying acorns. Some of these are retrieved and eaten at a later stage, but many are left to sprout and grow.

NESTING STRATEGIES

Many birds show distinctive coloration and subtle markings that give them a protective camouflage that blends with the textures and colors of native plants. Birds that mainly live in the foliage of trees generally have olive or gray upper parts, like the arboreal wood warblers. Kinglets, which are ground-dwellers, have earth-tone upper parts with patches of darker colors, enabling them to merge with stones, plant litter or dappled woodland shadows. Birds who live in grasslands generally have streaked plumage, like the meadowlarks and bobolinks. Protective coloration is one reason certain plant species may be preferred nesting plants for specific birds.

The breeding season of many birds coincides with the peak flowering or fruiting period of their favorite food source. With abundant food within easy reach, the adults can feed quickly, allowing more time to attend to the needs of the nestlings. For example, the nesting period of the red crossbill is determined by the availability of ripe pine seeds. The nesting of the cedar waxwing also tends to coincide with a plentiful supply of ripe fruits.

MIGRATION

Many species of birds are seasonal migrants — they move from place to place, rather than remaining in the same area all year. Migration is an evolutionary adaption that allows birds to escape unfavorable conditions — like the lack of food or cold winter weather — in an area by moving to a more favorable area during part of the year. Some migration may consist of mountain species moving to the lowlands for winter, while some species, such as the evening grosbeak, will move east or west across the United States to winter.

Many birds breed in northern areas in spring and summer, then retreat to warmer southern climates for fall and winter. For example, of the 215 bird species known to breed in Michigan, less than 20 of these species remain there year-round. Migrating birds have regular migration patterns, usually returning to the same breeding area each spring, returning to the same wintering area each year, and probably following the same migration route each year.

For some birds, migration is a long and wearying journey. It has been estimated that approximately 100 species of birds who spend the summer in the United States will winter in the West Indies or Central and South America, with the greatest winter concentration of birds in Mexico and over a range south to Panama. But other birds only migrate slightly south of their summer range. American goldfinches, dark-eyed (slate-colored) juncos, eastern bluebirds, yellow-rumped warblers, chipping sparrows, house wrens and some American robins and meadowlarks are among the northern species of birds that winter in the southern United States. The house sparrow, red-bellied woodpecker, downy woodpecker, pileated woodpecker, white-breasted nuthatch, tufted titmouse and cardinal may remain a resident in their territories all year-round.

Although the concept of "flyways" (or migratory "highways") is a well-established and long-standing theory, it is now thought that most species of nocturnally migrating songbirds spread out over a broad front during migration. The birds may follow a path marked by specific geographic features, such as a mountain ridge or a river, or may range widely across the countryside. However, waterfowl, shorebirds, and some raptors (birds of prey) are known to follow three main north-south flyways — the Pacific flyway, the Mississippi flyway and the Atlantic flyway, with some intermediate routes. During their migration period , great concentrations of birds can be found along their flyways. This makes the migration period a particularly exciting and rewarding time of the year for birdscapers.

BIRD
DIRECTORY

MOURNING DOVE

Zenaida macroura

The mourning dove takes its mournful name from its common call, a low-toned series of soft coos. The notes are uttered slowly and have a melancholy quality, as if the bird is mourning the loss of his mate rather than singing to her.

The bird has a long pointed tail and slim 12-inch body with gray-brown plumage. Due to the arrangement of the stiff wing feathers, the wings make a whistling sound when in rapid flight.

*A mourning dove
eating the seeds of
yellow wood sorrel (Oxalis stricta).*

Habitat

The mourning dove is widely adapted to varying habitats, including open fields, open deciduous and coniferous woods and windbreak trees on the Great Plains. The bird also inhabits both arid plains and mountains in the West.

The mourning dove is the most common native dove of parks and gardens in suburban areas throughout its range.

Migration and Winter Range

The birds reach their breeding grounds in the North between March and April.

The northernmost populations drift farther south to winter, with some remaining in the northern United States, but the greatest concentration winters from southern California east through Nebraska to New Jersey.

Breeding Range

The mourning dove has the greatest distribution of any North American game bird, breeding in all the continental United States.

The bird also breeds from southeastern Alaska, southern British Columbia, Alberta, Saskatchewan and Manitoba to southern Ontario, southern Quebec and southern New Brunswick, south to Baja California and through Mexico to western Panama and the West Indies.

Breeding Behavior

During the nesting season the birds are found in pairs. The birds indulge in an aerial courtship flight: After climbing steeply from a perch with vigorous wing-flapping, the wings clapping together with each downbeat, the birds sail with stiffly held wings like a small hawk and then glide back to their perch.

Mourning doves mate for life and, in the nesting season, become particularly devoted couples.

Nesting

A wide choice of nesting locations is used by the mourning dove, but they usually choose a horizontal branch of an evergreen tree 15 to 25 feet above the ground. The nest is sometimes built on the foundations of another species' old nest, or on the gutters of a house. The bird may occasionally nest on the ground, especially on the prairie.

A division of labor occurs during nest-building. The male brings building material to the site and the female constructs the nest. The birds build a loose, bulky platform of twigs; the female lays two (in rare cases, three or four) white eggs. Both sexes share in the 14- to 15-day incubation. The female usually sits from dusk to dawn and the male sits throughout the day. Both care for the young, brooding till near the end of nest life.

The young are fed on "pigeon milk" (regurgitated food taken from the parent's crop) and, later, weed seeds and insects. The young fly from the nest 14 or 15 days after hatching. A pair may raise two to five broods in one year.

Feeding Habits

Adult birds feed almost totally on seeds. Year-round, weed seeds are their principal food: 7,500 seeds of yellow woodsorrel were found in one bird's stomach, and 6,400 seeds of foxtail grasses were found in another. Mourning doves eat spilled grain as well as pine nuts and pokeberries.

Plants for food and shelter include:
Grasses (*Andropogon* spp.) (see page 157)
Sunflowers (*Helianthus* spp.) (see page166)
Spruces (*Picea* spp.) (see page 177)
Pines (*Pinus* spp.) (see page 178)

*A mourning dove on its nest in the protective spines of a tree cholla (*Opuntia imbricata*).*

The Inca dove eats the fruits
of prickly pear cacti, including this
plains prickly pear (Opuntia polyacantha).

INCA DOVE

Scardafella inca

The Inca dove is a familiar bird to be sighted often in parks and gardens of the West. Easily identified when in flight, the chestnut flash on the outer part of the wings may be revealed and the distinctive white margin of the long, square-ended gray tail is visible, helping to distinguish the 8¼-inch Inca dove from the similar ground dove. The dove's wings often make a twittering sound in flight. The song of the Inca dove is a repeated "coo-hoo."

Habitat

The Inca dove is an extremely tame bird, preferring areas of human settlement. The bird is extending its range north into settled areas, including suburban parks and gardens as well as ranches and fields.

Migration and Winter Range

The Inca dove is resident year-round within its range.

Breeding Range

The year-round range of the Inca dove includes Arizona, New Mexico, southeastern California and Texas, south to Costa Rica.

Breeding Behavior

When courting, male Inca doves strut around the females, cooing, with their tails raised almost vertically. If another male intrudes, the dove becomes pugnacious and a fierce fight may result with savage buffeting of wings. The birds also use their bills to peck each other on the head, often drawing blood. The mated pair show great affection, often indulging in mutual preening or caressing.

Nesting

The Inca dove prefers to nest near houses or barns close to human habitation. A horizontal fork or flattened tree limb is usually selected 4 to 25 feet above the ground. A variety of trees are used for nest sites, including cottonwoods, sycamores, elms, live oaks, mesquites and fruit trees. The birds will also nest in opuntia cacti. The nests of other birds, including the cactus wren, mourning dove and mockingbird, are sometimes used after repair and relining work has been done.

The nest is a small, compact platform 2 to 5 inches wide with a cavity about 1 inch deep. The nest is constructed of twigs, small rootlets, plant stems, grass and feathers. When building the nest, the male brings material to the female, then alights on her back and passes it down to her while she sits on the platform.

The female lays two whitish eggs. Both sexes incubate for about two weeks. In Arizona the Inca dove

An Inca dove with its young at the nest in a cholla cactus (Opuntia spinosior).

has the longest breeding season of any bird, often having four or five broods between January and November. Elsewhere two or more broods are common, and the birds often use the same nest twice. The previous year's nest is sometimes relined and used again.

The young birds leave the nest after two weeks. On leaving the nest, the young return and clamber over their parents' backs in order to huddle between them to roost at night.

Feeding Habits

Weed seeds form the bulk of the Inca dove's diet, though the birds sometimes eat spilled grain and poultry feed. Because of their dry seed diet, water is very important to the birds — in times of drought they extend their range in search of it, often staying in built-up areas.

Plants for food and shelter include:
Opuntia cacti (*Opuntia* spp.) (see page 175)
Western sycamore (*Platanus racemosa*) (see page 180)
Fremont cottonwood (*Populus fremontii*) (see page 181)
Live oak (*Quercus virginiana*) (see page 183)

GREATER ROADRUNNER

Geococcyx californianus

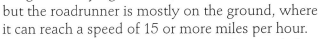

The greater roadrunner is a large (23-inch), streaky, brown and white bird with a long pointed tail and powerful pale blue legs. A patch of bare skin behind the eye ends in an orange-red spot. At close range, the plumage displays a variety of iridescent colors.

The bird's short rounded wings make flying an effort, but the roadrunner is mostly on the ground, where it can reach a speed of 15 or more miles per hour.

The bird's common name comes from its habit of running away rapidly when surprised on a road.

The greater roadrunner often nests in hawthorns, including the cockspur hawthorn (<u>Crataegus crus-galli</u>).

An extremely shy bird in the wild, it becomes tame in urban areas. In southern California, the birds often inhabit golf courses and pay little attention to the golfers.

The greater roadrunner is a member of the cuckoo family, and his voice reveals the affiliation. With his bill down, he starts with a high coo. With each coo, he raises his head and the pitch of the song becomes lower, until the bill points upward. "Coo, coo, coo, ohh, ohh, ohh," he sings with a mournful tone.

Other names of the greater roadrunner include chaparral cock, snake killer, cock of the desert, lizard bird and ground cuckoo. Mexicans refer to the bird as the loyal *paisano* (fellow countryman).

A roadrunner visiting a garden to search for insects.

Habitat
Possibly the most distinctive and well-known bird throughout its range, the greater roadrunner is common in desert scrub, chaparral and arid brush. It often inhabits farmlands and urban areas.

Migration and Winter Range
The bird is a year-round resident throughout its range.

Breeding Range
The roadrunner's range extends from north central California throughout the Southwest, east to eastern Oklahoma and northwestern Louisiana and south to central Mexico. It is the state bird of New Mexico and is resident in Nevada, Utah, Colorado, southwestern Kansas and Texas. The bird is extending its range east.

Breeding Behavior
In spring the male bird goes to the eastern rim of a mesa or climbs to the top of a high cactus or dead tree to greet the rising sun with song. This love song may be preceded by much strutting with the head held high and tail and wings drooping. During courtship greater roadrunners may indulge in a side-stepping dance, raising and dropping their head and wings.

Greater roadrunners mate for life and become year-round residents, developing a regular schedule in covering their area.

Nesting
The greater roadrunner places its 1-foot-diameter nest of coarse twigs lined with leaves, grass, feathers, rootlets and snakeskins in low, thorny growth such as cactus, mesquite or palo verde trees.

The female lays three to six white eggs at irregular intervals, usually between April and May. The female begins incubation after the first egg is laid, resulting in young birds in various stages of development in the same nest. Incubation takes about 20 days and the young birds fledge after 17 to 19 days.

Feeding Habits
The greater roadrunner's principal diet consists of lizards, grasshoppers and crickets. The birds may also eat scorpions, caterpillars, beetles, spiders, insects, seeds and fruit, including prickly pears. Roadrunners occasionally attack and eat mice, snakes (including rattlesnakes) and English sparrows, as well as other birds and their young. They have been recorded snatching swifts and sparrows out of the air. The roadrunner draws close to its prey, then with a quick dash and leap captures the airborne bird.

Plants for food and shelter include:
Plains prickly pear (*Opuntia polyacantha*) (see page 175)

ANNA'S HUMMINGBIRD

Calypte anna

The largest hummingbird in California, Anna's hummingbird is also the only hummingbird that winters in the United States and the only one that nests mostly within a single state. It is the only hummingbird in California that sings, delivering a series of thin, squeaky notes from a perch.

The 4-inch birds resemble living gems. Both sexes have a metallic green back. The male sports a brilliant iridescent pink-red crown and throat; the female usually has a few red feathers on her throat.

Like all hummingbirds, the bird is a master of flight. It can fly backward or hover in place as it takes nectar, pollen and insects from flowers. The wing beats of all hummingbirds are so rapid that they make a humming sound, giving the birds their common name. Anna's hummingbird was named

The female Anna's hummingbird builds up the sides of her nest while incubating the eggs. The nest is in a desert willow (Chilopsis linearis).

by the French naturalist René Lesson in 1879 to honor Anna, the Duchess of Rivoli, wife of Prince Victor Masséna.

In order to conserve energy, all hummingbirds, including Anna's, become sluggish in the evening. Their heart rate and body temperature reduce, and they enter a comatose state for several hours each evening. Because the bird has such high energy use and an inability to feed at night, this sluggish state saves it from starving to death by minimizing energy losses. The male's song is a repeated "chee-chee-chee."

Habitat

Anna's hummingbird is a common western garden bird and is also found in coastal woods.

Migration and Winter Range

Some birds migrate north to British Columbia or south as far as Arizona and Texas in fall, returning to California in December.

Breeding Range

Anna's hummingbird is a year-round resident bird within its breeding range, from northern Baja California and the coastal foothills of southern California north to southern Oregon. Summer pioneers reach British Columbia. In the 1960s they were seen wintering on Vancouver Island, and were later observed courting and carrying nest-building material.

Breeding Behavior

The male Anna's hummingbird does not rely on song to draw attention, but displays his superb mastery of the air to the object of his desire. The courtship flight consists of looping back and forth at high speed, climbing as high as 100 feet, tracing a towering U-pattern. The bird plummets to earth, keeping his eye on the female, and levels off at tremendous speed to pass over her, travelling into the sun so that his rose red throat glows in the sunlight. As he passes over her he produces an explosive "peek" sound by spreading out his specialized narrow tail feathers. This display flight is often also used to discourage intruders from entering his territory.

Nesting

In California, Anna's hummingbird begins nesting as early as December, often while snow and frost are still on the ground. A tiny cup-shaped nest made of plant down and lichen, bound together with spiderweb, is fastened to a sheltered horizontal limb. The female

The male Anna's hummingbird is a common visitor to California gardens.

often lays her two white eggs while the nest is still only a platform; the sides are built up during incubation and decorated with lichen.

Feeding Habits

Hummingbirds have evolved as efficient nectar-feeders, with their long, thin, needlelike bills and extendable tongue. Many flowers, in turn, have evolved to attract hummingbirds and are generally called hummingbird flowers. They are tubular flowers in open exposed groupings that allow the hummingbird to hover. As the bird feeds, pollen is deposited on its head and carried to the next plant. Anna's hummingbird also eats small insects and spiders.

Plants for food and shelter include:
Crimson columbine (*Aquilegia formosa*) (see page 158)
Desert willow (*Chilopsis linearis*) (see page 162)
Western hawthorn (*Crataegus douglasii*) (see page 164)
Ocotillo (*Fouquieria splendens*) (see page 165)
Scarlet lobelia (*Lobelia cardinalis*) (see page 170)
Twinberry (*Lonicera involucrata*) (see page 170)
Scarlet bugler (*Penstemon centranthifolius*) (see page 176)
Red shrubby penstemon (*Penstemon corymbosus*) (see page 176)
Firecracker plant (*Penstemon eatonii*) (see page 176)
Western azalea (*Rhododendron occidentale*) (see page 184)
Nootka rose (*Rosa nutkana*) (see page 186)
Soaptree yucca (*Yucca elata*) (see page 194)
California fuchsia (*Zauschneria californica*) (see page 195)

*The ruby-throated hummingbird sipping
nectar from blooms of cardinal flower (Lobelia cardinalis).*

RUBY-THROATED HUMMINGBIRD

Archiloctius colubris

The ruby-throated hummingbird is the only hummingbird that nests east of the Mississippi River. The birds are only 3 to 4 inches in length, with a long, needlelike bill. Metallic green above and gray below, the male has a brilliant iridescent metallic red throat. Constantly in motion, darting and hovering in flight, hummingbirds are the only birds that can fly backwards. The birds' insectlike flight is accompanied by a characteristic humming sound made by their rapidly beating wings.

In spite of their minute size, the birds' agility and speed of flight protects them from most enemies. In fact, the extremely feisty ruby-throated hummingbird will drive away much larger birds. It has been known to attack hawks, crows and eagles.

Habitat

These hummingbirds prefer suburban gardens, parks, woodland clearings and woods' edges, often near water. The birds may be found wherever nectar-bearing flowers are growing, especially if trees or thickets for shelter and perching or nesting are nearby.

Migration and Winter Range

The birds winter from northern Mexico and southern Texas south to Costa Rica. Some ruby-throated hummingbirds cross over 600 miles of ocean to reach the Bermudas, or cross the Gulf of Mexico to Yucatan and farther south.

Breeding Range

The birds' breeding range extends from Alberta eastward to Nova Scotia, south to the Gulf Coast and Florida and west to North Dakota, Nebraska, Kansas and central Texas.

Breeding Behavior

During courtship, the male performs display flights for the female. It loops backward and forward in a wide arc, as if hung from a pendulum, with a loud buzz from his wings at the bottom of the swing.

Nesting

The female builds a neat little cup-shaped nest of soft plant down and spiderwebs, 1 to 1 1/4 inches in diameter. The nest is built on a limb and covered with lichens. The female also incubates the eggs and raises the young alone. She lays two tiny white eggs and incubates them for 16 days. The young leave the nest when they are 20 to 22 days old. Two and sometimes three broods are raised in a season. The female apparently returns to the same nesting area each year.

Feeding Habits

Ruby-throated hummingbirds drink nectar from flowering plants and hummingbird feeders. They also eat tiny insects.

Plants for food and shelter include:
Columbines (*Aquilegia* spp.) (see page 157)
Trumpet vine (*Campsis radicans*) (see page 161)
Scarlet lobelia (*Lobelia cardinalis*) (see page 170)
Bee balms (*Monarda* spp.) (see page 173)

The ruby-throated hummingbird is attracted to red tubular flowers.

A male Costa's hummingbird
sips from the firecracker plant (<u>Penstemon eatonii</u>).

COSTA'S HUMMINGBIRD

Calypte costae

Like Anna's hummingbird, Costa's has a green back, but is distinguished by its slightly smaller size (3 inches) and brilliant violet crown and throat. The throat of this bird has distinctive streamers down the side of the neck. The female Costa's is smaller than the male and has a lighter gray underside than the female Anna's hummingbird.

The species name was given in 1839 by Jules Bourcier to honor Louis Costa, Marquis de Beau-Regard, who was the owner of a large collection of hummingbirds. The Costa's call is a "chip."

Habitat

Costa's hummingbird is a common bird of the southwestern deserts, preferring drylands inhabited by yucca, ocotillos and cacti, and open chaparral in southern California. In the spring and fall months it visits suburban parks and gardens.

Migration and Winter Range

Males migrate through the desert areas in late February and March while the ocotillos are in flower. By the end of May most birds have moved to coastal areas. The birds winter from southern California and southwestern Arizona south to Mexico.

Breeding Range

The bird nests from from central California, southern Nevada, southwestern Utah, southern Arizona and southwestern New Mexico to northwest Mexico and Baja California.

Breeding Behavior

Like Anna's hummingbird, the male Costa's performs amazing courtship display flights, preferring the towering U-pattern. Flying at speeds between 30 and 50 miles per hour, the bird climbs vertically to possibly 100 feet above the ground. The hummingbird turns and plummets toward the ground, turning at the last moment to climb again, tracing a U-pattern. As the bird loops back and forth, its outer tail feathers produce a high-pitched whirring sound as it dives. The female watches from a nearby perch.

Nesting

Nesting between February and June, Costa's humming-birds build a relatively loosely made cup-shaped nest 1 1/4 to 2 inches wide. They weave the nest from fine plant fibers bound with spiderweb and decorate it with leaves or lichens fastened to the outside. The birds line the nest with feathers.

The nest is usually built from 2 to 9 feet above the ground on a limb or twigs of oaks, alders, hackberry, willows or palo verde, or in sage, branching cacti or dead yuccas. The female continues to build up the sides of the nest during incubation until it is 1 1/4 to 1 1/2 inches high. The female lays two white eggs, which she incubates for 15 to 18 days. The young leave the nest after about three weeks. It is believed that only one brood is raised each year.

Feeding Habits

Like all hummingbirds, Costa's only feeds while hovering. Nectar, spiders and insects make up its diet. While eating, both sexes utter a light "chip" sound.

Plants for food and shelter include:
Desert willow (*Chilopsis linearis*) (see page 162)
Ocotillo (*Fouquieria splendens*) (see page 165)
Scarlet lobelia (*Lobelia cardinalis*) (see page 170)
Arizona honeysuckle (*Lonicera arizonica*) (see page 170)
Firecracker plant (*Penstemon eatonii*) (see page 176)
Soaptree yucca (*Yucca elata*) (see page 194)
California fuchsia (*Zauschneria californica*) (see page 195)

A Costa's hummingbird feeding on the nectar-rich flowers of Texas betony (Stachys coccinea).

COMMON FLICKER

Colaptes auratus

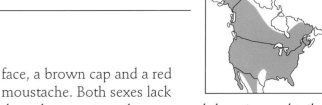

Because of their amusing antics, noisiness and abundance from Alaska to Mexico and coast to coast, the common flicker is probably the best-known woodpecker in North America. In different parts of its range, three color variations are found. All bear the signature white rump, which flashes when the bird flies up from the ground.

East of the Rocky Mountains and northwest into Alaska, the yellow-shafted flicker has a brilliant golden color on the underside of the wings and tail. The male has a black moustache and both sexes have a gray cap, a brown face and a red crescent on the nape of the neck.

An inhabitant of the Southwestern deserts, the gilded flicker has wings and tail similar to the yellow-shafted but has a brown cap, a gray face and a red moustache, and lacks the red nape.

The red-shafted flicker is the Western equivalent of the yellow-shafted flicker. The male has a gray face, a brown cap and a red moustache. Both sexes lack the red crescent on the nape, and the wing and tail linings are a salmon or scarlet-orange color.

The yellow-shafted and red-shafted races commonly interbreed where their ranges overlap in the Great Plains, resulting in hybrids that may show a mix of characteristics. Red-shafteds and gildeds hybridize where their ranges overlap in Arizona. Because of this interbreeding, all flickers were collectively grouped as the "common flicker" by the American Ornithologists Union in 1973.

The flicker is known by over 130 different common names, including "high-hole," "yellow hammer," "wake up," "high holder" and "yucker," attesting to its popularity. The genus name, *Colaptes,* is from the Greek *kolapter,* meaning a hammer or chisel, and *kolapto,* meaning to peck with the bill. The species name is Latin for gilded or lined with gold.

A common flicker digging for ants.
The wild strawberries (<u>Fragaria virginiana</u>)
nearby are another favorite source of food .

Habitat
Flickers are common birds in deciduous or mixed woodlands, parks and gardens, orchards and desert areas.

Migration and Winter Range
The bird winters from near the northern limits to the southern limits of its breeding range. In the fall and winter, many flickers move southward from their summer territory, while others remain resident year-round.

The spring migration begins in late winter, with the northern movement beginning as early as February and continuing until April. The birds travel in loose flocks, with the males arriving in their breeding territory several days ahead of the females. The birds are noisy on arrival and seem to alert the woodlands to the coming arrival of spring.

The male calls from a tall tree with a loud prolonged series of "wick, wick, wick, wick" or "yuck, yuck, yuck, yuck" and drums rapidly on a resonant limb, metal roof, utility pole or house. The drumming is a continuous roll, often waking people in the early hours of morning. These are challenge calls, establishing the bird's territorial boundaries, and are a preliminary to the courtship display.

Breeding Range
Flickers breed from Alaska to Mexico and from coast to coast.

Breeding Behavior
Flickers usually mate for life. Both sexes return to the same breeding area each year. The drumming and calling brings the pair together and, when they greet each other, the birds indulge in head-bobbing displays as well as the "frozen pose." During the head-bobbing display, the wings may be lifted and the tail spread to reveal the underwing and undertail colors and a soft musical call may be made. A competing suitor commonly appears early in the breeding season. The birds of the competing sex indulge in head bobbing and frozen pose displays. The males also chase each other, with the intruder generally being driven away.

Nesting
When the pair are united they begin nest-building. Flickers have slightly curved bills and are relatively poor excavators among woodpeckers. They tend to select dead trees, limbs with rotted wood or soft-timbered trees. Apple, sycamore, oak, cherry, elm, maple, beech, ash and pine trees are favorite trees for nesting. In the Southwest, the saguaro cactus is most commonly used.

Both sexes work on the excavation, beginning at first light and sometimes working until late at night. A number of extra holes are bored high up in trees before the final home is completed. Old fence posts, utility poles, the sides of buildings or a nest box may be selected from 2 to 60 feet above the ground. The cavity has an entrance hole 2 inches in diameter and the depth of the cavity may be from 10 to 36 inches deep. The birds will often make repairs to an old nest hole and reuse the nest.

The female usually lays six to eight white eggs. Both birds share the incubation, each feeding the other while it is on the nest. The birds display affection toward each other throughout the breeding season. After two weeks of incubation, the young birds are fed by regurgitation. The adult bird swallows the food and, when it is soft enough for the young, the adult bill is inserted into the baby's throat and the food pumped out. Young flickers in the nest become very noisy. If the nest tree is tapped, a loud buzzing sound can be heard from inside. The young leave the nest and fly about four weeks after hatching.

Feeding Habits
Unlike other woodpeckers, the flicker commonly feeds on the ground, probing for ants with its long, barbed tongue. Ants are an important part of the diet — flickers have been known to consume up to 5,000 ants at a feeding. Flickers also eat caterpillars, grubs and insects, and 25 percent of their diet consists of native fruits.

Plants for food and shelter include:
Serviceberries (*Amelanchier* spp.) (see page 156)
Hackberries (*Celtis* spp.) (see page 161)
Dogwoods (*Cornus* spp.) (see page 163)
Wild strawberry (*Fragaria virginiana*) (see page 166)
Pines (*Pinus* spp.) (see page 178)
Wild cherries (*Prunus* spp.) (see page 182)
Oaks (*Quercus* spp.) (see page 183)
Sumacs (*Rhus* spp.) (see page 185)
Viburnums (*Viburnum* spp.) (see page 193)

A common flicker at its nest hollow in a saguaro cactus (Carnegiea gigantea).

A male red-bellied woodpecker eating
the small red fruits of the tomatillo (Physalis ixocarpa).

RED-BELLIED WOODPECKER

Melanerpes carolinus

The male red-bellied woodpecker is a handsome bird, with its black-and-white barred back and wings, and scarlet head and nape. The female has a scarlet nape only. This woodpecker is sometimes called "zebra-back" or "zebra bird" because of the pattern and coloration of its feathers.

A noisy and conspicuous bird, the red-bellied woodpecker often visits parks and gardens. The birds have a repertoire of various churring, chattering calls, including a powerful and deliberate "chuck-chuck-chuck" descending in pitch.

Habitat

The red-bellied woodpecker prefers farmland woodlots and hedgerows, bottomland, swamps, mixed coniferous-deciduous woods and shade trees in suburban yards.

Migration and Winter Range

Usually a non-migratory permanent resident, the red-bellied woodpecker sometimes wanders outside its normal breeding range.

Breeding Range

This woodpecker breeds from southeastern Minnesota to Connecticut and south to southern Florida and western Texas.

Breeding Behavior

The red-bellied woodpecker becomes especially noisy during the breeding season as it selects a suitable nesting site.

Nesting

Dead trees or deciduous trees with softer wood, such as elm, maple, sycamore, poplar or willow, are usually selected for nesting. They may also nest in utility poles and fenceposts. A cavity 10 to 12 inches deep is excavated, usually less than 40 feet above ground. Both sexes assist in excaving the cavity and its 2-inch-diameter entrance hole. Manmade nest boxes may also be used.

The female lays four or five white eggs, which are incubated for 12 days by both sexes. Both sexes feed and care for the young, which leave the nest when 24 to 26 days old. Two or three broods may be raised in the South, while one brood is usual in the northern limits of the red-bellied woodpecker's range.

Feeding Habits

The red-bellied woodpecker eats wood-boring insect larvae as well as ants, beetles, grasshoppers and other insects. It also eats corn, beechnuts, pine seeds, acorns and fruits.

Plants for food and shelter include:
Dogwoods (*Cornus* spp.) (see page 163)
Cedars (*Juniperus* spp.) (see page 168)
Red mulberry (*Morus rubra*) (see page 171)
Bayberries (*Myrica* spp.) (see page 173)
Virginia creeper (*Parthenocissus quinquefolia*) (see page 175)
Pines (*Pinus* spp.) (see page 178)
Wild cherries (*Prunus* spp.) (see page 182)
Oaks (*Quercus* spp.) (see page 183)
Common blackberry (*Rubus allegheniensis*) (see page 187)
Elderberries (*Sambucus* spp.) (see page 188)
Fox grape (*Vitis vulpina*) (see page 194)

A male red-bellied woodpecker at his nest hollow.

Two red-headed woodpeckers
jostle playfully while eating the fruits
of Allegheny serviceberry (<u>Amelanchier laevis</u>).

RED-HEADED WOODPECKER

Melanerpes erythrocephalus

Usually very shy but amusing birds to watch, red-headed woodpeckers are often active and playful, chasing each other or drumming on dead limbs or tin roofs. When examining a tree for wood-boring insects, it will rap the timber sharply, then turn its head and listen carefully before deciding whether to continue drilling.

The species name is from the Greek *erythros,* red, and *kephale,* head, and refers to the bird's strikingly colored, entirely red head. With its bluish-black wings and tail and its white underparts, it is a conspicuously handsome bird. Other common names of this bird make reference to the striking plumage, including "red-head," "white wing," "flag bird," "patriotic bird," "shirt-tail bird" and "white-shirt". Red-headed woodpeckers range from 8½ to 9½ inches long.

Once a common bird throughout its range, the red-headed woodpecker has suffered through the clearing of dead trees required for nesting and the introduction of the European starling, which aggressively competes for the remaining nesting places. Many red-headed woodpeckers were shot over the years by fruit growers after the birds launched raids on cultivated fruit.

Habitat
The red-headed woodpecker inhabits open deciduous woods, farmlands with scattered trees, old orchards and suburban areas. The birds are uncommon in much of their range and populations are often very local.

Migration and Winter Range
In the extreme northern and western part of their range, the birds migrate south or southeast in autumn, wintering from the Great Lakes to the southern limits of the breeding range.

Breeding Range
Breeding range is from southern Saskatchewan east to New York and south to Texas, the Gulf Coast and Florida.

Breeding
A noisy bird in the breeding season, the red-headed woodpecker makes a variety of sounds, including a loud, rolling "ker-r-ruck, ker-r-ruck."

Nesting
A live tree, dead stub, utility pole or fence post is selected for a nest site in May. Both sexes excavate the hole — one bird excavates, then calls the other, who returns before the first leaves. The nest is located 8 to 80 feet above the ground and takes several days to complete. It has a 1¾-inch-diameter entrance and an 8- to 24-inch-deep cavity.

The female lays four to six round, glossy, white porcelain-like eggs. Both sexes share incubation for two weeks. In the southern parts of its range, the red-headed woodpecker may raise two broods.

Feeding Habits
The red-headed woodpecker has evolved flycatcher-like traits, and spends much of its time darting out into the air to catch flying insects. In one record of an adult bird feeding young, it was calculated that insects were being consumed at the rate of 600 per hour.

The bird eats fewer larvae and grubs than other woodpeckers. June bugs, weevils, ants, spiders, grasshoppers, crickets and caterpillars make up 50 percent of the bird's diet and give it an economic status in rural areas. The birds also eat corn, fruits and berries, and may visit feeding stations for seeds and suet.

Plants for food and shelter include:
Serviceberries (*Amelanchier* spp.) (see page 156)
Dogwoods (*Cornus* spp.) (see page 163)
Wild strawberry (*Fragaria virginiana*) (see page 166)
Red mulberry (*Morus rubra*) (see page 172)
Wild cherries (*Prunus* spp.) (see page 182)
Oaks (*Quercus* spp.) (see page 183)
Blackberries (*Rubus* spp.) (see page 187)
Elderberries (*Sambucus* spp.) (see page 188)

A red-headed woodpecker looks for wood-boring insects on the trunk of an American beech (Fagus grandifolia).

*An acorn woodpecker at his acorn
store in a California black oak (Quercus kelloggii).*

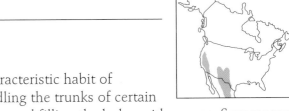

ACORN WOODPECKER

Melanerpes formicivorus

With its harlequin face, white eyes and red crown, the boldly patterned, 9-inch acorn woodpecker is a handsome bird. These birds are especially noisy in spring, calling loudly to mates with a "ja-cob, ja-cob" or "wake-up, wake-up." The birds also drum against dead limbs and noisily chase each other through the treetops.

The common name "acorn woodpecker" refers to the bird's fondness for acorns, which are the most important item in its diet. Some ornithologists call the bird the "California acorn-storing woodpecker," referring to the bird's characteristic habit of riddling the trunks of certain trees and filling the holes with acorns. Sycamores, black oaks, yellow pines and utility poles are usually selected. One old oak in California, with a trunk about 40 feet tall and 3 feet across, was completely covered with acorn holes, estimated to number 20,000 in all. The acorn woodpecker is also known as the "California woodpecker" because of its conspicuous presence in that state. Other names include "ant-eating woodpecker" and "Mearns' woodpecker."

Habitat

The acorn woodpecker is one of the most common and conspicuous birds throughout its range. It is found in valleys, foothills and oak and pine-oak canyons.

Migration and Winter Range

The acorn woodpecker is resident year-round throughout its range.

Breeding Range

Breeding range is from southwest Oregon south through California (west of the Sierra Nevadas), throughout Arizona, New Mexico and western Texas, and south to Colombia in Central America.

Breeding

Where food is plentiful, acorn woodpeckers live in loose colonies of 12 to 15 birds. The birds communally defend their territory. They also communally excavate the nest holes, incubate the eggs and care for the young.

Nesting

Both sexes excavate the nest hollow. Oak trees, sycamores, cottonwoods, willows and, more rarely, utility poles are excavated for nesting. The entrance hole is perfectly round, about 1¼ inches in diameter, with the chamber 8 to 24 inches deep. Usually nest holes are 12 to 60 feet above the ground.

The female lays three to four white eggs between April and May, which are incubated communally for about 2 weeks. Two and possibly three broods may be raised in one season.

Feeding Habits

Acorn woodpeckers harvest and store acorns in autumn, when they are plentiful. Acorns are an important food source from fall into spring. The storage holes made by a colony are reused each year and are not deep enough to damage the tree.

During the summer months, insects make up 30 percent of the bird's diet. Grasshoppers, ants, flies and beetles, along with fruit including cherries, apples and figs, are eaten. In June and July, the birds drill holes in the branches of oak trees and eat the sap.

Plants for food and shelter include:
Wild cherries (*Prunus* spp.) (see page 182)
Oaks (*Quercus* spp.) (see page 183)
Elderberries (*Sambucus* spp.) (see page 188)

This acorn woodpecker chooses a telegraph pole to excavate a nest hollow.

*A downy woodpecker eating the berries
of Virginia creeper (Parthenocissus quinquefolia).*

DOWNY WOODPECKER

Picoides pubescens

The most familiar bird in the woodpecker family, the downy woodpecker is also the smallest and tamest eastern woodpecker. When civilization spread across North America, the downy woodpecker adapted and is now commonly seen in settled areas. It is a small, black-and-white woodpecker with a broad white stripe that runs down the center of its back and a short, stubby bill. A distinguishing mark of the adult male downy woodpecker is the small, bright red patch on the back of his head.

Habitat
Downy woodpeckers are found in parks and gardens, farms, orchards, woodlots and open mixed deciduous and coniferous woodland. They prefer deciduous trees with shrubs nearby.

Migration and Winter Range
Downy woodpeckers usually remain in their breeding grounds all year, though a few birds move south from the northern limit of their range in autumn or early winter. Birds also move from higher to lower altitudes.

Breeding Range
The downy woodpecker breeds across most of the United States, ranging from southeastern Alaska across southern Canada to Newfoundland, and south to southern California, central Arizona and central Texas and along the Gulf Coast and Florida.

Breeding Behavior
In late winter, both sexes begin drumming, and males and females seek each other out for courtship. The male displays to the female by spreading his wings while facing the female on a limb. Another male may interrupt, courting the same female. Once the female has chosen the successful suitor, the search for a nest site begins. Some downy woodpeckers have remained paired for years.

Nesting
These woodpeckers nest in dead tree trunks or decaying branches. Nest boxes are also used. A gourd-shaped nesting cavity is chiseled out, and some wood chips are left on the floor.

The female lays four or five white eggs, which are incubated by both parents for 12 days. The young are fed insects and leave the nest when 21 to 24 days old. The young follow the parents around until they learn to find food for themselves. During the winter months, individual downy woodpeckers often join mixed flocks of chickadees, nuthatches and titmice.

Feeding Habits
Downy woodpeckers are particularly valuable in old orchards, since wood-boring larvae of insects that damage trees are a favorite food. The bird taps at a branch and lays its head along the limb, apparently listening to the movement of borers under the bark. The birds quickly chisel the bark and extract the borer. Beetles, moths, ants, spiders, snails, aphids and scale insects are included in the bird's diet. Wild fruits are also eaten.

Plants for food and shelter include:
Serviceberries (*Amelanchier* spp.) (see page 156)
Dogwoods (*Cornus* spp.) (see page 163)
Wild strawberry (*Fragaria virginiana*) (see page 166)
Virginia creeper (*Parthenocissus quinquefolia*) (see page 175)
Oaks (*Quercus* spp.) (see page 183)
Mountain ashes (*Sorbus* spp.) (see page 189)

A downy woodpecker searching for borers.

ASH-THROATED FLYCATCHER

Myiarchus cinerascens

The ash-throated flycatcher is a comparatively silent and shy flycatcher. The 8-inch bird has a pale sulphur-yellow belly, whitish throat, grayish-brown back, cinnamon-rust primaries and tail feathers and two wing bars. The bird's principal call notes includes a clear "huit, huit" repeated several times, and low whistled notes of "hip" and "ha-whip."

The genus name is from the Greek myia, fly, and archos, king or ruler. The species name means "turning ashy," referring to the ashy chest plumage.

An ash-throated flycatcher at his nest hollow in a Fremont cottonwood (Populus fremontii).

Habitat

The ash-throated flycatcher is found in western deciduous woods, mesquite and saguaros. The bird's favorite haunts are apparently not affected by climatic conditions, as it summers from altitudes of 9,000 feet in the southern Sierra Nevadas to below sea level in the broiling heat of Death Valley in California.

In Arizona the ash-throated flycatcher favors dense mesquite thickets in creek bottoms, oak canyons and dry brush. Along the Sacramento River in California, the flycatchers are found in sycamores, valley oaks, live oaks and dead trees close to the river. Farther east open woodland, pinyon-juniper forests and sagebrush are favored haunts.

Migration and Winter Range

The ash-throated flycatcher arrives on its nesting grounds between March and May. The birds winter in southern Arizona, California, Mexico and Central America. They move to their winter homes between late September and mid-October, where they linger among denser thickets of vegetation along streams or desert washes.

Breeding Range

The ash-throated flycatcher has a breeding range extending from southwestern Oregon and eastern Washington to southern Idaho, southwestern Wyoming, Colorado, New Mexico and north and central Texas to Baja California and Mexico.

Breeding

The ash-throated flycatchers arrive on their breeding grounds from mid-March in southern Texas to early May in Washington.

Nesting

Because of the shortage of protective concealing foliage in much of the bird's range, the ash-throated flycatcher has become a cavity nester, but still builds an elaborate nest inside the cavity. The bird usually selects a natural cavity or knothole in a mesquite, ash, oak, cottonwood, sycamore or juniper tree. In San Bernardino County in California, holes left by broken branches of Mojave yuccas and Joshua trees are frequently used. Old woodpecker holes are also used, and the flycatchers sometimes evict woodpeckers from their newly constructed cavity. The birds often nest near human habitation, using nest boxes, an empty mail box, old tin cans, a drainpipe or holes in a dead tree or post.

If the selected cavity is too large, the birds fill the extra space with grasses, rootlets, weed stems and dried animal dung. The cup-shaped nest is made of rabbit, deer or cattle fur on a foundation of grass. The nest is usually built 20 feet or less above the ground.

This ash-throated flycatcher forages for insects in a blue palo verde (Cercidium microphyllum).

The eggs are not the normal white eggs of a cavity-nester, but have the camouflage markings of a foliage-nesting bird, indicating that the species has adopted cavity-nesting comparatively recently. The female usually lays four or five eggs and incubates them for 15 days. The female often leaves the nest for several hours at a time in the warmer parts of the day, but remains close by the nest. Both parents feed the young with insects, often preparing the softer portions of larger insects by removing the wings and legs before feeding.

The young leave the nest when 16 or 17 days old and follow the parents around for some time, begging for food with quivering wings until they can care for themselves.

Feeding Habits

Unlike most flycatchers, the ash-throated does not usually return to the same perch after sallying forth to capture insects on the wing. The bird also forages among low shrubs eating caterpillars, grasshoppers, moths, bees, wasps and other insects. The birds also eat some berries.

Plants for food and shelter include:
Elderberries (*Sambucus* spp.) (see page 188)

This black phoebe eats the fruit
of blue elderberry (Sambucus caerulea).

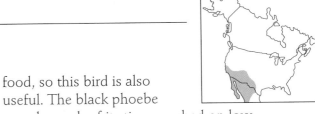

BLACK PHOEBE

Sayornis nigricans

The black phoebe is the only black-breasted North American flycatcher. The color pattern of the bird is like a junco's, although its posture and behavior mark it as a flycatcher. This 6- to 7-inch bird is slate-black with a white belly and outer tail feathers. Characteristic of the black phoebe are its erect posture and its habit of moving its tail in spasmodic jerks when perched. It is unusually gentle and unobtrusive for a member of the tyrant flycatcher family.

Seemingly unperturbed by human activity, the black phoebe has become a common suburban garden bird. Houseflies are a favorite food, so this bird is also useful. The black phoebe spends much of its time perched on low tree branches, stones, fenceposts or other low vantage points from which it sallies forth like a large butterfly, sailing in eccentric arcs to snap at insects.

The black phoebe's song is a repetition of "fi-bee, fi-bee," with the first two notes rising and the last two dropping in pitch. This song gives the bird its common name. The bird's common call is a sharp "tsip" or "chee," which it makes constantly in flight and whenever it alights.

Habitat

The black phoebe is partial to water and is usually found on the edge of mountain streams, irrigation ditches, ponds and lake banks. A watering trough will also attract it, and the bird is common in barnyards. In winter months it is often seen in city parks and gardens throughout its range.

Migration and Winter Range

The black phoebe is a year-round resident throughout its range.

Breeding Range

The black phoebe's breeding range is from California, southern Nevada, southwest Utah, Arizona, southern New Mexico and central Texas, south to Baja California, through Mexico and the Central and South American highlands to Argentina. The bird sometimes strays into Oregon and British Columbia, and it is a local resident in the bottom of the Grand Canyon in Arizona.

Breeding

The black phoebe is a solitary species, and apart from mated pairs in the breeding season is always seen alone. The birds often remain in their territory throughout the year, and return to the same nest site year after year.

Nesting

For nesting, the birds require a sheltered rock face or timber walls in the vicinity of a ready supply of mud. Bridges are favorite nesting sites, as are niches in the rocks along mountain streams and the rafters of barns. The nest is built of mud pellets, which are plastered to the vertical surface and mixed with grass, forming a strongly built cup 4 1/2 inches in diameter. The nest is lined with plant fiber and feathers.

The female lays three to six faintly speckled white eggs. She incubates the eggs for 15 to 17 days. The young leave the nest after about three weeks. Two or three broods may be raised in one year.

Feeding Habits

Insects form the bulk of the black phoebe's diet. The bird usually flies down from its perch and often dives towards water, almost skimming the surface, its bill clicking as it snaps at insects. Occasionally the bird will dip its belly beneath the water to bathe in flight. Large insects are taken back and tapped against the perch until they die. The bird also sometimes eats elderberries and pepperberries.

Plants for food and shelter include: Elderberries (*Sambucus* spp.) (see page 188)

The black phoebe is attracted to water.

A purple martin attracted to
big bluestem (Andropogon gerardii).

Purple Martin

Progne subis

The purple martin is the largest swallow in North America, and is noted for its apartment-style nesting in man-made community houses. Indians hung hollow gourds to be used as nesting sites by purple martins. Some people still hang gourds for martins, stringing them from trees or on a crosspiece. Many others put up multiroomed martin houses on tall poles.

Try building your own martin house. Martin houses can be built with compartments to accommodate 10 to 30 nesting pairs. Each room requires a 2¹/₂-inch-diameter entrance hole. The house should be placed on a pole 15 to 20 feet above ground, in a lawn or open area. But be warned— a martin house also provides ideal conditions for English sparrows and starlings. Many martin fanciers vigilantly remove sparrow or starling nests throughout the season.

The purple martin male is a glossy blue-black. Females and immature males are gray to white below and duller above. The bird's voice consists of loud and cheerful chirping notes and gurgles.

Habitat
Purple martins prefer open woodland, agricultural land, towns and lawns near lakes or ponds.

Migration and Winter Range
A summer resident, the purple martin arrives in North America from late January through April. In late August it begins the southward migration to winter in South America.

Breeding Range
Purple martins range across the United States, from southern Canada south to central Mexico, the West Indies and southern Florida.

Breeding Behavior
Males are usually the first to arrive at nesting sites and begin chirping loudly and defending a room in a martin house. The female arrives and chooses a room. The birds may nest alone, but usually nest communally.

Nesting
Both sexes gather material for their nests, and use grass, leaves, twigs, feathers and mud to line the martin house compartments. The female lays three to eight white eggs between March and July and incubates them for 15 or 16 days. The male guards the nest when the female is absent. When 28 days old, the young leave the nest. Both parents assist in the feeding and care of the young.

In August or September when the young can fly, the martins abandon their nest boxes and prepare for the southward migration. They gather in huge flocks in the evening, with as many as 100,000 birds in a roosting flock.

Feeding Habits
The purple martin takes almost all its food on the wing, consuming flying insects including flies, mosquitos and dragonflies. Enormous quantities of insects are fed to the young at the nest — parents may return to the nest as often as 205 times in a four-hour period. Because of their huge appetite for insects, purple martins are very beneficial to home gardeners and farmers.

Plants for food and shelter include:
Big bluestem (*Andropogon gerardii*) (see page 157)

Purple martins nest in man-made community houses.

A blue jay alights on a
red oak (Quercus rubra) to eat the acorns.

BLUE JAY

Cyanocitta cristata

A handsome, raucous, inquisitive bird, the blue jay is always active and usually noisy. Mostly blue above and gray below, with white patches on the wings and tail, this 11- to 12½-inch bird has a black necklace and a conspicuous blue crest. It is a strikingly beautiful bird and one of the most familiar birds of North America. The bird's call is a defiant "jay-jay," often sounded in a discordant chorus with other jays. The birds act as lookouts for danger, setting up a commotion of cries when a cat, snake, owl or other enemy is spotted. Blue jays also have an extensive repertoire of imitations and mimic other bird calls. In addition, the birds have a soft, sweet whisper song, a muted, barely audible piece sung only from a concealed perch.

Habitat
Originally a cautious bird of the oak forests, blue jays have become common in city parks and suburban yards, preferring areas with oak trees.

Migration and Winter Range
Although seen throughout the year, local populations seem to move south during winter and are replaced by birds from farther north, travelling in large, loose flocks in spring and fall.

Breeding Range
The blue jay's breeding range is east of the Rocky Mountains from southern Canada to Mexico.

Breeding
During the breeding period, blue jays are uncharacteristically quiet until the young birds have fledged. During courtship and at the nest, the male feeds the female selected morsels.

Nesting
Both sexes help to construct the nest. The birds break twigs and small branches from trees to build a bulky, untidy structure lined with grasses in the crotch of a tree or on a limb. Usually nests are 10 to 15 feet from the ground, although they can be placed as high as 50 feet.

Females lay four to six brown, spotted eggs and incubate them for 16 to 18 days. The devoted male feeds the female at the nest, approaching it quietly at a lower level and warily hopping in a spiral up to the nest. The young leave the nest when they are 17 to 21 days old. The adults fearlessly defend their nest and young by dive-bombing and pecking intruders.

Feeding Habits
The blue jay is omnivorous, eating insects, fruits, grain, eggs or young birds. Acorns and beechnuts are favorite foods when in season. Acorns are often stored in the ground, many of which sprout, helping to replant forests.

Plants for food and shelter include:
Sunflowers (*Helianthus* spp.) (see page 166)
Hollies (*Ilex* spp.) (see page 167)
Red mulberry (*Morus rubra*) (see page 172)
Wild cherries (*Prunus* spp.) (see page 182)
Oaks (*Quercus* spp.) (see page 183)
Sumacs (*Rhus* spp.) (see page 185)
Blackberries (*Rubus* spp.) (see page 187)
Blueberries (*Vaccinium* spp.) (see page 191)
Viburnums (*Viburnum* spp.) (see page 193)
Wild grapes (*Vitis* spp.) (see page 194)

A blue jay eats acorns from a southern red oak (Quercus falcata).

Steller's jay often nests in fir trees, including
the grand fir (Abies grandis), and eats seeds from the cones.

STELLER'S JAY

Cyanocitta stelleri

The Steller's jay is unmistakable with its large size (11½ inches), handsome blue to blue-black coat and prominent crest. It is the only crested jay in the West. Usually an extremely shy bird, it adapts to humans around picnic areas or at feeding stations, where it readily accepts handouts. Birds often roam together in small flocks.

Intelligent, cunning, alert and inquisitive, the Steller's jay is also a noisy, boisterous bird. Its low-pitched raucous screams and calls echo through the woodlands warning of an approaching intruder. It may imitate the screams of the golden eagle or red-tailed hawk, or call with a harsh rasping "shack-shack-shack-shack" or a mellow "klook-klook-klook."

The bird's genus name is from the Greek *kyanos,* blue, and *kitta,* meaning chattering bird. The species is named for Georg Steller, a German zoologist who obtained the first specimen for science in 1741 on the Alaskan coast.

Habitat

Steller's jay is a well-known bird throughout its range in coniferous and mixed forests, picnic grounds, orchards and gardens.

Migration and Winter Range

Steller's jay is resident year-round throughout its range. In fall and winter, small numbers of the birds often descend to the lowlands.

Breeding Range

The bird's breeding range extends from the Rocky Mountains west to the Pacific coast, from coastal Alaska south through California and Mexico to El Salvador and the highlands of Nicaragua, and east to southwestern Texas.

Breeding

The Steller's jay becomes very secretive during the breeding season. While nest-building or attending the nest they become silent and slip through the foliage, vanishing from sight.

Nesting

Both sexes share in nest-building. A large, well-made structure is constructed from twigs, cemented with mud and lined with rootlets and pine needles. The nest is commonly built in a spruce or fir tree (often a Douglas fir), usually 8 to 40 feet above the ground, but also as high as 100 feet or more. The nests are usually well concealed in dense conifers and, because of the secretive nature of the parents, are rarely found.

The female lays three to five greenish, spotted eggs and incubates them (mostly by herself) for about 18 days. The full-grown young join their parents in family groups for some time after leaving the nest, breaking up in early fall and scattering through the forest.

Feeding Habits

Vegetable food makes up over 70 percent of the Steller's jay's natural diet. Acorns and pine seeds are their main food source, and they sometimes raid the acorn woodpecker's stored supply. In winter they visit bird feeders and are attracted to sunflower seeds, corn and cracked nuts.

Steller's jay also eats beetles, grasshoppers, crickets, caterpillars, spiders, moths and sometimes snakes, and has a reputation for raiding other birds' nests and eating the chicks and eggs. Native fruits and some cultivated fruits are also in its diet, but the bird is too shy to visit the more established orchard areas.

Plants for food and shelter include:
Dogwoods (*Cornus* spp.) (see page 163)
Wild strawberry (*Fragaria virginiana*) (see page 166)
Pines (*Pinus* spp.) (see page 178)
Wild cherries (*Prunus* spp.) (see page 182)
Oaks (*Quercus* spp.) (see page 183)
Western raspberry (*Rubus leucodermis*) (see page 187)
Elderberries (*Sambucus* spp.) (see page 188)

A Steller's jay eats seeds from the cones of California red fir (Abies magnifica).

*A gray-breasted jay (Mexican race) eating
fallen acorns from Gambel oak (Quercus gambelii).*

GRAY-BREASTED JAY

Aphelocoma ultramarina

Also called the Mexican jay and Arizona jay, this large (11- to 13-inch) blue-gray jay without a crest is possibly the most interesting bird of the crow family. Gray-breasted jays usually live in flocks of 6 to 20 birds throughout the year. In contrast to the secretive nature of other nesting jays, the gray-breasted jays are semi-communal in the breeding season. If an intruder comes near the nest the whole colony will join in the defense, noisily screaming at the enemy while twitching their tails and bobbing their heads.

If a snake, hawk, fox or cat is found in their territory, 30 or 40 birds from the surrounding area may bond together to loudly scold the intruder. The bird's alarm call is a loud "wheat, wheat, wack, wack-wack." Call notes include a high-pitched "werk-werk-werk."

Habitat

Gray-breasted jays live in oak and oak-pine forests 2,000 to 9,000 feet in elevation, only occasionally descending to the lower zones.

Migration and Winter Range

The gray-breasted jay is a resident bird year-round within its range.

Breeding Range

The bird's breeding range is southern Arizona, southwestern New Mexico, western Texas (Chisos Mountains) and south to central Mexico.

Breeding

Two adult pairs of the flock construct separate nests while the rest of the flock maintains a communal interest, bringing nesting material and helping to build and defend the nests. The non-breeding birds also later assist in feeding the young.

Nesting

The nests are usually built 15 to 25 feet above the ground in oak or occasionally pine trees. The birds construct a bulky, very conspicuous basket of coarse sticks and leafy oak twigs that is held in place by the branches' crooked shapes. The jays always break twigs from trees rather than picking them up from the ground. The basket is lined with a closely woven cup of rootlets, animal hair and fine grasses.

Four or five green eggs are laid between March and July and incubated for 18 days. Young leave the nest 24 to 25 days after hatching.

Feeding Habits

Acorns provide the bulk of the gray-breasted jay's diet, and they are often seen hopping around under oak trees searching for food. When a jay finds an acorn, he holds it between his two feet and raps it with his bill to open the shell. If there is an abundance of acorns, the birds hide them under rocks or ledges for future eating. Jays play a role in the reforesting of burned or cut-over lands by burying a great many acorns that they cannot eat. Some of these acorns are eaten at a later stage, but many are left or forgotten, and they then sprout and grow into mature trees.

Wild fruits, grasshoppers and other insects are added to the diet as are smaller birds eggs and young. In many picnic areas the gray-breasted jay becomes tame, accepting handouts of food. It also visits garden bird feeders for suet or bread.

Plants for food and shelter include:
Oaks (*Quercus* spp.) (see page 183)

Gray-breasted jays live in communal groups of 6 to 20 birds.

*Black-capped chickadees eating
the fruits of California wax myrtle (Myrica californica).*

BLACK-CAPPED CHICKADEE

Parus atricapillus

Because of its friendliness, fearlessness and cheerful song, the black-capped chickadee is one of America's best-known and best-loved birds. Chickadees are cheerful little birds (4³/₄ to 5³/₄ inches long) with gray backs, white underparts and a black bib and cap. This good-natured bird with its cheery "chick-a-dee-dee-dee" call note brings joy to the spirit. The bird obtains its common name from its coloration and its "chick-a-dee" call.

Habitat
Mixed hardwood-coniferous forests, woodlots and suburban gardens are the preferred habitat.

Migration and Winter Range
The bird is mostly a year-round resident in its range; winter range extends slightly southward.

In the winter months, chickadees rove the woods in small, loose flocks in defined territories. The flock is formed in late summer after the young have dispersed. A hierarchical pecking order may develop within the flock, with a pair that nested successfully on the territory outranking the fall arrivals. The dominant pair dominate all others of their own sex and take precedence when food is found or a roosting place is decided. There are usually six to ten birds, and a feeding territory is established and defended against adjacent flocks. At the end of winter the original breeding pair remains while the others disperse.

Breeding Range
The breeding range extends from central Alaska and southern Canada south to northwestern California, northeastern Nevada, central Utah, northern New Mexico, northeastern Oklahoma, central Missouri, southern Ohio, eastern Tennessee, western north Carolina, western Maryland and northern New Jersey.

Breeding Behavior
In late winter, the male chickadee begins to give his "fee-bee" song, which is heard more often as the males define their breeding territory and the winter flocks break up. The birds form breeding pairs and become more shy and retiring as they establish a nesting site.

Nesting
Normally the birds excavate a nest cavity in partially rotten wood. Old woodpecker holes, natural cavities or bird boxes are sometimes used. Birch or pine trees are commonly selected, and the birds often use a woodpecker hole made while drilling the tree for insects. The hole is enlarged, with the birds scattering the excavated wood chips away from the nest site.

The female lines the nest chamber with plant fiber, insect cocoons and animal fur. She then lays five to ten lightly spotted white eggs. Both parents incubate the eggs and feed the nestlings. The young leave the nest after 14 to 18 days and are fed by the parents for another ten days. They disperse after a few weeks.

Feeding Habits
The chickadee eats enormous quantities of insect pests including aphids, scale insects, millipedes and snails. About 30 percent of its diet is vegetable, including the seeds of conifers and wild fruits. In winter, chickadees readily visit feeding stations for sunflower seed and suet.

Plants for food and shelter include:
Serviceberries (*Amelanchier* spp.) (see page 156)
Birches (*Betula* spp.) (see page 159)
Sunflowers (*Helianthus* spp.) (see page 166)
Winterberry (*Ilex verticillata*) (see page 167)
Bayberries (*Myrica* spp.) (see page 173)
Pines (*Pinus* spp.) (see page 178)
Hemlocks (*Tsuga* spp.) (see page 190)
Viburnums (*Viburnum* spp.) (see page 193)

A black-capped chickadee eating insects in the foliage of Canada hemlock (Tsuga canadensis).

*A mountain chickadee eats insects from the
foliage of Arizona mountain ash (Sorbus dumosa).*

MOUNTAIN CHICKADEE

Parus gambeli

The 5- to 5³/₄-inch mountain chickadee resembles the black-capped chickadee except for its white eye stripe, which is missing during summer molt. The mountain chickadee's call is "chick-a-dee-a-dee-a-dee." The bird also has a soft whistled call, whose tune resembles the first three notes of "Three Blind Mice." The species name of the mountain chickadee honors William Gambel, a nineteenth-century California ornithologist.

Habitat

During the breeding season and for much of the year, the bird's favorite habitat is the coniferous mountain forest of up to 10,000 feet elevation.

Migration and Winter Range

The bird is resident year-round throughout its range. In fall and winter loose flocks venture down to the valleys and foothills to forage in oaks, cedars and pines.

Breeding Range

The mountain chickadee breeds at higher altitudes from southeast Alaska, British Columbia and southwestern Alberta south to northern Baja California, Arizona, New Mexico and southwestern Texas.

Breeding

The birds move to the coniferous forests of the mountains and the males establish breeding territories with their distinctive call. Breeding pairs are formed and a nest site is selected.

Nesting

The mountain chickadee is similar to the black-capped chickadee in nesting habits. Like the black-capped chickadee, the mountain chickadee builds its nest in a hole it has excavated in rotten wood, or uses a natural cavity or abandoned woodpecker hole. The nest is lined with fur or hair. The female lays seven to nine plain white or spotted eggs. Both parents incubate the eggs and feed the nestlings. The young leave the nest after 14 to 18 days and are fed by the parents for another ten days. After a few weeks, the young leave the breeding territory.

Feeding Habits

Like all chickadees, the mountain chickadee is an arboreal acrobat, hanging head-down as he investigates twigs for insects. The mountain chickadee will readily visit bird feeders for sunflower seeds or baby chick scratch feed.

This mountain chickadee eats the tasty seeds of the piñon pine (Pinus edulis).

Plants for food and shelter include:
Sunflowers (*Helianthus* spp.) (see page 166)
Pines (*Pinus* spp.) (see page 178)
Oaks (*Quercus* spp.) (see page 183)

TUFTED TITMOUSE

Parus bicolor

The largest of the titmice, the 6-inch tufted titmouse has similar feeding and nesting habits to the related black-capped chickadee. The tufted titmouse is a plainly colored bird with a gray back and whitish belly. The flanks beneath each wing are tinged with a rusty brown. The bird has a prominent pointed crest which is raised up when the titmousebecomes excited. When the bird feels aggressive, the crest is flattened against its head.

Tufted titmice eating hackberry fruits (Celtis occidentalis).

A friendly and sprightly bird, the tufted titmouse flits through the foliage searching for insects, always alert and inquisitive. Possibly the bird's most distinguishing feature is its voice, a loud whistled series of four to eight notes, "peto-peto-peto," which both sexes sing (males much more than females) throughout the year. The bird is more often heard than seen, and in spring and early summer the call is incessant.

Tufted titmice, like other titmice and chickadees, are members of the titmouse family (Paridae), from the Latin word *parus,* titmouse. Titmouse is from the Old Icelandic word *titr,* small, and *mase,* an Anglo-Saxon word for bird, which was corrupted to mouse.

Habitat

The tufted titmouse is common in woodlands and clumps of large shade trees in suburban parks and gardens.

Migration and Winter Range

The tufted titmouse is a year-round resident throughout its range.

Breeding Range

The bird is a permanent resident from southeastern Nebraska (Missouri River), southern Wisconsin, central New York, southern Ontario and southwestern Connecticut south through the Mississippi valley to the Gulf Coast, southeastern Texas and central Florida. This titmouse has been spreading northward in large numbers.

Breeding Behavior

In early spring the birds separate into breeding pairs. The birds mate for life.

Nesting

The birds nest in cavities in trees, nest boxes or abandoned woodpecker holes 3 to 90 feet above the ground. The birds show a preference for hollows in dogwood and chinquapin oak trees. The unneeded cavity space is filled with bark strips, grass and leaves before the cup-shaped nest of animal fur, moss and fibrous bark is built. Shed snakeskins and hair are commonly used for nest lining. The tufted titmouse has been reported pulling hair from a human head for its nest.

The female lays four to eight brown-dotted white eggs. The male feeds the incubating female away from the nest after calling her. The female covers the eggs before leaving the nest hollow. The female sits closely on the eggs for about two weeks, fearlessly guarding her clutch against intruders, and the young leave the nest hollow when about 18 days old. Both parents feed the young long after they leave the nest. The birds travel around as a family group in early summer before joining mixed flocks for fall and winter.

Feeding Habits

The tufted titmouse's feeding habits endear it to gardeners. Caterpillars form half the bird's diet. Wasps, beetles, weevils, cockroach eggs, spiders, scales and snails make up another 17 percent of the diet. Titmice also eat wild fruits and nuts. Acorns are a favorite food. The titmouse carries the acorn to a suitable limb; then, holding it with both feet, cracks the nut with a fast hammering of its bill.

Throughout fall and winter, titmice roam around in small flocks searching for food and are often joined by other birds including nuthatches, kinglets, chickadees and the occasional brown creeper. During migration, the titmice are often joined by yellow-rumped warblers, perhaps because of their knowledge of food-gathering. Titmice visit bird feeders for suet, sunflower seeds and nutmeats.

Plants for food and shelter include:
Serviceberries (*Amelanchier* spp.) (see page 156)
Hackberries (*Celtis* spp.) (see page 161)
Sunflowers (*Helianthus* spp.) (see page 166)
Red mulberry (*Morus rubra*) (see page 172)
Bayberries (*Myrica* spp.) (see page 173)
Pines (*Pinus* spp.) (see page 178)
Oaks (*Quercus* spp.) (see page 183)
Common blackberry (*Rubus alleghertiensis*) (see page 187)
Elderberries (*Sambucus* spp.) (see page 188)
Wild grapes (*Vitis* spp.) (see page 194)

A tufted titmouse eating a sunflower seed (Helianthus annuus).

A bridled titmouse in the branches of one of
its favorite trees, a silverleaf oak (Quercus hypoleucoides).

BRIDLED TITMOUSE

Parus wollweberi

Named for the black-and-white stripes on the head that resemble a horse's bridle, the bridled titmouse is the most beautiful of the crested titmice. This 5¼-inch bird has a small black bib, setting off his whitish belly and gray back. The call of the bridled titmouse is a rapid, squealing "chick-a-dee-dee-dee" or a high-pitched, repeated, quick "fee-bee."

Habitat
The bridled titmouse inhabits the evergreen-oak woodlands in mountain foothills up to 6,000 feet in elevation.

Migration and Winter Range
A resident bird throughout its range, the bridled titmouse roams in small flocks except during the breeding season. In winter, the bird may move down to wooded valleys and streamsides.

Breeding Range
The bridled titmouse breeds from central and southeastern Arizona and southwestern New Mexico south to the highlands of western Mexico.

Breeding
Little is known about breeding behavior.

Nesting
The birds nest in tree cavities, bird boxes or old woodpecker holes like the tufted titmouse. The female lays five to seven white eggs. Family groups are formed in late August after the young have left the nest. The young birds are taught to forage in oak trees before joining larger flocks in the fall.

Feeding Habits
Bridled titmice search out insects, insect eggs and larvae in oak branches and bark crevices.

Plants for food and shelter include:
Oaks (*Quercus* spp.) (see page 183)

A bridled titmouse foraging for insects in an Emory oak (Quercus emoryi).

Verdins at their nest in a western hackberry (<u>Celtis reticulata</u>).

VERDIN

Auriparus flaviceps

The verdin is a very small bird (4½ inches) with a yellow head and bright reddish-chestnut shoulder epaulettes. This bird has a very distinctive voice, calling in a loud, piping whistle which is quite out of proportion to its size. The common call is heard as a staccato "tsit, tsit, tsit." The common name "verdin" is derived from the French and means "yellow hammer." Verdins are seen to be very similar to the chickadee family in their habits.

Habitat
The verdin is a conspicuous resident of the low brushy desert scrub and mesquite thickets.

Migration and Winter Range
The bird is a year-round resident in its range.

Breeding Range
The verdin's range extends from southeastern California, southern Nevada, southwestern Utah, Arizona, New Mexico and Texas south to southern Baja California and central Mexico.

Breeding Behavior
Verdins are sociable during the winter months, roaming the desert in small family groups. They become shy and secretive during the breeding season, hiding in dense thickets.

Nesting
The birds build a large, round nest 3 to 10 feet above the ground in a desert shrub or cactus. Mesquite, hackberries, desert willow, palo verde, cholla and creosote bush are among the preferred shrubs. The ball-shaped nest is surprisingly large for such a small bird, measuring about 8 inches across. Usually placed at the end of a low limb in a conspicuous position, the nest is built of up to 2,000 thorny twigs, making it possibly the most labor-intensive nest of all North American birds. The thorny twigs are interlaced so that the free ends stick out from the nest, quill-like, protecting it from intruders. Coarse grass, leaves and plant stems are also used in the construction, and spiderweb is used to help bind the nest together. Spiderweb and plant fibers are used to block up holes in the nest. The nest is lined with grass, leaves and feathers, which are also bound together with spiderweb.

The resulting nest is a strong, compact structure able to withstand the fiercest sandstorms. The nest is well insulated and able to protect the young from desert heat. The nests last for many years after use and, along with the birds' habit of also building roosting or winter nests, may give a false impression of the verdin population in an area. The female lays three to six spotted, greenish eggs between March and June and incubates them for about 10 days. The young leave the nest at 21 days, returning to the nest to sleep.

The verdin builds separate winter homes for protection and warmth. The female's winter nest is better lined than the male's, and she may often use the breeding nest for her winter home. The male builds himself a smaller and less comfortable structure close by.

Feeding Habits
The verdin flits around like a chickadee, hanging upside down from a twig as it seeks out insects, and inspecting under leaves and in bark crevices. It eats insects and their larvae, as well as wild fruits and berries, including hackberries. Verdins sometimes nest 10 miles away from a water supply.

Plants for food and shelter include:
Hackberries (*Celtis* spp.) (see page 161)
Desert willow (*Chilopsis linearis*) (see page 162)
Opuntia cacti (*Opuntia* spp.) (see page 175)

A verdin eating from the flowers of an ocotillo (Fouquieria splendens).

A wrentit eating the fruits
of the snowberry (Symphoricarpos albus).

WRENTIT

Chamaea fasciata

The wrentit is the only species in the only family of birds that is solely North American (Muscicapidae), and it shows no close relationship to any of the other North American songbirds. It has a small, thick bill similar to a chickadee; in coloration, scolding behavior and long tail it resembles a wren. The wrentit is 6½ inches long, with a dark gray-brown back and cinnamon-brown belly. It has a streaked breast and very noticeable white eye.

An elusive bird, seldom showing itself in the open, wrentits keep to the security of low dense cover. The wrentit is a weak flier and usually it chooses to hop through the vegetation rather than navigate the air. Mature birds establish their territories of about 2½ acres and maintain them for most of their lives. It is not very often that wrentits can be observed because they will rarely leave the cover of a dense shrub.

The bird's call consists of six or more loud ringing whistles that are delivered in the same tone. Beginning slowly the notes of this call speed up and finally run together in a trill. When angry make a distinctive low-pitched chatter when angry.

Habitat
Wrentits are found in chaparral and other brushy growth and in suburban gardens and parks.

Migration and Winter Range
Wrentits are resident year-round within their established territory.

Breeding Range
The bird's breeding range is from western Oregon to northern Baja California.

Breeding Behavior
Defense of the territory is more vigorous during the breeding season. Pairs mate for life and live together all year long. The couple feed together, roost together and often preen each other. Their interest in each other is heightened as nest-building begins, when the male chases the female in rapid flight.

Nesting
A compact cup of coarse bark, grasses and plant fibers, bound with spiderweb, is built in a low dense shrub by both sexes. Three to five greenish-blue eggs are incubated for 15 to 16 days, with the young leaving the nest when 15 to 16 days old.

Feeding Habits
The wrentit eats insects on shrubs, feeding on caterpillars, ants, wasps, beetles, flies and spiders, as well as fruits, especially from low-growing bushes. Wrentits may visit feeding stations for bread crumbs.

Plants for food and shelter include:
Bayberries (*Myrica* spp.) (see page 173)
Common blackberry (*Rubus allegheniensis*) (see page 187)
Sumacs (*Rhus* spp.) (see page 185)
Elderberries (*Sambucus* spp.) (see page 188)
Twinberry (*Lonicera involucrata*) (see page 170)
Grasses (for nesting) (*Andropogon* spp.) (see page 157)

A wrentit feeding in the foliage of a birchleaf mountain mahogany (Cercocarpus betuloides).

A pair of white-breasted nuthatches
at their nest hollow in a sugar maple (Acer saccharum).

WHITE-BREASTED NUTHATCH

Sitta carolinensis

Dressed in its Confederate military uniform with plumage of gray-blue, the white-breasted nuthatch is the common nuthatch of the eastern United States. This 5³/4-inch bird also has a black cap and some rust under the tail.

The nuthatch, a relative of the chickadees and titmice, has adapted to a life on tree trunks. The bird usually feeds head-down, moving down tree trunks, a position that may help it find food overlooked by creepers and woodpeckers that forage going up the trunk. The nuthatch will also climb upward or sideways in its search for insects and nuts. In spring the bird's distinctive call is most noticeable, a nasal "yank, yank, yank." can be heard. This is supplemented with various other calls, including a soft "hit, hit" and the bird's song which is a hollow whistled "tew, tew, tew, tew" sound.

The common names "nuthatch" and "nuthacker" refer to the way the bird takes a nut in his claws and hacks at it with his bill or wedges it in the bark of a tree and hacks it with hard strokes to break it open.

Habitat
The white-breasted nuthatch is a common bird of mature deciduous woodlands, woodlots, mixed forests and large shade trees in residential areas.

Migration and Winter Range
The bird is resident year-round throughout its range.

Breeding Range
This nuthatch is found from southern Canada (British Columbia, Ontario and Nova Scotia) south to Florida, the Gulf Coast and southern Mexico. The bird is not found in most of the Great Plains of the United States.

Breeding Behavior
The birds mate for life and travel singly or in pairs throughout the winter. As spring approaches the male becomes more attentive to the female, often shelling seeds and tenderly feeding her or chasing her with short careening flights.

Nesting
The favorite nesting trees of the white-breasted nuthatch are native oaks, chestnuts and maple trees. A natural cavity, old woodpecker hole or nest box is selected 15 to 50 feet above the ground. The birds sometimes excavate a hollow in a decaying limb. The cavity is lined with shreds of bark, rootlets, animal fur, grasses and feathers.

The female lays 5 to 10 (usually 8) spotted, white eggs. Both parents incubate the eggs for 12 days and tend the young, who leave the nest in about two weeks. The birds stay together as a family group until winter, when they scatter to roam the woods, often in mixed flocks with chickadees, woodpeckers and the occasional brown creeper.

Feeding Habits
Insects form the bulk of the diet in spring and summer. The enormous quantities of caterpillars (including codling moth larvae), woodborers, aphids and other pests devoured make these valuable birds. They are quite tame and are regular visitors at bird feeders, enjoying sunflower seeds and suet.

The white-breasted nuthatch also eats acorns, beech-nuts, hickory nuts, sunflower seeds and corn. If food is plentiful, the nuthatch will store supplies in crevices in the bark of trees and, when icestorms freeze his normal supply of seeds and acorns, he will raid his larder.

Plants for food and shelter include:
Maples (*Acer* spp.) (see page 154)
Sunflowers (*Helianthus* spp.) (see page 166)
Pines (*Pinus* spp.) (see page 178)
Oaks (*Quercus* spp.) (see page 183)
Elderberries (*Sambucus* spp.) (see page 188)

This white-breasted nuthatch is foraging for insects in the rough bark of an Arizona white oak (Quercus arizonica).

RED-BREASTED NUTHATCH

Sitta canadensis

The red-breasted nuthatch is an extremely active little bird that spends most of its life in the northern coniferous forests. It differs from the white-breasted nuthatch (*Sitta carolinensis*) in its small size (4½ inches), chunkier appearance and red-brown underparts. This is the only North American nuthatch with a broad black line through the eye and a white line over it.

The red-breasted nuthatch has a high-pitched, nasal, slightly drawled call, "yna, yna." It also makes a high-pitched "ank, ank, ank."

A red-breasted nuthatch leaving
his favorite food tree, black spruce (Picea mariana).

Habitat

The bird's preferred habitats are the coniferous forests of balsam and spruce in the north and the fir forests of the Pacific coast. Ornamental conifers in suburban gardens are often used for nesting.

Migration and Winter Range

Considered a resident bird, the red-breasted nuthatch usually winters in the coniferous forests within its breeding range. Irregular migrations about every two years, which are thought to occur when northern cone-bearing trees fail to produce a crop of seeds, spur the birds to travel south, where they winter from southern Canada to northern Mexico and the Gulf Coast.

Breeding Range

The species name, *canadensis,* is Latin for Canada, and the bird has a breeding range from the Upper Yukon Valley, northern Manitoba, southern Québec and Newfoundland south to northern Minnesota, Michigan, Indiana, the mountains of New York and Massachusetts in the East south to the mountains of California, Arizona and New Mexico in the West, and from the Alleghenies to North Carolina. The bird in recent years has begun extending its range southward into eastern New York and Pennsylvania.

Breeding Behavior

Like the white-breasted nuthatch, the diminutive red-breasted nuthatch mates for life.

Nesting

In the breeding season both sexes excavate a nesting hole, usually in a dead coniferous tree, a stump or the dead wood of a living cottonwood or oak. The nest hollow has an entrance diameter of 1 1/2 inches, slants for 3 to 4 inches, then goes down vertically for about 4 inches. It is built 5 to 40 feet above ground level. The birds begin building by marking out the entrance hole with a series of small holes to form a circle before excavating. Deserted woodpecker holes and nest boxes are also used. A nest of gasses, rootlets, mosses and shreds of bark is built inside the excavated cavity.

The red-breasted nuthatch always smears pitch around the entrance hole. In the northern woods balsam fir and spruce pitch is preferred, while farther south pitch is gathered from pine trees. The pitch is carried on the tip of the bird's bill in little globules and tapped in place around the entrance. It is thought that the pitch may help keep insects, other birds and small predators from entering the hole. On entering the cavity the bird usually flies straight in to avoid the pitch. On rare occasions, birds have been found caught in the pitch and unable to escape.

The female lays four to seven spotted, white eggs, which are incubated by both sexes for 12 days. The young leave the nest after about three weeks.

A red-breasted nuthatch, suspended upside down, pries an insect from the bark of a sycamore tree (Platanus spp.).

Feeding Habits

When eating, the red-breasted nuthatch seems to prefer smaller outer branches rather than the tree trunk, hunting insects including beetles, woodborers, wood lice, caterpillars, spiders and scales. It often spirals around branch tips or darts out into the air and captures flying insects like a flycatcher.

Seeds of pines, spruces, firs and other conifers are the nuthatches' favorite food and, in parts of their range, (such as the North Adirondacks) the seed of the black spruce makes up almost the total diet. The bird often clings upside down to the extreme tips of branches while eating, and may often be seen hovering around cones searching for a convenient foothold from which to reach their food source. When food is plentiful, the birds store seeds in larders that are sometimes some distance from the food source.

The red-breasted nuthatch visits bird feeders for sunflower seeds, suet and chopped walnut and pecan kernels. It can be hand-tamed with patience.

Plants for food and shelter include:
Firs (*Abies* spp.) (see page 154)
Spruces (*Picea* spp.) (see page 177)
Pines (*Pinus* spp.) (see page 178)

A pygmy nuthatch eating insects
in the bark of a Ponderosa pine (Pinus ponderosa).

PYGMY NUTHATCH

Sitta pygmaea

The pygmy nuthatch is a noisy, gregarious little bird, most abundant in Ponderosa pines from 3,500 feet to 10,000 feet in elevation. The bird's species name is from the Latin pygmaeus, pygmy, referring to its small size—only 3½ inches long. This is the smallest of the North American nuthatches, and the western counterpart of the brown-headed nuthatch, which it resembles in habits and appearance.

Pygmy nuthatches are most conspicuous in fall and winter, when they travel through the woods flying in flocks of up to 100 birds. As they drift through the tops of the pine trees the birds keep in contact with their ceaseless chatter. They call each other with a high staccato "ti-di, ti-di, ti-di" and while in flight utter a soft "kit, kit, kit." The flock is often joined by other species of native birds including chickadees, titmice, warblers and the occasional smaller woodpecker or white-breasted nuthatch.

Habitat

The birds are found in Ponderosa pines in the Rockies, also in the juniper-pinon belt in Arizona and Ponderosa and other pines of the Pacific coast.

Migration and Winter Range

The bird is a year-round resident in mountainous areas. During winter, the pygmy nuthatch may drift to lower elevations and forage among oaks and in the juniper-pinon belt, returning to the pines in early spring.

Breeding Range

Pygmy nuthatches range from mountainous areas of the southern interior of British Columbia, western Montana and southwestern South Dakota south to northern Baja California, Arizona and the central plateau of Mexico to Morelos and Puebla.

Breeding Behavior

In spring, the nuthatches pair off from the winter flock.

Nesting

Both sexes help excavate a nest hollow, usually high up in a dead pine. Deserted woodpecker holes and nest boxes are also used. The birds dig with their bills and carry the wood chips and dust to the entrance, then shake the bill, flinging the contents to the wind. The nest cavity is 8 to 10 inches deep and is lined with shreds of bark, fur, feathers and bits of cocoons.

The female lays four to nine speckled, white eggs. Eggs are incubated for 14 days, mostly by the female. Both parents feed the young, who leave the nest after 22 days. The young travel with their parents as a family group, later joining other families to form the large flocks of fall and winter.

Pygmy nuthatches roost communally at night in cavities in trees or nest boxes. A hollow trunk of a dead Ponderosa pine reportedly held over 150 pygmy nuthatches roosting together.

Feeding Habits

The pygmy nuthatch moves with short hops, exploring branches, cones and outermost twigs for insects. It also feeds on bark insects, moving head-down as it descends the trunk in true nuthatch fashion or, on occasion, head-up. Insects account for over 80 percent of the pygmy nuthatch diet, including wasps, ants, grasshoppers, spiders, moths, caterpillars and beetles.

The pygmy nuthatch also eats pine seeds, cracking the nut with its powerful little bill to release the seed.

Plants for food and shelter include:
Firs (*Abies* spp.) (see page 154)
Pines (*Pinus* spp.) (see page 178)

A pygmy nuthatch at its nest hollow in a Ponderosa pine (Pinus ponderosa).

HOUSE WREN

Troglodytes aedon

The busybody of the avian world, the house wren is the most common wren in the eastern states. An aggressive, enterprising midget with boundless energy, it bustles around the garden examining each twig and leaf for insects and scolding all the time. The tyrant of the garden is possibly best known for his bubbling joyous song. House wrens are 4 3/4-inch brownish birds with barred wing and tail feathers.

The house wren's genus name, *troglodytes,* is Greek for "creeper into holes." The species name, *aedon,* is from Greek mythology: Aedon, the Queen of Thebes, was changed into a nightingale by Zeus, probably alluding to the bird's song. The bird's common name refers to its habit of residing near houses.

A house wren eating insects attracted to a twinberry (Lonicera involucrata).

Habitat

House wrens are found in woodland edges, city parks and residential areas.

Migration and Winter Range

The male birds arrive at their breeding grounds in the United States before the females. Although the birds do not travel in large flocks, their scolding chirrs announce their presence in the brush. The birds return to the previous year's breeding territory, an area usually between 1/4 and 3/4 acre in size.

In summer after breeding, the house wren leaves the vicinity of houses and becomes a shy, secretive bird, frequenting low bushy areas of woodlands. On migrating south these birds become forest birds, skulking among the undergrowth and rarely singing or coming near human habitation.

The bird winters from southern California east across the United States to Georgia, Virginia, southern Florida, the Gulf Coast and into Mexico.

Breeding Range

The bird has a breeding range from southern Canada south to northern Baja California, southeastern Arizona, northern Texas, northern Arkansas, Tennessee and northern Georgia.

Breeding Behavior

Almost immediately after his arrival, the male wren begins to sing, his whole body quivering as he delivers his rather loud melodious trill, rising and falling in pitch. The song is repeated constantly as part of territory formation and is delivered from two or three prominent perches within the territory.

Other acts of territory formation include making claim to all available nest sites. The nest hollows are cleaned of the previous year's nesting material and then refilled with twigs to form a foundation for new nests. During the initial cleaning stage, the house wren empties all nesting cavities in his territory and, if the contents include other birds and their eggs or young, these may be evicted. Birds as large as a flicker may be driven away by a wren dropping twigs into its cavity nest and covering its eggs.

The male wren patrols his territory, guarding against intruding males. Other males often enter adjoining territory to locate new nest sites or nest material, and are driven out by the defending male flying at the intruder with tail lowered and spread out.

Finally the female arrives and the male's song changes its tone to a harsher sound with high-pitched squeaks added. The song is accompanied by much wing and tail quivering at this point and, as the male becomes increasingly excited, his tail becomes more erect.. It is ordinarily in the lowered position.

Nesting

Wrens are well known for their odd nesting sites. Birds have been reported nesting in watering cans, old hats, flowerpots, old shoes, laundry pockets and other bizarre sites. They also favor nesting boxes.

The female begins inspecting the partially built nests and, once she has decided on a site, she lines the rough twigs with a soft lining of grass, fur and feathers. The house wren lays six to eight pinkish-white eggs, which the female incubates for about two weeks. Both parents feed the young, who leave the nest when about 17 days old. After leaving the nest the young stay with the parents for up to two weeks, when the female leaves to start a second brood.

If house wrens fail to raise a brood of their own or fail to obtain a mate, they may care for the young of other species. They have been recorded feeding the nesting adults and young of rose-breasted grosbeaks and English sparrows.

Feeding Habits

Spiders, grasshoppers, crickets, caterpillars, wasps, flies and many other insects make up 97 percent of the house wren's diet.

Plants for food and shelter include:
Poplars (*Populus* spp.) (see page 181)
Oaks (*Quercus* spp.) (see page 183)
Grasses (for nesting) (*Andropogon* spp.) (see page 157)

A house wren taking nesting material to a garden nest box.

CACTUS WREN

Campylorhynchus brunneicapillus

The cactus wren is the largest wren in the United States (8½ inches) and is the state bird of Arizona. The brown-backed bird has a conspicuous long, white eye stripe and heavily spotted breast.

The cactus wren is a common bird among thorny shrubs and cholla cactus in deserts and arid hillsides in the Southwest. This bird will also live in shade trees and open mesquite close to human habitation.

The bird's genus name, *camphylorhynchus,* is from the Greek, meaning curved beak. The species name, *brunneicapillus,* is from the Latin *brunneus,* brown, and *capillus,* hair, referring to the bird's streaked brown crown and back.

The cactus wren peering from an old woodpecker hole in a saguaro cactus (<u>Carnegiea gigantea</u>).

Habitat

The cactus wren frequents deserts and arid hillsides where thorny shrubs and trees offer secure nesting sites. It is also found in shade trees and near buildings in towns.

Migration and Winter Range

The cactus wren is resident year-round within its range.

Breeding Range

The bird's range is from southern California south to southern Baja California, southern Nevada, southwestern Utah, central and southern Arizona, southern New Mexico and central Texas to central Mexico.

Breeding Behavior

The male bird sings from a prominent perch to advertise his territory. The voice, although described as an unmusical deep, throaty, prolonged churring, is a sound evocative of the desert.

Nesting

Although cactus wrens are generally shy birds that skulk away when encountered rather than flying off, they have conspicuous, bulky nests. The nests are usually placed in the tops of cholla cacti, but mesquite, hackberry, yuccas or other prickly shrubs are also used. Backyard specimen cacti are appreciated as nesting sites, and some nests are placed in building cornices.

The nest is a football-shaped mass of coarse grass stems and fine plant fiber lined with feathers and soft plant fiber. The nest has an inside diameter of about 6 inches and an overall length of about 12 inches. It is placed horizontally with access via a long passageway up to 14 inches long, built of grass stems usually supported by a horizontal branch. In the many-branched chollas, the entrance is often woven between the spiky branches to achieve encircling support.

Nests not only are for breeding purposes but are used throughout the year for weather protection and evening roosting. If a storm erupts, the wren seeks shelter in his nest and, in one report, a nest was examined following a 2-inch rainstorm and was found to be quite dry inside. The wrens keep their nests in a state of good repair, rebuilding where necessary. Before the onset of cold weather, they reline their nests and replenish the straw entrance passageway. Each pair of wrens has several roosting nests, and new nests are built in spring and summer for breeding purposes. The number of nests in an area can give a false impression of population density.

The female lays three or four dotted, pinkish eggs, which are incubated for 16 days. Both parents share the nesting duties, bringing worms and insects to the young, who leave the nest after about three weeks. The young stay together for several weeks after leaving the nest, exploring their surroundings as a group before dispersing. The parents remain together throughout the year.

On leaving the nest, the young birds soon begin making their own individual roosting nests if sufficient sites are available. In an area that provides nesting opportunities, many nests may be seen in close proximity. In one record, 12 nests were built in a single mesquite bush. If the first brood is successful, the cactus wrens will build a new nest and raise a second brood, adding even more nests to the count.

Feeding Habits

The cactus wren usually searches for food among fallen leaves and twigs on the ground, carefully inserting its bill under an object and lifting one side as it peers for insects, then quickly snatching its prey. Beetles, ants, wasps, weevils, grasshoppers and spiders make up over 80 percent of the cactus wren diet. Cactus fruit, elderberries and other fruits are also eaten, and occasionally a small lizard or tree frog.

The birds visit bird feeders and are especially fond of young sweet corn (if the husks are stripped off) and pieces of raw apple.

Plants for food and shelter include:
Saguaro (*Carnegiea gigantea*) (see page 160)
Hackberries (*Celtis* spp.) (see page 161)
Opuntia cacti, including cholla (*Opuntia* spp.) (see page 175)
Sumacs (*Rhus* spp.) (see page 185)
Elderberries (*Sambucus* spp.) (see page 188)
Soaptree yucca (*Yucca elata*) (see page 194)

A cactus wren attracted to ocotillo (Fouquieria splendens).

A mated pair of blue-gray gnatcatchers
at their nest in live oak (<u>Quercus virginiana</u>).
The male assists the female (below) in feeding the nestlings.

BLUE-GRAY GNATCATCHER

Polioptila caerulea

Gnatcatchers are small active birds with thin bills, members of the Old World Warbler family Sylviidae (from the Latin *sylva,* a woods). The blue-gray gnatcatcher is often described as a tiny (4½-inch) mockingbird, with its blue-gray back and wings, white breast and belly and long tail, which is often cocked like a wren's. A fidgeting midget, the gnatcatcher is constantly flicking its tail upward or jerking it from side to side as it forages for insects in the upper branches of tall trees.

The bird's common call, which is heard constantly as it forages for food and tends the nest, is a thin "ting" like the twang of a banjo string. The gnatcatcher's habit of constantly calling as it works through the trees makes it easy for the birderscaper to spot him.

The gnatcatcher's genus name, *Polioptila,* is from the Greek *polios,* gray, and *ptilon,* feathers. The species name, caerulea, is Latin for blue.

Habitat

These gnatcatchers prefer deciduous woodland, live oaks, chaparral and piñon-juniper chaparral.

Migration and Winter Range

The birds winter from Virginia along the Atlantic Coast south into Mexico, Cuba and Guatemala.

Breeding Range

The blue-gray gnatcatcher ranges from northern California, Utah, eastern Nebraska, southern Wisconsin, southern Ontario and New York south to central Mexico.

Breeding Behavior

In common with many of the smaller bird species there seems to be no definable courtship ritual. The male birds defend a territory with extremely active fidgeting, bloodless combat and constant chattering and singing. A mate is selected in a short time and breeding commenced.

Nesting

The mated pair construct their beautiful nest together. Apart from hummingbirds' nests, this is the daintiest nest in the woodlands. The nest is usually on a horizontal branch, often in an oak. In South Carolina, the gnatcatchers prefer live oaks, while in Florida and Alabama scrub oaks are preferred. A cup-shaped nest of plant fibers bound together with spiderweb is lined with bark strips, fine grass and feathers. Lichen is fastened to the outside of the nest with spiderweb or caterpillar silk, giving the nest the appearance of a lichen-covered knot on a limb. Because the birds are so active and noisy, even during nest-building, it is often easy to find the location of a nest.

The female lays four to five pale blue eggs, most of them spotted with red-brown, and both sexes share the incubation for about 13 days. The nestlings are fed small insects, and leave the nest after 10 or 12 days.

Feeding Habits

The blue-gray gnatcatcher's diet consists of insects and spiders. The birds glean the insects from leaves and outer twigs, but may also flit from the foliage like a flycatcher for flying insects or hover like a hummingbird. The birds sometimes visit bird feeders and have been known to eat suet mixed with grated carrot.

Plants for food and shelter include:
Oaks (*Quercus* spp.) (see page 183)

The blue-gray gnatcatcher resembles a miniature mockingbird.

*A black-tailed gnatcatcher feeding
in the foliage of a red-osier dogwood (Cornus sericea).*

BLACK-TAILED GNATCATCHER

Polioptila melanura

In the Southwest, the ranges of the blue-gray gnatcatcher and the black-tailed gnatcatcher overlap, making identification difficult. However, the tail of the blue-gray is mainly white when viewed from below, while the black-tailed is black underneath with white only on the outer web and tip. The male black-tailed gnatcatcher has a glossy black cap from late February to August, while the male blue-gray has only a black forehead stripe and black stripe over the eyes. Black-tailed gnatcatchers are 4½ to 5 inches long.

The call of the black-tailed gnatcatcher is less plaintive and more wrenlike than the blue-gray's. It is a repeated, "pee-ee-ee," whereas the blue-gray gnatcatcher usually gives a single note.

Habitat
The black-tailed gnatcatcher lives throughout the year in mesquite thickets in desert country.

Migration and Winter Range
The black-tailed gnatcatcher is resident year-round throughout its range.

Breeding Range
The birds range from southern California, Nevada, Arizona, New Mexico and Texas south into Mexico and Baja California.

Breeding Behavior
The birds are permanently mated and may begin nest building long before the breeding season, often building several nests that are later deserted or destroyed before the final nest is constructed.

Nesting
For nesting, the black-tailed gnatcatcher prefers medium-size shrubs such as buckthorn and laurel, sumac, sagebush or cactus. The nest is a small, deep cup of plant fiber, sage leaves, plant down and spiderweb. It's usually built low — only 2 to 4 feet above the ground.

The female lays three or four spotted, pale blue eggs, and both sexes incubate for 14 days. The young leave the nest after 9 or 10 days.

Feeding Habits
Insects make up the bulk of the black-tailed gnatcatcher's diet. Small amounts of seeds are also eaten.

Plants for food and shelter include:
Sumacs (*Rhus* spp.) (see page 185)

The black-tailed gnatcatcher eating insects that are attracted to the flowers of creosote bush (Larrea tridentata).

BROWN THRASHER

Toxostoma rufum

The brown thrasher gets its name from its brown color and its habit of "thrashing" in leaf litter with its long, curved bill as it searches for insects. The bird has a long, graceful tail, and is bright reddish-brown above with white or pale buff, heavily streaked underparts and two white wing bars. The eyes of adult birds are yellow in color.

A member of the mockingbird family, the similar to that of the catbird and mockingbird, family, the brown thrasher's spring song is a loud, melodious carol often with phrases repeated in

A brown thrasher driving
a snake away from its nest area.
The native grass is Indian rice (Oryzopsis hymenoides).

pairs. The call of the male bird may be heard up to half a mile away.

The brown thrasher is a shy and elusive bird and is more often heard than seen. When approached, the bird will retreat into dense shrubbery.

Habitat
Brown thrashers prefer deciduous thickets, woodland borders and bushy fields.

Migration and Winter Range
The brown thrasher winters from eastern Oklahoma east to north Carolina and south to southern Florida. Some birds remain in the northern parts of the breeding range over winter.

Breeding Range
The brown thrasher breeds east of the Rockies, although it may occasionally wander west of the mountains. It nests from Alberta to Québec and south to Texas and Florida.

Breeding Behavior
In early spring the male sings from a perch in the top of a tree or large bush to attract the female. Courtship occurs near the ground in dense shrubbery and is not easily observed. The male often struts gracefully around the female with his lowered tail touching the ground. The male's song becomes subdued and soft. After the nest is completed, the male's full voice returns and hesings loudly once again.

Nesting
Both sexes of brown thrasher share nest-building, constructing a large, bulky nest loosely built of twigs, leaves, paper and grass. The nest is lined with a cup made of rootlets. It is built in thickets or a garden shrub or small tree, usually within 10 feet of the ground, but occasionally on the ground.

The female lays four or five pale blue to white, brown-dotted eggs, which are incubated by both sexes for 12 to 14 days. The birds are extremely clean around the nest. When 9 to 13 days old, the young leave the nest. Two broods are raised each season.

Feeding Habits
Thrashers spend most of their time on the ground. They run or hop, foraging for insects. In spring, spiders and insects, especially caterpillars, make up most of the bird's diet. In summer and autumn, the main food is wild fruit. Brown thrashers also eat snakes, lizards, cicadas and tree frogs.

Plants for food and shelter include:
Serviceberries (*Amelanchier* spp.) (see page 156)
Dogwoods (*Cornus* spp.) (see page 163)
Wild strawberry (*Fragaria virginiana*) (see page 166)
Hollies (*Ilex* spp.) (see page 167)
Red cedar (*Juniperus virginiana*) (see page 168)
Red mulberry (*Morus rubra*) (see page 172)
Bayberries (*Myrica* spp.) (see page 173)
Virginia creeper (*Parthenocissus quinquefolia*) (see page 175)
Wild cherries (*Prunus* spp.) (see page 182)
Oaks (*Quercus* spp.) (see page 183)
Sumacs (*Rhus* spp.) (see page 185)
Common blackberry (*Rubus allegheniensis*) (see page 187)
Elderberries (*Sambucus* spp.) (see page 188)
Blueberries (*Vaccinium* spp.) (see page 191)
Viburnums (*Viburnum* spp.) (see page 193)
Fox grape (*Vitis vulpina*) (see page 194)

A brown thrasher feeding its young in a nest that has been built on the ground.

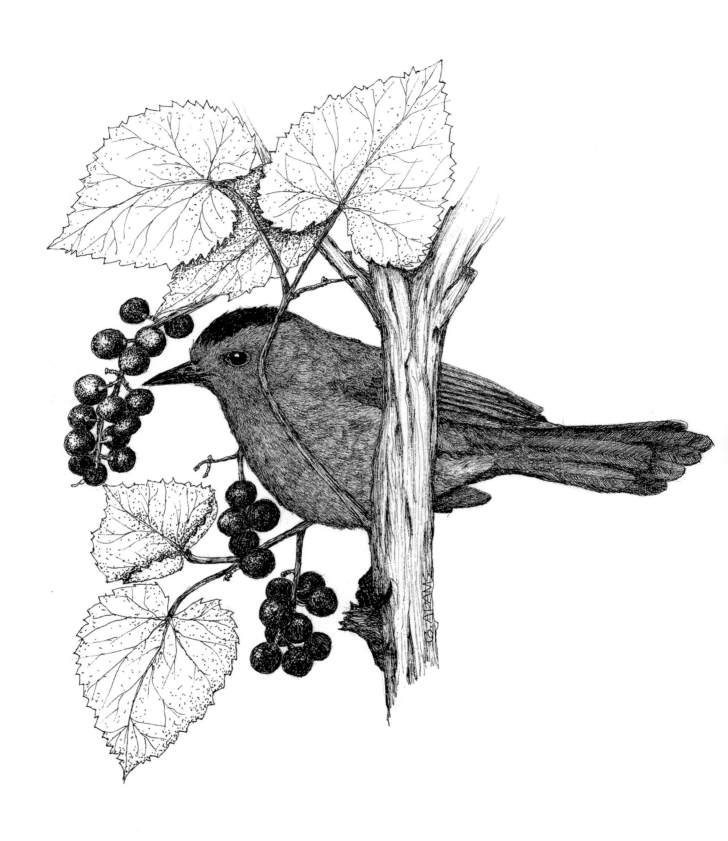

*A gray catbird eating
the fruits of fox grape (Vitis vulpina).*

GRAY CATBIRD

Dumetella carolinensis

The gray catbird is a bird of shady thickets. It may sing its varied and delightful song from an open perch but, when disturbed, it will dart into a thicket and remain hidden from view. Male and female birds are similar in appearance: 9-inch-long slate-gray birds with a black cap and chestnut undertail coverts.

The catbird's song is a melody of various phrases, some musical, others discordant, punctuated by short pauses and often containing some mimicry of other bird songs. The song of the gray catbird is similar to that of the mockingbird, but the catbird does not normally repeat its phrases. A complaining call note, a nasal cat-like "mew," which gives the bird its name, is usually included in the complete song. The catbird also often sings at night.

Habitat

Catbirds can be found in low, dense, deciduous thickets, preferably at streamsides and damp forest edges. They are also often found in bushes and hedges in gardens, sometimes very close to houses.

Migration and Winter Range

Catbirds migrate at night. Most catbirds winter in the southern United States and Central America.

Breeding Range

Catbirds breed from southern British Columbia to Nova Scotia, south to eastern Oregon, central Arizona, Texas and central parts of the Gulf states.

Breeding Behavior

The females appear at the breeding ground just after the males, and courtship antics begin. The male sings, pausing to dash off in pursuit of the female. The male struts with lowered wings and erect tail, wheeling around and exhibiting the chestnut patch on his undertail coverts.

Nesting

The nest is a coarse, bulky structure of sticks and twigs, neatly lined with fine rootlets and bark shreds. An average of four blue-green eggs are laid and incubated for about 12 to 13 days. The young leave the nest when about 10 to 15 days old. Two broods are often raised. The male feeds the female at the nest and guards the nest when the female leaves to feed herself.

Feeding Habits

About half of the gray catbird's diet is insects, including crickets, grasshoppers, beetles (especially Japanese beetles and June beetles), caterpillars and cicadas. The catbird also eats many kinds of fleshy fruits.

Catbirds prefer a shady section of the garden.

Plants for food and shelter include:
Serviceberries (*Amelanchier* spp.) (see page 156)
Hackberries (*Celtis* spp.) (see page 161)
Dogwoods (*Cornus* spp.) (see page 163)
Hollies (*Ilex* spp.) (see page 167)
Red mulberry (*Morus rubra*) (see page 172)
Bayberries (*Myrica* spp.) (see page 173)
Wild cherries (*Prunus* spp.) (see page 182)
Sumacs (*Rhus* spp.) (see page 185)
Common blackberry (*Rubus allegheniensis*) (see page 187)
Elderberries (*Sambucus* spp.) (see page 188)
Mountain ashes (*Sorbus* spp.) (see page 189)
Highbush blueberry (*Vaccinium corymbosum*) (see page 191)
Viburnums (*Viburnum* spp.) (see page 193)
Wild grapes (*Vitis* spp.) (see page 194)

Mockingbird

Mimus polyglottos

Once considered a Southern bird, at home among the moss-covered live oaks and flowering magnolia trees, the mockingbird has adapted very well to civilization and has increased its range northward and westward. A slender, long-tailed, 10-inch gray bird with white patches on the tail and wings. The popular, melodious mockingbird is recognized as the state bird of Arkansas, Florida, Tennessee, Texas and Mississippi.

A mockingbird eating the fruits of Saskatoon serviceberry (Amelanchier alnifolia).

As the bird's scientific name, *Mimus polyglottos,* (mimic of many tongues) suggests, the mockingbird is noted for its ability to repeat the songs of other bird species as well as its own delightful song. One observer recorded 39 bird songs and 50 bird calls, plus the calls of a cricket and a frog. The mockingbird's call consists of stanzas of repeated phrases, loud, melodious and impassioned song which is often poured out on a warm spring moonlight night from conspicuous places such as housetops, treetops and flagpoles. The birds are never still when singing, raising a foot or changing perches, singing a rapturous flight song continuously.

This mockingbird is attracted to the fruits of 'First Lady' flowering dogwood (<u>Cornus florida</u> 'First Lady').

Habitat

The birds are frequently seen in shrubbery, tangles, hedges, city parks and gardens. Suburban gardens provide ideal habitat.

Migration and Winter Range

Mockingbirds usually live as year-round residents within their range.

Breeding Range

Mockingbirds breed from southern Canada south to the Caribbean.

Breeding Behavior

The mockingbird's courtship performance is unique. As spring approaches the male pauses from his song and, raising his wings above his head, exposes his large white wing markings. This is repeated several times. The courtship antics include a nuptial dance. A pair of birds may face each other a foot apart, hopping up and down and moving from side to side with their heads and tails held high and feathers depressed.

Nesting

Both birds share in the nest-building. The completed nest is a coarse, bulky structure usually built of small dead twigs and lined with grass and rootlets. The nest is usually 3 to 10 feet above the ground in a bush or low tree, but may be as high as 50 feet.

The female lays three to five green eggs with brown spots and incubates them for 12 days. Young birds leave the nest when 10 to 12 days old. Two or three broods may be raised in one season.

After breeding, the parents establish and defend their winter territories.

Feeding Habits

During spring and early summer, mockingbirds are mainly insectivorous. But as wild fruits ripen, they are eaten with relish, making up nearly half of the diet. During winter, the bulk of the diet consists of fruits. Mockingbirds sometimes visit feeders for raisins and other soft foods.

Plants for food and shelter include:
Serviceberries (*Amelanchier* spp.) (see page 156)
Hackberries (*Celtis* spp.) (see page 161)
Dogwoods (*Cornus* spp.) (see page 163)
Hollies (*Ilex* spp.) (see page 167)
Red cedar (*Juniperus virginiana*) (see page 168)
Red mulberry (*Morus rubra*) (see page 172)
Bayberries (*Myrica* spp.) (see page 173)
Wild cherries (*Prunus* spp.) (see page 182)
Sumacs (*Rhus* spp.) (see page 185)
Blackberries (*Rubus* spp.) (see page 187)
Elderberries (*Sambucus* spp.) (see page 188)
Viburnums (*Viburnum* spp.) (see page 193)
Wild grapes (*Vitis* spp.) (see page 194)

EASTERN BLUEBIRD

Sialia sialis

Henry David Thoreau described the bluebird as the bird of heaven and earth because of its sky-blue and earth-red coloration. A member of the thrush family, this beautiful bird with its musical song is generally regarded as the beloved herald of spring. The eastern bluebird has an intensely blue head, back, wings and tail, a reddish-brown breast and a white belly. It is very similar to its western counterpart, the western bluebird.

Eastern bluebirds at their nest hollow in an abandoned woodpecker hole in a western sycamore (Platanus racemosa).

Bluebirds are cavity nesters. The practice of removing dead wood in orchards and other woodlots, the use of metal fence posts rather than wood, the use of pesticides, and the introduction of English sparrows and starlings, which aggressively compete for available hollows, have all contributed to the decline of the bluebird population. "Bluebird trails" and backyard birdwatchers who add nest boxes to their yards have done a lot to increase the bluebird population. Eastern bluebirds are also susceptible to the vagaries of climate: Many adults are killed during harsh late winter weather, and early spring nests may not survive.

Habitat

The eastern bluebird is found in open woodlands, old orchards, parks, gardens and around farms where old trees, fenceposts or nest boxes provide nesting sites.

Migration and Winter Range

The birds winter from south of the Ohio Valley and the middle states south into Mexico, the Gulf Coast and southern Florida. Some northern birds remain on their nesting grounds all winter. During fall and winter, the birds form loose flocks of from 6 to 25 birds.

Breeding Range

The birds breed from the Atlantic coast to the Rockies and from southern Canada south through Mexico to Nicaragua, the Gulf Coast and southern Florida.

Breeding Behavior

The male birds usually arrive first, but sometimes pairs arrive together. Some pairs remain year-round on the breeding territory. Courtship may involve a display flight by the male, fluttering high above his treetop perch and sailing back to the perch, singing his soft warbled call while in flight.

Nesting

A nesting site adjacent to an open grassy area is preferred. Old woodpecker holes and natural cavities in old trees, stumps or fenceposts are selected. Bluebird nest boxes are welcomed. The female builds a nest of grasses, fine twigs and weed stems, lined with fine grasses, hair or feathers. Between March and July, she lays four to six pale blue eggs. The female incubates for 13 to 16 days, and the young leave the nest when they are 15 to 20 days old. Both parents feed the young and keep the nest clean. Two broods are usually raised.

A male eastern bluebird feeding its young at the nest it has built in an old tree stump.

Feeding Habits

Bluebirds eat insects, waiting on a low perch, then flying to the ground after their prey. The bird also flies out from a high perch to snatch flying insects or hovers above foliage to catch disturbed insects. Grasshoppers, caterpillars, beetles, ants, spiders, earthworms and snails make up over 70 percent of the bird's diet. The balance is made up mostly of native fruits.

Plants for food and shelter include:
Serviceberries (*Amelanchier* spp.) (see page 156)
Hackberries *(Celtis* spp.) (see page 161)
Dogwoods (*Cornus* spp.) (see page 163)
Hollies (*Ilex* spp.) (see page 167)
Red cedar (*Juniperus virginiana*) (see page 168)
Virginia creeper (*Parthenocissus quinquefolia*) (see page 175)
Sumacs (*Rhus* spp.) (see page 185)
Elderberries (*Sambucus* spp.) (see page 188)
Fox grape (*Vitis vulpina*) (see page 194)

AMERICAN ROBIN

Turdus migratorius

The familiar adult robin is 9 to 11 inches long, with a gray back and brick red breast. Males have a black head and tail, while females, which are generally paler in color overall, have a gray head and tail. Although the robin's cheerful song is looked for as the harbinger of spring, it is not generally known that many robins spend the entire winter in the northern latitudes, frequenting cedar bogs and swamps away from civilization.

An American robin at its nest in a lodgepole pine (Pinus contorta).

Robins may live to be more than 17 years old in the wild. Domestic cats are the bird's greatest enemy, with one estimate that, on average, a cat will capture 50 birds in one season, mainly helpless young birds.

The robin's song is the first one heard in the morning and the last heard in the evening. "Cheer-up, cheer, cheer, cheer-up" is sung in long choruses of rising and falling phrases. The song has a joyous liquid quality.

Habitat
City parks and suburban yards, open woodland and orchards are the robin's preferred habitat.

Migration and Winter Range
Flocks form in fall. Robins winter from southern Canada and the northern United States south to Baja California, the Gulf Coast and Florida, and as far south as Guatemala.

Breeding Range
American robins breed from the treeline in Alaska and across Canada south to southern Mexico and the Gulf Coast.

Breeding Behavior
Robins remain in flocks throughout winter and disperse in spring, signaling the beginning of the breeding season. The male bird becomes less tolerant of other males and generally restricts its own movements to within an area of about one acre. The male returns to the same breeding area each year. With the arrival of the females, the males begin their familiar caroling.

Nesting
Robins are one of the earliest birds to nest in North America, with evergreen trees often selected for protection of early nests. Later nests may be in maples and other deciduous trees, or around buildings. A tree fork or horizontal branch is selected or a horizontal ledge on a building is used. A deep, cup-shaped nest of mud and grasses, lined with fine grasses, is constructed by the female. The female may carry mud in her bill from up to a quarter of a mile from the nest site, and molds the nest shape by sitting inside and pushing against the edges with her breast.

Three or four blue eggs are usually laid and are incubated by the female for about two weeks. The nestlings are fed vast quantities of insects and worms. In one report it was calculated that the parents fed

An American robin eating the fruits of 'Sparkleberry' winterberry holly (Ilex verticillata 'Sparkleberry').

their young 3.2 pounds of food over the two weeks that they were in the nest.

Young robins have speckled breasts, indicating their family relationship to thrushes. The young follow the parents around, demanding to be fed. The female often leaves to begin nest-building and to raise another brood, leaving the male to feed the fledglings.

Feeding Habits
Robins are a familiar sight on suburban lawns in spring, eating earthworms. They also eat beetles, weevils, grasshoppers, termites, cutworms and other insect pests. Robins also eat fruit, especially in winter. Many native trees and shrubs are planted by robins scattering the seed as a result of their fruit- and berry-eating.

Plants for food and shelter include:
Serviceberries (*Amelanchier* spp.) (see page 156)
Hackberries (*Celtis* spp.) (see page 161)
Dogwoods (*Cornus* spp.) (see page 163)
Hawthorns (*Crataegus* spp.) (see page 164)
Hollies (*Ilex* spp.) (see page 167)
Red cedar (*Juniperus virginiana*) (see page 168)
Red mulberry (*Morus rubra*) (see page 172)
Bayberries (*Myrica* spp.) (see page 173)
Wild cherries (*Prunus* spp.) (see page 182)
Sumacs (*Rhus* spp.) (see page 185)
Common blackberry (*Rubus alleghveniensis*) (see page 187)
Elderberries (*Sambucus* spp.) (see page 188)
Mountain ashes (*Sorbus* spp.) (see page 189)
Viburnums (*Viburnum* spp.) (see page 193)
Grasses (for nesting) (*Andropogon* spp.) (see page 157)

The fruits of pin cherry
(Prunus pensylvanica) are favored by the wood thrush.

WOOD THRUSH

Hylocichla mustelina

Possibly the best known of the North American spotted brown thrushes and the only one that commonly nests in parks and gardens, the 8-inch wood thrush is noted for its incredibly musical song, a flutelike "ee-oh-lay."

The wood thrush is known by several other names, including "bellbird," in reference to its clarion-like song. "Song thrush," "swamp angel," "swamp robin" and "wood robin" are other common names. The bird's genus name, *Hylocichla,* is from the Greek words *hyle,* wood, and *kickle,* thrush. The species name is Latin, pertaining to weasel (the color of the bird's back).

Habitat

The wood thrush is usually a bird of cool, moist deciduous woodlands with tangled undergrowth and sapling growth, as well as parks and gardens.

Migration and Winter Range

The wood thrush begins its spring migration in March. By the end of April, the thrushes have reached Connecticut, and by May 19 they have progressed to the northern limit of their range. The birds winter from southern Texas and southern Florida south to Panama.

Breeding Range

The wood thrush is found from southern Ontario, southwestern Québec, southwestern New Brunswick and Nova Scotia in Canada throughout most of the eastern half of the United States, south to Florida and the Gulf of Mexico.

Breeding Behavior

The male bird arrives in his breeding territory before the female. The breeding territory may be from 1/5 to 2 acres. The first evidence of the bird's arrival is his song. Song is used to challenge an intruder into the territory, and one such song is reported to have lasted for 10 minutes. The male may also chase an intruder, attack or simply raise his head feathers in threat.

The females arrive two or three days after the males. Courtship displays include the male chasing the female in six or seven circular flights; then the birds eat together. The male bird also sings to impress his loved one.

Nesting

A nest is built in a sapling or bush, usually 5 to 15 feet above the ground. Nests are similar to robin nests, with the addition of dead leaves and mosses, and are lined with rootlets. Maple, witch hazel, hawthorn, elm and birch trees are among the trees selected for nest sites.

Three or four pale blue or blue-green eggs are laid and incubated by the female for about two weeks. The nestlings are fed by both parents. Mulberries, honeysuckle berries, caterpillars and small insects are fed to the young, who leave the nest when 12 or 13 days old. Two broods are usually raised.

The wood thrush nest is frequently parasitized by cowbirds. Squirrels may eat the eggs and cats also take their toll, but if these hazards are escaped the birds may live for more than eight years.

Feeding Habits

Wood thrushes obtain a large part of their food from scratching around the roots of shrubs. Animal matter including moths, grasshoppers, beetles, ants and worms make up about 60 percent of the bird's diet, and the balance is made up of fruit.

Plants for food and shelter include:
Serviceberries (*Amelanchier* spp.) (see page 156)
Dogwoods (*Cornus* spp.) (see page 163)
Hollies (*Ilex* spp.) (see page 167)
Honeysuckles (*Lonicera* spp.) (see page 170)
Red mulberry (*Morus rubra*) (see page 172)
Wild cherries (*Prunus* spp.) (see page 182)
Common blackberry (*Rubus allegheniensis*) (see page 187)
Elderberries (*Sambucus* spp.) (see page 188)
Highbush blueberry (*Vaccinium corymbosum*) (see page 191)
Viburnums (*Viburnum* spp.) (see page 193)
Wild grapes (*Vitis* spp.) (see page 194)

The wood thrush prefers a cool, moist, overgrown garden corner.

CEDAR WAXWING

Bombycilla cedrorum

Waxwings get their name from the red waxy droplets on the tips of the secondary wing feathers. This 7-inch bird is robed in soft, silky, harmoniously colored plumage. With his slim appearance, conspicuous crest, rich grayish-brown upper parts, black mask and chin, greenish-yellow belly and yellow-tipped tail, he looks like the perfect gentleman of the bird world. His refined appearance matches his dignified manner. A polite, gentle, sociable bird, he often sits motionless with an erect bearing.

The waxwing's crest is used to express emotion. When pointing backward, it signifies that the bird is unperturbed. If the bird is disturbed, the crest is erect; if it's frightened, the crest is pulled flat.

Cedar waxwings may suddenly appear in an area where their favorite wild fruits are abundant and just as quickly disappear. They travel in groups of up to 20 birds. The birds fly in close ranks at treetop level and suddenly, when in full flight, may wheel around and dive to a tree to feed. On alighting, the

A cedar waxwing eating the berries of an Eastern red cedar (Juniperus virginiana).

birds remain perfectly still and are often very difficult to detect.

Among French Canadians, the bird is called *recellet,* as the color of the crest resembles the color of the hood of a religious order of that name. The bird's genus name, *Bombycilla,* is combined Greek and Latin meaning "silky-tailed;" the species name, *cedrorum,* is Latin meaning "of cedars," referring to the bird's fondness for cedar berries.

Habitat
Cedar waxwings prefer open and sparse woodlands, orchards, second-growth stands on the edges of rivers, swamps or dams, and parks and gardens with berry-producing trees and shrubs.

Migration and Winter Range
Cedar waxwings winter from the southern part of their breeding range south to Mexico and as far as northern South America. Migration is often erratic.

Breeding Range
The bird's breeding range extends from southeastern Alaska, north-central British Columbia and northern Alberta east across Canada to Newfoundland and south to northern California, northern Utah, northwestern Oklahoma, southern Illinois, northern Alabama and northern Georgia.

Breeding Behavior
During courtship, the male may approach the female carrying a flower petal or berry in his bill, hopping sideways along the branch. A responsive female may take the offering and hop once to the side, standing erect. After a short pause she returns to the male, who takes the offering and hops away with one hop, pauses and hops back. The dance is repeated several times and has a dignified rhythm and precision about it.

Nesting
The birds are late nesters, usually beginning nest-building in June or as late as September. Since the young are fed on fruit, the birds may time their nesting to coincide with a plentiful supply of ripe fruits. The birds nest in deciduous or coniferous trees or shrubs, usually at the extreme end of a horizontal branch 6 to 40 feet above ground.

A bulky, loosely woven cup of twigs, dry grasses, rootlets, bark strips, mosses, pine needles and lichens is built. The female lays three to six pale gray or blue-gray eggs, marked with black dots. She incubates them for 12 to 16 days. The young are fed small fruits and insects. The parents often return to the nest with their gullets bulging with food.

Feeding Habits
Adult birds eat mostly fruit and berries. They are especially fond of mountain ash berries and cherries. When eating, the birds may gorge themselves until they are unable to fly. The birds may also sit in a row and politely pass a cherry from one to the other along the line and back again several times before one will eat it.

In some areas, the waxwing is known as the "cankerbird" because of its fondness of cankerworms. The bird is a major foe of the elm leaf beetle and also eats weevils, scale insects, cicadas, carpenter ants and other insects. In late summer and early fall, the cedar waxwings become adroit flycatchers, sallying from a high perch to catch insects in midair.

The birds are often seen pecking at the blossoms of fruit trees in spring and scattering the petals. Scientists disagree over whether the birds are after the petals or the insects that infest the blossoms.

Plants for food and shelter include:
Serviceberries (*Amelanchier* spp.) (see page 156)
Hackberries (*Celtis* spp.) (see page 161)
Dogwoods (*Cornus* spp.) (see page 163)
Hawthorns (*Crataegus* spp.) (see page 164)
Black crowberry (*Empetrum nigrum*) (see page 164)
Hollies (*Ilex* spp.) (see page 167)
Cedars (*Juniperus* spp.) (see page 168)
Crabapples (*Malus* spp.) (see page 171)
Red mulberry (*Morus rubra*) (see page 172)
Bayberries (*Myrica* spp.) (see page 173)
Virginia creeper (*Parthenocissus quinquefolia*) (see page 175)
Spruces (*Picea* spp.) (see page 177)
Wild cherries (*Prunus* spp.) (see page 182)
Nootka rose (*Rosa nutkana*) (see page 186)
Common blackberry (*Rubus allegheniensis*) (see page 187)
Elderberries (*Sambucus* spp.) (see page 188)
Mountain ashes (*Sorbus* spp.) (see page 189)
Viburnums (*Viburnum* spp.) (see page 193)

A cedar waxwing eating insects attracted to paper birch (Betula papyrifera).

BLACK-AND-WHITE WARBLER
Mniotilta varia

The black-and-white warbler is one of the 56 species of the American Wood Warbler family found in North America. They are second only to the Finch family in number of species among North American songbirds. This handsome 4½- to 5½-inch bird has black stripes running horizontally along its head, back and wings, with a whiter breast and belly.

Once called the "black-and-white creeper," the black-and-white warbler displays even more agility than the brown creeper when eating. The warbler creeps over the trunks and larger branches of trees and shrubs, gleaning insects from crevices in the bark. As he feeds, he flits from tree to tree creeping around the trunk. The black-and-white warbler

Black and white warblers probe for insects in the bark of white ash (Fraxinus americana).

may move up the trunk like a creeper, vertically down like a nuthatch or spiral around the trunk pursuing an insect and catching it in flight like a flycatcher.

Although called a warbler, like other warblers the black-and-white is not particularly noted for its song. The song is an attenuated high-pitched squeaky "weesy-weesy-weesy-weesy," sung as it searches the bark for insects and occasionally during flight.

The black-and-white warbler takes its genus name, *Mniotilta,* from the Greek words *mnion,* moss, and *tillein,* to pull out. The species name, *varia,* is Latin for variegated, referring to the bird's plumage stripes of black and white.

A black-and-white warbler eating insects in the bark of a balsam poplar (Populus balsamifera).

Habitat
The black-and-white warbler is usually common in deciduous and mixed woodlands, preferring damper areas. During migration it is common in parks and gardens throughout its range.

Migration and Winter Range
One of the earliest warblers to arrive in spring, the black-and-white is most conspicuous when most deciduous trees are just beginning to sprout the first light green leaflets.

The fall migration is a slow drift to the south. Black-and-white warblers often remain in New England until mid-October, long after the frosts have arrived in that area.

The bird winters from southern Baja California, Mexico, southern Texas, central Florida and the Bahamas south to the West Indies and central America to Ecuador, Columbia and northern Venezuela.

Breeding Range
The black-and-white warbler breeds from northeastern British Columbia across central and southern Canada to Newfoundland and south to central Texas, southeastern Louisiana, eastern Montana, central Alabama, central Georgia and southeastern North Carolina.

Breeding Behavior
After the arrival of the females, the males often flutter their black-and-white plumage, indulge in frequent song, periodically chase the female and warn off other males before settling down with their partners.

Nesting
A cup-shaped nest of dry leaves, rootlets, bark strips and pine needles is built on the ground, usually hidden from the top under a log or against a tree or shrub. The birds sometimes nest in a low stump or under the roots of a fallen tree. The female builds the nest, lines it with fine grass, then incubates her four or five purple-spotted white eggs for 11 or 12 days. The young leave the nest 8 to 12 days after hatching and soon ascend a nearby tree, where they are fed by the parents.

Feeding Habits
The black-and-white warbler mainly eats insects that are harmful to trees, as well as spiders and daddy longlegs. They are attracted to rough-barked trees where insects are likely to be found.

Plants for food and shelter include:
Maples (*Acer* spp.) (see page 154)
Pines (*Pinus* spp.) (see page 178)
Oaks (*Quercus* spp.) (see page 183)

YELLOW WARBLER

Dendroica petechia

The most widespread of the wood warblers, the 5-inch yellow warbler is also the easiest to recognize, with its seemingly all-yellow plumage. At closer range the male bird's reddish-streaked breast can be observed. This little ray of sunshine is represented by seven distinct subspecies in North America with each subspecies varying in intensity of color from orange-yellow to pale yellow.

During courtship, the male sings every minute or two with a high-pitched melodious "sweet-sweet-sweet-sweeter-than-sweet." One male has been recorded as having sung 3,240 times in one day at the peak of the mating season.

*On finding a cowbird egg in
its nest, this yellow warbler has built
another layer on the nest and laid more eggs.
The nest is in common blackberry (Rubus allegheniensis).*

Habitat

These birds prefer shrubby areas in open country or roadside thickets, the edges of streams and ponds, hedges, parks and gardens. Yellow warblers favor willow thickets, but often can be found wherever patches of trees and shrubs grow.

Migration and Winter Range

The yellow warbler begins its southern migration early, with some birds crossing the Gulf of Mexico in mid-July. By mid-August, most of the breeding birds have left the northern states. The bird winters from southern Baja California, central Mexico and the Bahamas south to Peru and Brazil.

Breeding Range

The yellow warbler has a vast breeding range stretching from Alaska near the treeline across Canada to Newfoundland and south to southern Baja California, central Peru, coastal Venezuela, Trinidad, the Antilles, Bahamas, Galapagos Islands and Florida Keys.

Breeding Behavior

Soon after their arrival to their breeding grounds, the male birds select a territory and defend it against other males. The territory may be about 150 feet in diameter. The male courts the female with singing and persistent chasing.

Nesting

Nest-building is mainly done by the female, though she is attended by the male. Favorite nesting sites are in moist thickets, along small streams and brooks and on the edge of swamps among alders, willows and blueberry and elderberry bushes. Overgrown fences and cut-over areas with regrowth of wild raspberry, blackberry or low shrubs are also selected. In Iowa, it is reported that the bird most frequently nests in the wolfberry bush, a prairie shrub with leathery leaves and pale pink flowers. A strong, compact, cup-shaped nest of plant fibers, grasses and plant down is fastened to a fork of a sapling branch, shrub or bramble from 7 to 12 feet above the ground. The birds are fairly tame and don't mind a human audience, even when building their nest, so you can often get a close look at the process. The female lays three to six brown-spotted pale blue eggs and incubates them for 11 to 12 days. The young leave the nest after 9 to 12 days.

The yellow warbler is one of the most frequent hosts of cowbirds. A large majority of nests in areas where cowbirds are common will be visited at least once by these parasitic birds, who lay their eggs in the warbler's nest. Many yellow warblers have learned to circumvent the cowbird by building another nest on top of the first. The cowbird's egg is left to cool off in the basement. This process may be repeated several times if the cowbird persists and, in one record, a six-storied nest was constructed, each nest containing a cowbird's egg. When yellow warblers nest in swampy areas inhabited by colonies of red-winged blackbirds, they may be protected from the cowbirds since the blackbirds won't tolerate cowbirds in their territory.

Feeding Habits

The yellow warbler is a very beneficial bird whose diet consists almost entirely of insect pests, including caterpillars, which make up 67 percent of the diet when plentiful. Gypsy moth and brown-tail moth caterpillars, cankerworms, tent caterpillars, bark beetles, borers, weevils, aphids and grasshoppers are included in the warbler's diet.

Plants for food and shelter include:
Elderberries (*Sambucus* spp.) (see page 188)

A male yellow warbler displaying its fine reddish-streaked breast plumage.

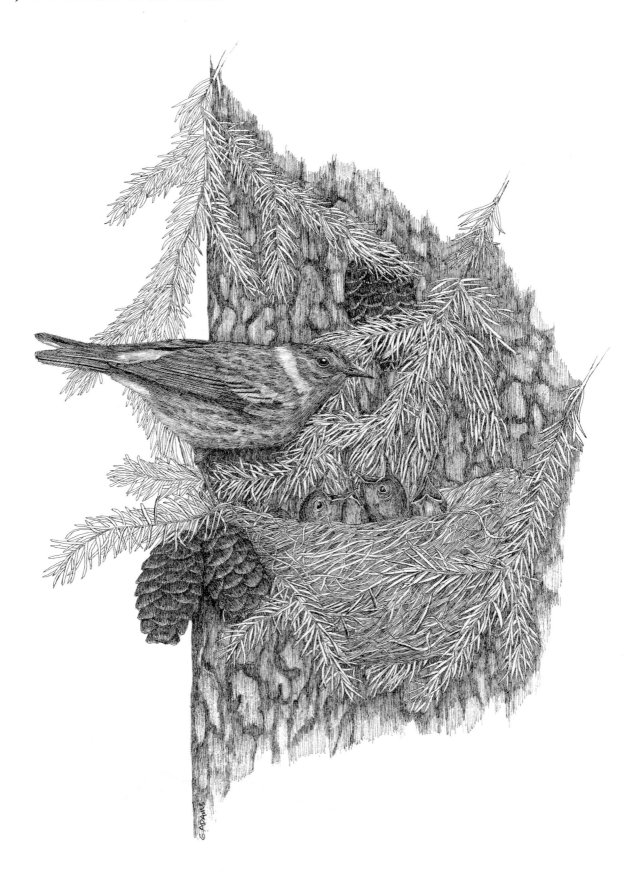

*The Cape May warbler often nests
in the foliage of red spruce (<u>Picea rubens</u>).*

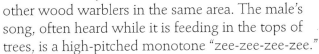

CAPE MAY WARBLER

Dendroica tigrina

he Cape May is one of the most beautiful of the warblers. It is uncommon, although often seen in migration. The male bird in breeding plumage has chestnut cheeks and a white wing patch, and is yellow below with heavy black streaks. The female has a much duller coloration but retains a suggestion of the cheek patch. Both are 5 inches long.

Like most of the wood warblers, the Cape May occupies his own ecological niche in the forest, so his feeding habits and nesting sites don't compete with other wood warblers in the same area. The male's song, often heard while it is feeding in the tops of trees, is a high-pitched monotone "zee-zee-zee-zee."

The Cape May warbler takes its common name from Cape May, New Jersey, where the first scientifically described specimen was obtained in 1811. The species name, *tigrina,* is from the Latin *tigrinus,* meaning "striped like a tiger."

Habitat

During migration, the Cape May may be seen passing through coniferous or deciduous woods or suburban parks and gardens. On its breeding grounds it prefers open, parklike stands of large mature spruce and fir trees, or the edge of forests or forest openings with a mixture of tall birch and hemlock trees.

Migration and Winter Range

The main fall migration flight is east of the Mississippi, and the birds winter in Mexico and in the West Indies.

Breeding Range

The breeding range of the Cape May warbler is from Alberta east to Nova Scotia and south to northeastern North Dakota, Minnesota, northern Wisconsin, northern Michigan, southern Ontario, northeastern New York, central and eastern Vermont and southern Maine.

Breeding Behavior

Little is known of the Cape May warbler's courtship behavior. It has been observed that the male chases the female and, by the following day, the female has apparently completed the nest-building.

Nesting

Black spruce, red spruce and fir trees are preferred nesting trees. The female builds a compact, cup-shaped nest of moss, grass and twigs near the top of the tree 30 to 60 feet above the ground. Six to seven heavily spotted cream-white eggs are laid. Nesting information is limited due to the birds' habit of nesting high up in treetops and the fact that much of its breeding range is beyond settled areas.

Feeding Habits

The birds feed in the tops of trees, often darting into the air to catch insects. The birds eat beetles, crickets, caterpillars, spruce budworms, flies, ants, wasps and spiders. The Cape May warbler also punctures grapes to drink the juice and drinks sap from holes drilled by sapsuckers.

Plants for food and shelter include:
Firs (*Abies* spp.) (see page 154)
Spruces (*Picea* spp.) (see page 177)
Wild grapes (*Vitis* spp.) (see page 194)

A Cape May warbler eating insects attracted to the foliage of a speckled alder (Alnus rugosa).

YELLOW-RUMPED WARBLER
(MYRTLE RACE)

Dendroica coronata

The yellow-rumped warbler species has two distinct forms: the myrtle race and the Audubon's race. The myrtle warbler was named for its fondness of bayberries or wax myrtles. It is one of the first birds to arrive in North America in spring. The yellow-rumped warbler is one of the few warblers that can survive on berries and seeds alone for a long period.

Second only to the yellow warbler as the best-known American warbler, the yellow-rumped is the most numerous of all the American wood warblers. The 5- to 6-inch bird is easily identified by its four distinct patches of yellow which are found on the crown, rump and each side of the breast. True to its name, this bird is the only white-throated, yellow-rumped warbler.

The fruits of the southern bayberry (Myrica cerifera) are particularly atttractive to the yellow rumped warbler. This bird is the myrtle race.

The bird has a distinctive song, a juncolike trill described as something like the tinkling rattle of a small chain. The ordinary call note is a sharp "chek." The species name, *coronata,* is Latin for "crown," referring to the bird's yellow-crowned head. The yellow-rumped (myrtle) warbler is sometimes called the "golden-crowned warbler" or "myrtle bird."

Habitat
Yellow-rumped warblers prefer coniferous and mixed forests. They are widespread during migration.

Migration and Winter Range
In spring, the birds pass over the Rio Grande into Texas and move up the coast, with waves of birds drifting through the tall deciduous woods of Massachusetts by about mid-April.

The myrtle warbler is one of the last of the warblers to begin the fall migration. The birds drift south during September, October and much of November. The numbers now are swelled by the young birds, and the birds are becoming even more abundant. The winter range extends from the northern and north-central United States south to central Panama and the Greater Antilles.

As the birds drift south, they may stop off where food supplies are abundant and spend the winter not much farther south than the southern limit of their breeding range. Many birds remain in coastal areas where the bayberries provide winter food. The myrtle warbler is the only warbler that regularly winters in the northern states. Myrtle warblers apparently return to winter in the same place each year.

Breeding Range
The birds move into the northern areas to breed, from north-central Alaska and across Canada throughout much of the forested areas to Labrador and Newfoundland and south to northern British Columbia, central Alberta, northern Minnesota, central Michigan, eastern New York, eastern Pennsylvania and Massachusetts.

Breeding Behavior
As summer approaches the males begin to court the females, following them and displaying their beauty spots by fluffing out their side feathers, erecting the crown feathers and raising their wings.

Nesting
The birds build a relatively bulky and loose nest for warblers. The female does most of the building, with the male occasionally bringing nesting material to the site but mostly encouraging her with singing and companionship. The nest is built of twigs, rootlets and grass interwoven

Yellow-rumped warbler (myrtle race) showing its distinctive patches of yellow.

with animal hair, and is usually 5 to 50 feet up on a horizontal branch of a spruce, red cedar or pine tree.

Between May and June, three to five brown-spotted white eggs are laid and are incubated by the female for 12 to 13 days. The young leave the nest 12 to 14 days after hatching. Like the other wood warblers, the juvenile plumage is kept for only a short period and by August the young birds have acquired their first winter plumage.

Feeding Habits
The myrtle warbler's favorite food is bayberries. Dogwood, red cedar, viburnum, honeysuckle, mountain ash and Virginia creeper berries are also eaten. In the South Atlantic states, the berries of the native tree palms or palmettos are eaten. During the winter, poison ivy berries are a favorite.

During spring and summer insects are the preferred food, and the bird flits around bushes taking beetles, weevils, wood borers, scale insects and aphids from the foliage and bark. It often flutters above the foliage to catch mosquitos, gnats or flies.

The seeds of grasses, sunflower seeds and goldenrod seeds are also eaten. The birds may visit bird feeders for suet or a peanut butter mixture.

Plants for food and shelter include:
Dogwoods (*Cornus* spp.) (see page 163)
Sunflowers (*Helianthus* spp.) (see page 166)
Red cedar (*Juniperus virginiana*) (see page 168)
Honeysuckles (*Lonicera* spp.) (see page 170)
Bayberries (*Myrica* spp.) (see page 173)
Virginia creeper (*Parthenocissus quinquefolia*) (see page 175)
Pines (*Pinus* spp.) (see page 178)
Sumacs (*Rhus* spp.) (see page 185)
Mountain ashes (*Sorbus* spp.) (see page 189)
Viburnums (*Viburnum* spp.) (see page 193)
Grasses (for nesting) (*Andropogon* spp.) (see page 157)

*The Blackburnian warbler usually nests in
hemlocks such as this eastern hemlock (Tsuga canadensis).*

BLACKBURNIAN WARBLER

Dendroica fusca

The Blackburnian warbler is considered to be the most brilliant of all the wood warblers, with the bright plumage of a tropical bird. The male Blackburnian warbler in breeding plumage has a vivid orange throat, a large white wing patch and distinctive black head markings. The female and young have similar but paler markings. The 5-inch bird's beauty is best appreciated seen in its forest home against a backdrop of dark conifers.

The song is a thin, very high-pitched "zip, zip, zip, zip, zeeeeee." The Blackburnian warbler is one of the first birds to stop their singing in summer.

It was named for Mrs. Anna Blackburne, an eighteenth-century English botanist who collected stuffed birds, a patron of ornithology. The species name, fusca, is Latin for dark or dusky. Other names are "firethroat" and "hemlock warbler."

Habitat
The Blackburnian warbler is an arboreal bird, usually keeping well concealed in the foliage of the tall spruce, pine and hemlock trees that it prefers. The bird's high-pitched song is usually the only indication of its presence. It often uses the very tip of a tall tree for a singing perch.

Migration and Winter Range
The Blackburnian warbler is known only as a migrant throughout most of the eastern United States. By late summer, most of the birds have left their breeding grounds and, throughout August and September, are seen drifting through the deciduous woods in mixed flocks with other warblers. By early October most Blackburnian warblers have left the United States en route to their winter range from Guatemala south to central Peru and Venezuela.

Breeding Range
The bird's breeding range covers the mature and well-developed second-growth coniferous and mixed wood-lands of the lower Canadian and upper transition zones from central Saskatchewan east to the Gaspe Peninsula and Nova Scotia and south to central Minnesota, central Wisconsin, central Michigan, northeastern Ohio, southeastern New York, Massachusetts and the Appalachian Mountains to northern Georgia and South Carolina.

Breeding Behavior
The male bird characteristically frequents the tops of tall trees in his breeding area, facing his colorful breast into the sunlight. A glimpse of the vivid orange shows why this bird is also called "firethroat."

Nesting
The birds nest in coniferous trees, including hemlock, fir, pine and cedar. The bird's fondness for hemlocks has earned it the name of "hemlock warbler." A nest of small twigs, dry grasses and soft plant down or lichen is constructed on a horizontal branch well out from the trunk and 5 to 85 feet above the ground. Other than hemlocks, the bird will also nest in spruces, pines, firs and tamaracks. The nest is lined with lichens, mosses, rootlets and hair.

The female lays four or five brown-spotted white eggs. The male may occasionally share the incubation duties, which last for 11 or 12 days. Both parents feed the young.

Feeding Habits
The Blackburnian warbler is insectivorous like other wood warblers. It eats beetles, crane flies, ants and small caterpillars and also will eat berries.

Plants for food and shelter include:
Elderberries (*Sambucus* spp.) (see page 188)
Hemlocks (*Tsuga* spp.) (see page 190)

The Blackburnian warbler displaying his breeding plumage.

An American redstart eating
insects attracted to the red flowers
of the Arizona honeysuckle (<u>Lonicera arizonica</u>).

AMERICAN REDSTART

Setophaga ruticilla

With its fluttering motions and bright patches of orange on the wings and tail, the American redstart is commonly referred to as "the butterfly of the bird world." The male is unmistakeable, with the orange patches contrasting with the black body and white belly. Females and young are olive-gray above, with yellow tail and wing patches.

The American redstart can also be recognized by its habit of spreading its tail and drooping its wings. The song is high-pitched and varies in its pattern; one sounds like "tseet, tseet, tseet."

Habitat
The redstart's preferred habitat includes open deciduous and mixed woodlands, tall shrubbery and woodlots. During migration, the birds may be found in almost every habitat.

Migration and Winter Range
The American redstart can be found from Mexico to South America during winter.

Breeding Range
The American redstart breeds from southeastern Alaska east to Newfoundland and south to eastern Oregon, northern Utah, northern Colorado, southeastern Louisiana and central Georgia.

Breeding Behavior
The males arrive before the females and defend a chosen territory, advertising their presence by singing. The males aggressively defend their territories. When the females arrive, the males posture for them and flash their colors.

Nesting
The female bird builds the neat, cup-shaped nest from grass, rootlets and bark fiber bound with spiderweb and ornamented with lichens. The nest is built in the crotch of a deciduous tree or shrub, usually 10 to 20 feet above ground. Four whitish eggs speckled with gray and brown are laid and incubated by the female for 12 days. Both parents feed the young, who leave the nest after 8 or 9 days.

Feeding Habits
The American redstart eats forest insects, including beetles, borers and caterpillars, as well as flies, aphids, spiders and moths. This bird is attracted to insects that live in most garden trees and shrubs.

Plants for food and shelter include:
Maples (*Acer* spp.) (see page 154)
Alders (*Alnus* spp.) (see page 156)
Birches (*Betula* spp.) (see page 159)
Elderberries (*Sambucus* spp.) (see page 188)

A female American redstart eating insects in the foliage of a spicebush (Lindera benzoin).

EASTERN MEADOWLARK

Sturnella magna

This beautiful grassland bird has a bright yellow breast marked with a striking black V. Its back is mottled brown, and its tail shows distinctive white outer feathers in flight. Despite its name, the meadowlark is not a lark but a member of the blackbird family, related to the starling. The bird resembles the starling in the way it walks with a swaggering gait, and in flight it has the same flapping then gliding action of the starling.

An eastern meadowlark probing the ground for insects.

The eastern meadowlark is almost identical in appearance to the western meadowlark. The mottled back of the eastern species is darker than the back of its western cousin. The two birds are similar in appearance, habits, and haunts, but when the two sing, the difference is apparent.

The western species is by far the better musician, possibly unequalled in quality of song among North American birds. The song of the eastern meadowlark is a plaintive, slurred whistle usually rendered as "spring-o-the-year." The song is one of the earliest to be heard in spring. The bird also has a harsh, chattering, guttural alarm call, and male birds perform a bubbling, tinkling flight song.

Habitat
Eastern meadowlarks are found in open grasslands, prairies and fields with shrubby borders.

Migration and Winter Range
In fall the birds leave the northern limits of their range, though some winter as far north as southern Ontario and part of New England. In winter, meadowlarks roam in loose flocks of several families.

Breeding Range
The eastern meadowlark breeds from southeastern Ontario and Nova Scotia through the prairie country of Canada, and south through the central and eastern United States to Arizona, New Mexico, Texas and the Gulf states to northern South America. The birds are early spring migrants, with the males arriving first at the breeding territory.

Breeding Behavior
Nesting begins early. The male bird defends his breeding territory with song, advertising to other males that the area is occupied. Males may have more than one mate. The territory is usually about 7 acres, and intruding meadowlarks are chased to the borders.

Nesting
The female builds a beautiful nest in a 1- to 3-inch-deep depression in the ground in meadows, pastures, the edges of a marsh or any open grassy area. Damp or wet ground is often preferred. She lines the depression with coarse, dry grass, then with fine grasses, forming a grassy saucer. The nest is often given a dome-shaped roof made of grass interwoven with surrounding vegetation. The entrance to the nest is on the side. The nest is well concealed and very hard to detect. The bird's coloration helps it blend with its surroundings.

Three to seven (usually five) whitish-pink eggs, speckled with brown and lavender, are laid and incubated by the female for 13 to 15 days. The young leave the nest when they are 11 or 12 days old and wander around in the grass with their parents until they are able to fly. The birds then roam the countryside in small family groups.

Feeding Habits
Apart from all their other attributes, meadowlarks are very beneficial birds to farmers, with insect pests making up 70 percent of their diet. Beetles, weevils, cutworms, crickets and their eggs, caterpillars and snails are all eaten in great quantities. They also eat spilled grain, weed seeds and grass seeds, as well as some wild fruits.

Plants for food and shelter include:
Big bluestem (*Andropogon gerardii*) (see page 157)
Wild strawberry (*Fragaria virginiana*) (see page 166)
Sunflowers (*Helianthus* spp.) (see page 166)
Common blackberry (*Rubus allegheniensis*) (see page 187)

An eastern meadowlark displaying its bright yellow breast plumage.

Brewer's Blackbird

Euphagus cyanocephalus

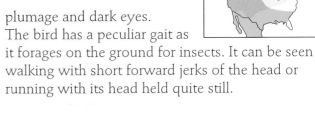

The Brewer's blackbird is a robin-size (9-inch) bird. In spring, the male is dressed in glossy greenish-black plumage with a purplish-black head and neck and yellow eyes. The female Brewer's blackbird has a more subdued brownish-gray plumage and dark eyes.

The bird has a peculiar gait as it forages on the ground for insects. It can be seen walking with short forward jerks of the head or running with its head held quite still.

A male Brewer's blackbird courts a female eating in a bunchberry (<u>Cornus canadensis</u>).

An extremely sociable bird, it commonly flocks with red-winged blackbirds, tricolored blackbirds or brown-headed cowbirds. In summer, fall and winter, these flocks may contain 40 to 100 Brewer's blackbirds plus the other species. The flocks roost communally in groves of trees and in marshes. The common call note is a harsh "check."

Brewer's blackbird is named after Dr. Thomas M. Brewer, a nineteenth-century Boston physician and ornithologist.

A Brewer's blackbird drinking from a garden pond.

Habitat
Brewer's blackbird is a common bird around ranches, prairies, roadside shrubbery, golf courses, parks and lawns.

Migration and Winter Range
Brewer's blackbird has a winter range from southwestern Canada, Montana, Kansas, Arkansas, Tennessee, Mississippi and Alabama south to southern Baja California, central Mexico, the Gulf Coast and east to western Florida.

Breeding Range
The bird's breeding range extends from British Columbia east to southern Manitoba, northern Minnesota, western Ontario and northern Wisconsin south to Baja California, central California, southern Nevada, southwestern and central Utah, central Arizona, western and south central new Mexico, northern Texas, Oklahoma, northern Iowa, southern Wisconsin, northeastern Illinois, northwestern Indiana and southwestern Michigan.

The bird first appeared in Washington State at the turn of the century, and is also a recent arrival in Ontario. It is extending its range east, with numerous sightings in Maryland, Delaware, southern New Jersey and southeastern Pennsylvania, including flocks seen on Christmas bird counts in the 1960s.

Breeding Behavior
In spring, the flocking behavior is modified as the birds begin to associate in pairs within the flock. The birds indulge in an elaborate display during the breeding season, with both sexes fluffing out their feathers while spreading the tail and wings and cocking the tail with the bill held upward and the wings quivering. The courting male's song is a creaky, wheezing "que-ee." The pair remain together as they walk or perch. The male becomes very protective of the female, driving away an intruder by flying directly at him or blocking his path.

A nest site is selected and aggressive behavior may result from competition with other pairs for possession of the site. The birds may nest in loose colonies of from 6 to 30 or more pairs.

Nesting
Accompanied by the male, the female constructs the sturdy nest of interlaced twigs and coarse grass reinforced with mud or dried cow dung and lined with rootlets and fine grass and hair. The nest may be on the ground (common in the East) in thick weedy vegetation, in marshes, in windbreaks or in tall conifers up to 150 feet above the ground. Nests are usually between 20 and 40 feet above ground.

The female lays three to seven (usually five or six) blotched, light gray eggs and incubates them for 12 to 14 days. While the female is incubating, the male spends less time guarding her and, if an unmated female is present, he may mate with her also. The male in this case guards both nests and later helps feed both sets of nestlings. The young birds fly 13 or 14 days after hatching, and juveniles have plumage similar to the female's.

Feeding Habits
The Brewer's blackbird's diet consists of 32 percent insects and 68 percent fruits and vegetable matter. Grasshoppers, crickets, forest tent caterpillars, aphids and cankerworms are eaten, as are waste grain and weed seeds, which are mainly eaten in winter. The bird has been reported as eating commercial cherry crops, and it also eats other fruit. Brewer's blackbird frequents freshly plowed fields to eat the disturbed insects and grubs.

Plants for food and shelter include:
Sunflowers (*Helianthus* spp.) (see page 166)
Wild cherries (*Prunus* spp.) (see page 182)
Grasses (for nesting) (*Andropogon* spp.) (see page 157)

A male orchard oriole (top) and
a female orchard oriole eating
the fruits of the red mulberry (<u>Morus rubra</u>).

ORCHARD ORIOLE

Icterus spurius

The 6- to 7-inch orchard oriole is a gentle, sociable and friendly bird that spends much of its time out of sight in the dense foliage of shade trees as it flits around searching for insects. The adult male is the only brick-red oriole and the only eastern oriole with a solid black tail. The head, back and wings (with a single white bar) are black. The female is the only eastern oriole with a greenish-yellow breast.

In spring the attractive song of the orchard oriole is often heard. A rapid musical warble with piping whistles interspersed and ending in a loud slurred "wheer," the song is delivered from a perch or on the wing. The song rhythm approximates "look here, what cheer, what cheer, whip yo, what cheer, wee-yo," and can be heard from the bird's arrival through to early summer.

Habitat

As you might expect from the bird's common name, orchards are a favorite haunt, but roadside shade trees and scattered garden trees are also suitable. The bird avoids densely wooded areas.

Migration and Winter Range

The orchard oriole reaches the United States in March or early April, mainly moving up the Mississippi Valley where it remains common. The birds reach the northern limits of their range in early May. It is one of the first birds to return south to its winter range, leaving in mid-July for southern Mexico, Colombia and Venezuela.

Breeding Range

The orchard oriole breeds in most of the eastern United States, from southern Manitoba to Massachusetts south to southern Texas, northern Mexico, the Gulf Coast and northern Florida, and west to central Nebraska and northeastern Colorado.

Breeding Behavior

During courtship the male bird often flies high above the foliage and then sings as he descends to his sheltered perch.

Nesting

The orchard oriole often nests in loose colonies. In the Delta Wildlife Refuge in Louisiana, a total of 114 nests were recorded in a 7-acre area. Throughout their range, orchard orioles prefer oak trees for nesting, but willow, elm, cottonwood, magnolia, hackberry, mesquite, honey locust and old apple trees are among other trees used frequently. The nest is a beautifully woven basket of grasses suspended from a horizontal fork in a branch of a tree or shrub, usually 10 to 20 feet above the ground.

The female constructs the nest and lines it with finer grasses and a thick padding of plant down.

The female lays three to six (usually four or five) whitish eggs with purple marks and incubates them for 11 to 14 days. The male feeds the female while she is on the nest and both sexes tend the young, who fly 11 to 14 days after hatching.

Feeding Habits

The orchard oriole's diet is about 90 percent insects, including ants, grasshoppers, crickets, mayflies, caterpillars, boll weevils and spiders. The bird also eats fruit, especially its favorite, red mulberries.

Plants for food and shelter include:
Wild strawberry (*Fragaria virginiana*) (see page 166)
Red mulberry (*Morus rubra*) (see page 172)
Wild cherries (*Prunus* spp.) (see page 182)
Common blackberry (*Rubus allegheniensis*) (see page 187)
Viburnums (*Viburnum* spp.) (see page 193)
Wild grapes (*Vitis* spp.) (see page 194)

A male orchard oriole eating insects.

HOODED ORIOLE

Icterus cucullatus

One of the brightest birds in the Southwest, the hooded oriole's brilliant orange "hood" and black throat seem emphasized by desert sunshine. The only oriole in the United States with an orange crown, the 7- to 7³/₄-inch hooded oriole is more slender than other orioles. The female is olive-gray above and olive-yellow below. Both sexes have a thin, black, slightly downcurved bill.

They sing in a warbling, throaty whistle, interspersed with a chatter or rattle. The call note is a liquid whistled "wheet."

A male hooded oriole feeding on nectar and insects in the blossoms of soaptree yucca (Yucca elata).

Habitat
The hooded oriole is a common bird in suburban parks and gardens with suitable shade trees and open woodlands, especially near streams. Although regarded as a shy, quiet bird, the hooded oriole is well known because it has found congenial surroundings among the palm plantations and ornamental shrubs of suburban areas and ranches.

Migration and Winter Range
The hooded oriole arrives in California and Texas in March and in Arizona in April. The bird has usually left his summer range by late August, with some immature birds remaining until early September before moving into Mexico. The hooded oriole sometimes winters in southern Texas, and there are numerous winter records for southern California as far north as Pasadena and Los Angeles.

Breeding Range
The hooded oriole is the most common breeding oriole in southern Texas. The bird's breeding range extends from central California, southern Nevada, central and southeastern Arizona, southern New Mexico and western and southern Texas south to southern Mexico, Baja California, Guatemala and Belize. The bird is extending its range north, and has been reported recently breeding in southwestern Utah.

Breeding Behavior
In late April the male hooded oriole begins courting, chasing the female and advancing toward her with exaggerated bows.

Nesting
The female constructs the well-built, basket-shaped nest from shredded palm or yucca fibers suspended from the underside of a palm leaf in a bunch of Spanish moss or mistletoe. Hackberry, mesquite and sycamore trees and yuccas are also used for nesting, and occasionally the nest is attached under the eaves of a house. In California, the nests are commonly fastened to the underside of a leaf of the California fan palm. The palm leaf provides shelter from rain and sun as well as concealment. This nesting habit has earned the bird its other common name, "palm-leaf oriole."

Three to five spotted blue-white or gray-white eggs are laid and incubated by the female for 12 to 14 days. Young leave the nest about 14 days after hatching, but are fed and cared for by the parents for some time later. The young birds resemble the female, though the young males have a black throat. Two or three broods a year are not uncommon.

Feeding Habits
The bird spends most of its time restlessly gleaning insects from the dense foliage of large trees and rarely descends to the ground. The oriole searches for

A female hooded oriole constructing its nest in a desert fan palm (Washingtonia filifera).

caterpillars on the undersides of leaves, often hanging upside down like a chickadee. Insect larvae and grasshoppers are also included in the diet.

Hooded orioles enjoy nectar, and much time is spent probing tubular flowers such as agaves, aloes and lilies for their nectar. Larger flowers are often punctured at the base and robbed of nectar. The birds also feed on berries and fruits, including cherries and loquats, and visit feeders to eat sugar-water syrup, bread and fresh or dried fruits.

Plants for food and shelter include:
Wild cherries (*Prunus* spp.) (see page 182)
Elderberries (*Sambucus* spp.) (see page 188)
Soaptree yucca (*Yucca elata*) (see page 194)

NORTHERN ORIOLE (BALTIMORE RACE)

Icterus galbula

The northern oriole species includes the Baltimore and the western Bullock's races. With the planting of trees across the Great Plains, the Baltimore race has extended its range west to meet the western Bullock's oriole.

The two birds (Baltimore and western Bullock's race) interbreed freely where ranges overlap and, in 1973, they were made subspecies of the northern oriole by the American Ornithologists Union (A.D.U.).

A female northern oriole (Baltimore race) leaving her nest in an elm (Ulmus spp.) the oriole's favorite nesting tree.

The Baltimore race is a brilliantly colored melodious oriole and is the state bird of Maryland. The male is black above and orange below, while the female is olive above and yellow-orange below; both birds have white wing bars and are 7 to 8½ inches long. The oriole's song is flutelike, a low "hew-li."

The Baltimore oriole takes its common name from Sir George Calvert, first Baron of Baltimore, whose land grant north of the Potomac became the state of Maryland. Sir George's coat of arms bore the orange and black colors of the male oriole, and the early settlers named the bird in his honor.

Habitat
The Baltimore oriole prefers places where large trees are present in relatively open areas, such as shade trees along country roads, orchards, city parks and suburban areas.

Migration and Winter Range
The bird usually winters from southern Mexico to Colombia and Venezuela, though it is sometimes found in south-eastern Canada and the eastern United States. In mid-August, about two weeks before it migrates south, the bird's song is often heard, especially in the early morning.

Breeding Range
The bird's breeding range extends from central Alberta east to central Nova Scotia and south to west-central Oklahoma, northeastern Texas, southeastern Louisiana, north-central Georgia, western South Carolina, central Virginia and Delaware.

Breeding Behavior
The males arrive at the breeding grounds several days before the females. On the female's arrival, the male begins a series of displays of his brilliant plumage. First he raises his wings and spreads his tail as he shows off his orange breast, then in bright sunlight he shows off his brilliant black, orange and white upperparts, all the while uttering low, sweet, seductive whistling notes. Once mated, the pair remain constantly together.

Nesting
The Baltimore oriole's nest is probably the most beautiful of all North American bird nests. The nest is a well-woven, deep, silvery pouch suspended by the rim from the end of long, drooping branches. It is often placed 25 to 30 feet above the ground, where it tosses in the wind. Elms, poplars, maples, birch and oak trees are used.

The nest is woven of plant fibers, string, cloth and hair. Many people enjoy supplying the birds with short lengths of string or yarn. The nest is lined with wool, hair and fine grasses. The female lays four (sometimes five or six) dark brown- and black-marked grayish eggs, which are incubated for 12 to 14 days. The young fly from 12 to 14 days after hatching. The young join their parents and wander in family groups, eating wild fruits and berries. The birds seem to return to the same nesting site year after year.

Feeding Habits
The birds spend much of their time in the dense foliage of shade trees, gleaning insects from the leaves and twigs. Caterpillars are an important food source, usually making up over 33 percent of the total diet. The bird has been known to eradicate local infestations of orchard tent caterpillars. Moths, beetles, ants, bugs, scale insects, aphids and wood borers are among other food insects. Wild fruits, garden peas and flower nectar are also consumed. Nectar feeders and oranges cut in half attract orioles to feeding stations.

Plants for food and shelter include:
Serviceberries (*Amelanchier* spp.) (see page 156)
Red mulberry (*Morus rubra*) (see page 172)
Wild cherries (*Prunus* spp.) (see page 182)
Highbush blueberry (*Vaccinium corymbosum*) (see page 191)

*A male northern oriole, Baltimore race, eating insects from the flowers of the Canada plum (*Prunus nigra*).*

Flowering dogwood (Cornus florida)
is a common nesting tree for the summer tanager.

SUMMER TANAGER

Piranga rubra

The male summer tanager retains his bright rose-red color and brown flight feathers throughout the year, while the female is olive-green above and a deep yellow below. Both sexes are 7 to 8 inches long. The summer tanager has a long yellowish-brown bill in the breeding season, which changes to a darker color in the fall and is a dusky color in young birds. The bird's common call is a distinctive rattling "chicky-tucky-tuck."

Though the plumage of the male summer tanager is unmistakeable, like the scarlet tanager it is difficult to detect the bird in the dense concealing foliage of the woodland trees that he inhabits. The summer tanager is a solitary bird in its habits and deliberate in its movements.

Habitat
Summer tanagers prefer mature trees in the dry oak and mixed forests in the South, and cottonwood and willow thickets along streams in the Southwest.

Migration and Winter Range
The summer tanager is one of the many North American species that migrate across the Gulf of Mexico from Central America to the Gulf States. A common summer resident of the southern states, the summer tanager arrives in Florida as early as late March. The main northern migration occurs throughout April, with the birds reaching the northern limit of their breeding range by early May.

The migration south begins as early as late August and continues until mid-October, as the birds return to their Central and South American winter haunts. The bird winters from northern Mexico south to Bolivia and Brazil.

Breeding Range
The bird's breeding range extends from southeastern California, New Mexico, Nebraska, Iowa, central Ohio, Maryland and Delaware south to southern Florida, the Gulf Coast and northern Mexico.

Breeding Behavior
The male proclaims his territory with a rich, varied musical song similar to the scarlet tanager's, but sweeter and less harsh. The female is attracted to the song, and the male spreads his wings and tail with his bill pointed vertically as part of a courtship display.

Nesting
The female constructs the flimsy, shallow, cup-shaped nest from stems, grasses, bark and leaves. Nests are usually near the tip of a limb 10 to 35 feet above the ground. In northwestern Florida, the flowering dogwood is a common nesting tree. Turkey oak and Jack oak, as well as other oaks, are also favored trees, since the nests become very difficult to locate among the large leaves. Pine trees are sometimes also used for nesting.

Three or four brown-spotted blue-green eggs are laid and incubated by the female for 11 or 12 days. Both sexes feed the young.

Feeding Habits
Insects, beetles, wasps, spiders and worms are included in the summer tanager's diet. The bird often catches insects on the wing, like a flycatcher. The bird's habit of catching bees and eating soft larvae of wasps out of their nests has earned it the common name of "beebird" in some southern parts of its range. Wild fruits such as blackberries are also eaten, and garden feeding stations are visited for peanut butter and cornmeal mixture.

Plants for food and shelter include:
Red mulberry (*Morus rubra*) (see page 172)
Wild cherries (*Prunus* spp.) (see page 182)
Common blackberry (*Rubus allegheniensis*) (see page 187)

A male summer tanager showing his yellow-brown bill, which will darken after breeding season.

Scarlet Tanager

Piranga olivacea

The tanager family is represented by 236 species found only in the western hemisphere. Only four species regularly migrate to North America while a fifth species of tanager, the blue-gray tanager, has been introduced in Miami, Florida.

The scarlet tanager's brilliant plumage is unrivaled among North American birds. Seen in sunlight, the male in breeding plumage is a brilliant scarlet with black wings and tail. The female has an olive-green back, brown wings, and yellow breast and belly; both birds are 7½ inches long. Between July and August, the male scarlet tanager adopts a winter plumage that is similar to the female's, of dull green above and yellowish below, but retains his black wings and tail.

A male scarlet tanager
displaying his scarlet plumage while
courting a female in staghorn sumac (Rhus typhina).

Although the male's breeding plumage is hard to miss at close range, the scarlet tanager is an arboreal bird and tends to remain hidden in the trees. The tanager's song is like a robin's in style, a repetitive caroling with a husky quality, sounding like "querit, queer, queery, querit, queer." The call note is a nasal "chick-kurr." Its voice is often confused with that of the American robin. The bird is therefore often thought to be rare, when "unseen and unheard" would be a more accurate description.

Habitat

The preferred habitat is mature deciduous woods of oak, tulip tree, hickory and ash, but it often frequents mixed woods of pine and hemlock, wooded parks and large shade trees in suburban areas.

Migration and Winter Range

The scarlet tanager arrives in the United States in April and drifts into the northern parts of its range in early- to mid-May. It has usually left the United States by mid-October for its winter haunts in South America. The bird winters in South America from Colombia to Bolivia.

Breeding Range

The bird's range extends from southeastern Manitoba east to New Brunswick and the east central United States and south to eastern Oklahoma, central Alabama and northern Georgia.

Breeding Behavior

The male bird arrives several days before the female and claims his territory, warning off other males with frequent singing from the tops of tall trees. The female is attracted to the song, and the male courts her by positioning himself on a lower branch and spreading his wings to display the gorgeous scarlet plumage of his back. This plumage is normally hidden from view when his wings are folded.

Nesting

The female constructs a small, flat, cup-shaped nest from twigs, rootlets and grass lined with finer grasses or pine needles, usually far out on the limb of a large tree. The nest is usually 8 to 75 feet above the ground. Three to five brown-spotted greenish eggs are laid and incubated by the female for 13 or 14 days. Both parentshelp to feed the young, who leave the nest about 9 to 11 days after hatching.

The female scarlet tanager. These colorful birds are not as uncommon as had been thought.

Feeding Habits

Scarlet tanagers are drawn to oaks because of their many insect pests. Insects make up over 80 percent of the bird's diet. Aphids, weevils, wood borers, scale insects, ants, termites, caterpillars, slugs, snails and worms are all on the menu. Tanagers are particularly beneficial birds in orchards, where they can control outbreaks of the small caterpillars of the gypsy moth. It has been estimated that two scarlet tanagers could destroy over 14,000 of these caterpillars in one week. The rest of the scarlet tanager's diet consists of wild fruits such as huckleberry, mulberry, bayberry, sumac, blackberry, elderberry and blueberry.

Plants for food and shelter include:
Serviceberries (*Amelanchier* spp.) (see page 156)
Dogwoods (*Cornus* spp.) (see page 163)
Red mulberry (*Morus rubra*) (see page 172)
Bayberries (*Myrica* spp.) (see page 173)
Wild cherries (*Prunus* spp.) (see page 182)
Sumacs (*Rhus* spp.) (see page 185)
Common blackberry (*Rubus alleghaniensis*) (see page 187)
Elderberries (*Sambucus* spp.) (see page 188)
Highbush blueberry (*Vaccinium corymbosum*) (see page 191)

LARK BUNTING

Calamospiza melanocories

A characteristic bird of the open prairie grasslands and weed-grown pastures of southern Canada and the west-central United States, the lark bunting is a stocky, thick-billed finch. The male in breeding plumage is a black bird with conspicuous white wing patches, which are most noticeable in flight. The female all year and the male in winter are dull brown, 7-inch birds striped with darker brown above and white with brown streaking on the undersides.

Because of the lack of trees and elevated song perches on the prairies, the lark bunting indulges in spectacular song flights over the breeding grounds that have given it the name of "lark." Its song is a flutelike series of whistles, trills, and slurs. The call note is a soft whistled "hoo-ee."

A male lark bunting at his nest on the ground under common sagebrush (Artemisia tridentata).

In North Dakota, farmers once looked on the arrival of the lark bunting as an indication of a period of warm, settled weather and as the optimum time for planting frost-tender crops. If the flocks were large it indicated a good season ahead; if the numbers were small a poor harvest could be expected.

The bird's genus name is from the Greek *kalamos,* a reed, and *spiza,* a finch. The species name is Latin, from the Greek *melanos,* black, referring to the male's plumage, and *korus,* lark, referring to its larklike song.

Habitat
A bird of the drier treeless plains and prairies, the lark bunting shows a preference for regions where the grasses contain clumps of sagebrush.

Migration and Winter Range
The lark bunting begins its northern migration in early March, drifting into southwestern Kansas from late March on and reaching central Nebraska in the first week of May. They continue their journey, slowly reaching the northern limits of their breeding range in southern Canada by the first of June. The birds travel in flocks sometimes numbering several hundred.

The southward migration begins in late July or early August, with stragglers still seen in New Mexico as late as the last week in October. The bird winters from southern California, central Arizona and north-central Texas south to central Mexico.

Breeding Range
The state bird of Colorado, the lark bunting is found east of the Rocky Mountains. Its breeding range extends from southern Alberta, southern Saskatchewan, southwestern Manitoba, southeastern North Dakota and southwestern Minnesota and west-central Montana to southeastern New Mexico, northern Texas, western Oklahoma and south-central and eastern Kansas.

Breeding Behavior
Courtship takes place during pauses in the northward migration. The male birds sing to their chosen mates, leave a perch near ground level and, with a conspicuous fluttering of the wings, rise above the prairie. They hover about 15 feet up, then descend, all the while pouring out their rich, modulated warbling that is rather like a canary singing. Sometimes up to 100 males may be airborne at the same time, filling the air with their music.

On arrival at their breeding grounds, the flocks disperse into mated pairs. The birds remain sociable during the breeding season, often nesting in small colonies.

Nesting
The nest is built in a simple depression in the ground, with the rim level with or slightly raised above the ground. The nest is made of grasses, rootlets and weed stems and lined with plant down. The nest is often sheltered by prairie plants or plant debris such as tumbleweeds or sagebrush.

Three to six light blue eggs are laid and incubated by the female for about 12 days. The male sings to his mate constantly throughout the incubation period and may sometimes share these duties with her. Both parents care for the nestlings, feeding them large quantities of insects.

At the end of the breeding season, the male adopts his sparrowlike winter plumage and ceases his glorious song. The birds gather together in large flocks and wheel in unison across the prairies, feeding in weed patches and grassy areas.

Feeding Habits
The lark bunting diet consists of 79 percent insects, including grasshoppers, beetles and weevils, and 21 percent seeds which are mainly weeds including pigweed, knotweed, dandelion, Russian thistle, verbena and goosefoot.

Plants for food and shelter include:
Grasses (for nesting) *(Andropogon* spp.) (see page 157)

A small flock of lark buntings on their northern migration.

DARK-EYED JUNCO

Junco hyemalis

In 1973, the American Ornithologists Union determined that several geographical forms of junco should be considered one species, the "dark-eyed junco". The white-winged race, the slate-colored race and the Oregon race were previously regarded as separate species, but are now regarded as subspecies.

The slate-colored race is the most widespread.

Common in winter in the East and across most of the United States, the male slate-colored junco has slate-gray upper parts and breast, which are sharply defined against the white underparts and white outer tail feathers that are usually shown in flight. The female is similar but a paler gray.

Dark-eyed juncos eating the fruits of the sweet birch (Betula lenta). The slate-colored junco is shown at top and the Oregon junco is shown at bottom.

The Oregon race is the western subspecies, abundant in suburbs, fields and gardens in winter. The Oregon male junco has a black hood and chestnut mantle with white underparts, buff sides and white outer tail feathers. Females have a gray hood and are less colorful.

The white-winged race is an isolated population confined to the Black Hills of South Dakota and eastern Montana. It is similar to the slate-colored junco, but is distinguished by its two white wing bars and extensive white outer tail feathers. In all three races, both sexes are 5 1/2 to 6 3/4 inches long.

The male dark-eyed junco sings with a ringing metallic trill. The call note is a constant "chip" sound.

All subspecies have dark eyes, giving the bird its common name. The genus name is thought to be from the Latin *juncus,* rush-colored; the species name is from the Latin *hiemalis,* pertaining to winter.

In the East, the junco is known as the "snow bird" because in the winter birds retreat from the weedy breeding areas and seek refuge in gardens near houses with the appearance of the first snowstorm.

Habitat
Many of the subspecies vary slightly in their habits, with most preferring openings and edges of coniferous and mixed woodlands in the nesting season. They are often found in weedy patches in fields, along roadsides and in gardens in winter and during migration.

Migration and Winter Range
When the first wintry blasts arrive in the northern forests, the juncos begin their winter migration, forming large flocks. Slate-colored juncos winter from southern Canada to the southern limits of the United States; Oregon juncos winter in the western half of the country, south to Mexico; and white-winged juncos winter in the Southwest and south into Mexico.

Breeding Range
The slate-colored junco's breeding range extends from the wooded areas of Alaska to Newfoundland and across the northern United States. The Oregon junco's range extends along the Northwest Coast south to Baja California. The white-winged junco's breeding range is confined to the Black Hills of South Dakota and eastern Montana.

Breeding Behavior
On arrival at his nesting grounds, the male dark-eyed junco proclaims his territory by singing from the treetops. The male may continue singing for several days before a female arrives in his territory. The birds' courtship display involves hopping around each other with wings dropped and the tail fanned showing the white outer feathers. The pair stay close to each other throughout the day.

Nesting
The female constructs a deep, cup-shaped nest of mosses, twigs, rootlets and grasses. She usually builds the nest on the ground, well concealed under tree roots, overhanging vegetation, an overhanging bank or a rock ledge. Three to six (usually four or five) blotched, bluish-white eggs are laid and incubated by the female for 11 or 12 days.

Both parents care for the young. The young are fed regurgitated food for the first few days; later, green caterpillars form the main course. The birds leave the nest when 12 or 13 days old, but remain partially dependent on the parents for three more weeks.

Feeding Habits
Juncos are mainly ground-feeding seed eaters, preferring weed seeds that they forage for by scratching among leaf litter under bushes or shrubs. Grass and weed seeds and the seeds of conifers are eaten. Seed-bearing annuals such as cosmos and zinnias provide food in the garden. In summer, various insects make up about half of the juncos' diet. In gardens they usually feed on the ground under bird feeders, picking up seed dropped by other birds.

Plants for food and shelter include:
Firs (*Abies* spp.) (see page 154)
Birches (*Betula* spp.) (see page 159)
Tamarack (*Larix laricina*) (see page 169)
Honeysuckles (*Lonicera* spp.) (see page 170)
Pines (*Pinus* spp.) (see page 178)
Sumacs (*Rhus* spp.) (see page 185)
Hemlocks (*Tsuga* spp.) (see page 190)

A dark-eyed junco eating the seed of western hemlock (Tsuga heterophylla).

CARDINAL

Cardinalis cardinalis

Once known exclusively as a southern bird, the cardinal was trapped and exported to Europe as a cage bird, the "Virginia nightingale," and hunted and killed to provide feather trimmings for ladies' hats. Now protected, the bird has extended its range north, becoming abundant, and is breeding in areas where it was once only a casual visitor.

The cardinal was named after the scarlet robes worn by cardinals of the Roman Catholic church.

The male has true red plumage, with a black bib and narrow area surrounding its bill. The female is olive-gray or brownish, with a touch of red on the crest, wings and tail. Both sexes are 8 to 9 inches long. The birds have a prominently crested head and use their crests to indicate annoyance. Another characteristic is their heavy grosbeak-like red or orange bill.

*A male cardinal (top) helping the female
care for their young in a nannyberry (Viburnum lentago).*

A member of the Finch family, the cardinal is one of the rare songbirds that sing throughout the year. The male sings with a loud, clear, rich whistle: "what-cheer, cheer, cheer; purty-purty-purty-purty," and "sweet-sweet-sweet-sweet." If disturbed at night, the cardinal will often erupt into song, and there are at least 28 different songs in his repertoire. Both sexes sing, sometimes together, the female slightly more softly than the male. The common call is a sharp metallic "tsip."

This brilliantly colored bird, often seen in the leafless winter shrubs of a snow-covered landscape, brings life to a seemingly lifeless world.

Habitat
The cardinal is a year-round inhabitant of tangled shrubby growth, preferring dense thickets, hedges, woodland borders and bushy swamps. It is a common resident in parks and gardens where suitable dense hedges or shrub borders are grown, and in bushy areas around houses.

Migration and Winter Range
Cardinals are year-round residents in their range. In winter months, cardinals often gather in flocks of up to 70 birds, and are found in the more sheltered areas of their range in dense shrubby growth and bushy thickets.

Breeding Range
The cardinal is a permanent resident from southeastern South Dakota, southern Ontario and Nova Scotia south to the Gulf of Mexico and southern Florida; and from southeastern California, central Arizona, southern New Mexico and central Texas south to Mexico and Belize.

Breeding Behavior
With the coming of spring, the male begins to accompany the females more frequently and singing by both sexes increases, often being heard at almost all hours of the day. The male becomes very defensive of his breeding territory, flying at other intruding males. The male often feeds the female as part of the courtship.

Nesting
The male follows the female while she constructs the nest, often singing to her in his most melodious voice. The nest is built in tall shrubs or small trees usually from 2 to 8 feet above the ground. Popular nest sites include dense thickets, blackberry or gooseberry bushes, rose canes or honeysuckle vines and saplings of hackberry, elm, hawthorn or locust. The nest is a loosely built, bulky, bowl-shaped structure of twigs, shredded bark, weed stems and grass rootlets, lined with finer grasses and hair.

Two to five (usually three or four) red-brown-spotted pale green eggs are laid and incubated by the female for 12 or 13 days. The male lovingly delivers morsels of food to the female while she performs the incubation duties. Both parents care for the young, who leave the nest when 10 to 11 days old. When the young birds can fly, the female leaves them in the care of the male while she attends to a second brood. The male fusses over the young birds, becoming a restless and anxious guardian as he conducts his family around the nest area. The young are guarded for three weeks or more, and two or three (sometimes four) broods are raised in a single year.

Feeding Habits
The bird's diet consists of about 30 percent insects and 70 percent vegetable matter. The bird feeds while hopping on the ground or moving through the trees and shrubs, eating many of the worst agricultural pests, including codling moths, cotton cutworms, scale insects, cotton bollworms, grasshoppers, aphids, snails and slugs. Almost 40 species of weed seeds, 33 species of wild fruit and spilled grain are eaten.

Plants for food and shelter include:
Hackberries (*Celtis* spp.) (see page 161)
Dogwoods (*Cornus* spp.) (see page 163)
Hollies (*Ilex* spp.) (see page 167)
Red mulberry (*Morus rubra*) (see page 172)
Wild cherries (*Prunus* spp.) (see page 182)
Sumacs (*Rhus* spp.) (see page 185)
Elderberries (*Sambucus* spp.) (see page 186)
Viburnums (*Viburnum* spp.) (see page 193)

A male cardinal eating the fruits of Carolina rose (Rosa carolina).

RED CROSSBILL

Loxia curvirostra

The red crossbill is known for its distinctive crossed bill and parrot-like behavior. The bill tips are elongated and cross each other like shears. A sparrow-size member of the finch family, the male red crossbill has brick-red plumage that is brighter on the rump, and dusky brown back, wings and tail. The female red crossbill is a dull olive-gray, yellowish on rump and breast, with dusky brown wings and tail. Both male and female birds measure 5¼ to 6½ inches long. Immature birds resemble the female in coloration.

The bird's song is a sweet, twittering "chipa, chipa, chipa, chee-chee, chee-chee." The normal call of the red crossbill is a sharp "jip, jip."

Red crossbill eating seeds from the cones of a tamarack (Larix laricina).

Habitat
The birds live in flocks and are usually found in mixed and coniferous forests and in suburban areas with ornamental conifers.

Migration and Winter Range
Crossbills wander erratically in winter. It seems their influx into an area is due to the abundance of a favorite food in that region or the population density in their usual range. They may be present one winter in the frozen forests of the North, and spend the next winter in the South. Winter flocks visiting New England travel from as far away as the Rocky Mountains, with the abundance or scarcity of pine cones largely guiding their movements.

Breeding Range
The range extends from southeastern Alaska east to Newfoundland and south through the Sierra Nevada to northern Baja California and northern Nicaragua. In the east, the range extends to northern Wisconsin and the Appalachian Mountains to Tennessee and North Carolina. The bird's erratic wandering continues after the breeding season is over.

Breeding Behavior
The red crossbill has an erratic breeding period, which may occur from as early as January to as late as August, apparently determined by the pine cone crop. If the pine seeds are available in winter, the birds may nest while the trees are mantled with snow in January. If the cone crop fails, the birds may breed later in the year in the sunny southern regions where food is abundant. In northern areas, pairs may form in mid-January and perform a brief courtship, which includes much singing and a courtship flight. The female may sit in the top of a tree while the male circles her constantly with vibrating wings, singing his melodious song. The male then swoops across to the top of an adjacent tree and is followed by the female.

Nesting
A loosely built, bulky, shallow, saucer-shaped nest is constructed from twigs, rootlets, bark strips, lichens and grass and lined with moss and plant down. The nest is placed far out on a horizontal limb 10 to 40 feet above the ground in a pine, cedar or spruce tree.

Three to five (usually four) lightly spotted, pale blue-green eggs are laid and incubated by the female for 12 to 14 days. The female may be fed on the nest by the male, and when she is brooding the newly hatched nestlings she may feed them by regurgitation. Both parents feed the young directly when they are older. The young leave the nest when they are about 17 days old, though their bills do not cross until some time later. Only one brood is raised each season.

A male red crossbill alights on piñon pine (Pinus edulis). The seeds of this tree are also eaten.

Feeding Habits
The seeds of conifers are the crossbill's favorite food. The birds use their specialized bill to force and hold the pinecone scales apart while they extract the seeds with their tongue. Crossbills also eat seeds of birch, alder, willow and other trees. In late spring and summer some insects are eaten, including caterpillars, aphids, beetles and ants. During winter, the birds frequently visit gardens with fruiting larches or spruces, and will remain until the cones have been emptied of their seed. They are also fond of salt.

Plants for food and shelter include:
Firs (*Abies* spp.) (see page 154)
Maples (*Acer* spp.) (see page 154)
Alders (*Alnus* spp.) (see page 156)
Birches (*Betula* spp.) (see page 159)
Tamarack (*Larix laricina*) (see page 169)
Spruces (*Picea* spp.) (see page 177)
Pines (*Pinus* spp.) (see page 178)
Hemlocks (*Tsuga* spp.) (see page 190)

HOUSE FINCH

Carpodacus mexicanus

As their name implies, house finches often inhabit cities and residential areas, commonly nesting near houses. As with other red finches, there is considerable variation in the intensity of color in these birds. The head, chest and rump of the male house finch can be bright red, orange-red, dull orange or even dull yellow. The rest of the plumage is streaked grayish-brown. The plumage of the female house finch is streaked with gray-brown all over. Both the male and the female birds measure 5 to 5¾ inches long.

The fruits of wild sweet crab (Malus coronaria) attract the house finch.

The male house finch is a tireless singer, his song a joyous, spirited warble delivered from an elevated perch for prolonged periods. The female bird also sings, even when on the nest. The call note is "queet."

A native of the West, the house finch has benefited from the clearing of land for agriculture, extending its range and increasing in numbers. In 1925, this finch became a breeding bird in the Oklahoma panhandle and in 1937 Victoria, British Columbia, was added to its breeding range. In 1940, California cage-bird dealers shipped numbers of house finches to New York for illegal sale as "Hollywood finches." Agents of the Fish and Wildlife Service were alerted to this violation of the International Migratory Bird Treaty Act, and many dealers released their birds to avoid prosecution. The birds survived on Long Island, and in May 1943 the first nesting was recorded. By 1953, the house finch had spread around new York City and in 1971 was established as an urban New York City bird. The house finch then spread north into Connecticut, New Hampshire and Maine and south into Pennsylvania, Maryland, Virginia and North Carolina.

A house finch eating the seeds of brittlebush (Encelia farinosa).

Habitat
House finches are found in open woods, around farms, around buildings in towns and cities and in coastal valleys, chaparral, deserts and orchards.

Migration and Winter Range
The bird is a permanent resident within its range. In late summer, the birds gather in flocks and roam the countryside seeking more open feeding areas, and are less conspicuous around built-up areas.

Breeding Range
In very recent years, the house finch has expanded its breeding range so that it is now found across the continent. Ornithologists attribute its successful spread across the final barrier of the Great Plains to ornamental plantings of blue spruces, which provide ideal nesting and shelter for the birds.

Breeding Behavior
In March and April, flocks of house finches break up into pairs, and the male may be seen following the female around while singing and fluttering his wings.

Nesting
The female builds the nest, which is a well-made, compact, cup-shaped structure of twigs, grass and rootlets. It is made in a shrub, in a natural cavity, in a bird box, or on a building projection or ledge. Hanging baskets on an open porch are also a favorite nest site. Nests may be anywhere — old cliff swallow, towhee, oriole and phoebe nests are sometimes used, or the birds may build in cholla cacti, vines or shrubbery around houses.

Four or five lightly spotted, pale blue eggs are laid and incubated by the female for about 13 days. The male feeds the incubating female by regurgitation. The young birds leave the nest 11 to 19 days after hatching.

The birds are sociable while nesting, with one record in California of nine pairs nesting in plastic strawberry baskets placed under the eaves of one house. The birds appear to return to the same nest for a second brood and also in subsequent years.

Feeding Habits
The house finch eats mainly weed seeds, which make up 86 percent of its diet. Thistle, dandelion and other noxious weeds' seeds are eaten. In some fruit-growing areas, house finches damage crops by puncturing the skin of ripe fruits.

Plants for food and shelter include:
Honeysuckles (*Lonicera* spp.) (see page 170)
Pines (*Pinus* spp.) (see page 178)
Western sycamore (*Platanus racemosa*) (see page 180)
Sumacs (*Rhus* spp.) (see page 185)
Elderberries (*Sambucus* spp.) (see page 188)
Grasses (for nesting) (*Andropogon* spp.) (see page 157)

*A male American goldfinch perched
on a favorite food source, a sunflower (Helianthus spp.).*

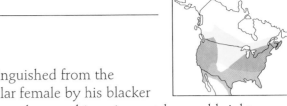

AMERICAN GOLDFINCH

Carduelis tristis

The familiar "wild canary" seems like the happiest of all birds. Its bouncy, undulating flight in flocks, its lively effervescent song and its amiable nature seem to be a celebration of life.

The male in summer has a yellow body and a black cap, wings and tail, with white wing bars, tail coverts and tips of the outer tail feathers and a yellowish bill. In winter the male is a dull olive-yellow without a black cap, and can be distinguished from the similar female by his blacker wings, clearer white wing patches and bright yellow wing coverts. Both sexes are 5 inches long.

The goldfinch song is a sweet high-pitched warble similar to a canary's song, and is sung by males from an exposed perch. A light gentle twittering can be heard throughout the year as the birds fly; it is heard on the upswing of their bouncy flight.

Habitat

The birds prefer weedy grasslands and brushy thickets not far from the edge of woods, or patches of woods. When nesting, they are found around open deciduous shrubs.

Migration and Winter Range

Goldfinches are believed to be year-round residents, but there is seasonal movement in spring and fall in flocks of between ten and several hundred birds. Their winter range is from southern Canada and the northern United States to Mexico and the Gulf Coast.

Breeding Range

The bird's breeding range is from central Canada south to southern California, Utah, Colorado, northeast Texas and the Midwest east to South Carolina.

Breeding Behavior

In spring the males burst into warbling songs. Males begin to chase the females, and short fights may break out between males. During the summer, goldfinches break up into smaller groups and become less conspicuous, with pairs forming long before nest-building begins.

Nesting

The goldfinch is one of the latest birds to nest, usually at the end of July through September, which coincides with the ripening of thistledown, which is used to line the nest. The birds construct a well-made, delicate, cup-shaped nest of grasses and plant down, usually placed only a few feet off the ground in the forked stem of a shrub. Four or five pale blue eggs are laid and incubated by the female for 12 to 14 days. The male feeds the female at the nest. The young leave the nest when 12 to 16 days old.

Feeding Habits

A small quantity of aphids and caterpillars are eaten, but the birds are primarily seed-eaters. Goldfinches commonly feed in flocks. Weed seeds are consumed in vast quantities. The goldfinch hulls the seeds before eating them. Seeds of lettuce and thistles are favorites, and goldfinches feed readily at bird feeders when thistle seed is offered.

Plants for food and shelter include:
Maples (*Acer* spp.) (see page 154)
Alders (*Alnus* spp.) (see page 156)
Asters (*Aster* spp.) (see page 158)
Birches (*Betula* spp.) (see page 159)
Sunflowers (*Helianthus* spp.) (see page 166)
Tamarack (*Larix laricina*) (see page 169)
Honeysuckles (*Lonicera* spp.) (see page 170)
Spruces (*Picea* spp.) (see page 177)
Pines (*Pinus* spp.) (see page 178)
Western sycamore (*Platanus racemosa*) (see page 180)
Oaks (*Quercus* spp.) (see page 183)
Hemlocks (*Tsuga* spp.) (see page 190)

An American goldfinch feeding in a weedy patch in the lawn.

A pine siskin eating white alder (Alnus rhombifolia) seeds.

PINE SISKIN

Carduelis pinus

The pine siskin is a brown, dark-streaked finch with a sharply pointed bill, a notched tail and yellow on the wings and tail. The yellow color is not as evident on female siskins. Both sexes are 4½ to 5 inches long.

The siskin's call resembles a hoarse goldfinch call and is a loud "clee-ip," "bzzzt" or "shree." This bird is noted for its erratic wanderings. It may be plentiful in an area one year and absent the next; its movements are apparently governed by the abundance of the seed crop in the boreal forests.

The pine siskin is an extremely sociable bird. Breeding individuals form social flocks of up to six birds away from the breeding territory, and from late summer to late winter form mixed flocks with redpolls, goldfinches, crossbills, purple finches, cedar waxwings and juncos. Flocks of between 50 and 200 birds are common. These flocks may break up whenever they take flight.

The pine siskin is often very tame and trusting of human beings.

Habitat

Pine siskins prefer coniferous and mixed woods, ornamental groves and shade trees in towns, alder thickets and bushy pastures.

Migration and Winter Range

The pine siskin appears to migrate to the southern areas of its range in autumn and to move north in spring. Winter wanderings are erratic and unpredictable. The usual winter range is from southeast Alaska and southern Canada south in the mountains to Baja California and the Gulf Coast, but the birds can turn up practically anywhere.

Breeding Range

The bird's breeding range extends from Alaska, Mackenzie and central Québec south through the higher mountains of the western United States to southern California, southeastern Nebraska and the mountains of North Carolina.

Breeding Behavior

Larger flocks break up by late January into social groups. A pair bond forms within the social group, with symbolic feeding and flight song displays before breeding.

Nesting

The nesting area is unpredictable; pine siskins may nest in one area one year and not return to the area the next year. The birds often nest in loose colonies.

A nest of twigs, moss and bark strips lined with down, fur, hair and feathers is usually placed in a conifer 6 to 40 feet above the ground. The female lays three or four lightly speckled, pale green eggs. The male feeds the female during the 13-day incubation period and for about 10 days thereafter. The young leave the nest when they are 15 days old. Two broods are sometimes raised.

Feeding Habits

Pine and alder seeds form a large proportion of the bird's diet, along with other tree seeds, insects and weed seeds. The pine siskin often hangs upside down when eating in a tree or forages on the ground for seed. Pine siskins visit bird feeders for sunflower seeds.

Plants for food and shelter include:
Maples (*Acer* spp.) (see page 154)
Alders (*Alnus* spp.) (see page 156)
Birches (*Betula* spp.) (see page 159)
Sunflowers (*Helianthus* spp.) (see page 166)
Red cedar (*Juniperus virginiana*) (see page 168)
Honeysuckles (*Lonicera* spp.) (see page 170)
Spruces (*Picea* spp.) (see page 177)
Pines (*Pinus* spp.) (see page 178)

Pine siskins eating the seeds of vine maple (Acer circinatum).

Indigo buntings eating the seeds
of the New England aster (Aster novae-angliae).

INDIGO BUNTING

Passerina cyanea

The adult male indigo bunting in full breeding plumage is the only small North American finch that appears blue all over. In fact, the bird has no blue pigment at all — light refraction gives the feathers a blue coloration. The bird is usually seen singing from a high perch or in poor light and appears as a black silhouette, relying on perfect lighting conditions to reveal his bright turquoise-blue color. The female is a drab brown with indistinct streakings. Both sexes are 5½ inches long.

The song is a fast, excited warble, the rhythm suggested by "sweet-sweet, where-where, here-here, see-it, see-it." The bird sings throughout the day from his arrival in spring until mid-August and sometimes later. The bunting also has a flight song, usually sung at dawn and twilight. The flight song may last for eight seconds or more and has an effervescence similar to a leisurely goldfinch song. The call note is "tsick."

Habitat

The birds prefer a combination of dense concealing cover for nesting and moderately high perches for singing. Woodland edges and openings, abandoned farmland, cornfields, shrubby roadsides, open brushy fields and hedgerows are among its preferred habitats. The birds avoid mature forests.

Migration and Winter Range

When the young have grown strong and the male is dressed in his brown fall plumage, the birds leave for central Mexico and the West Indies and head south to central Panama.

Breeding Range

The bunting's breeding range is from southwestern South Dakota and southern Manitoba east to Maine and south to southwestern Oklahoma, southeastern Texas, the Gulf States and northern Florida.

Breeding Behavior

The males appear in their nesting areas several days before the female birds. The male soon begins singing in defense of his territory, warning other males to keep away. When the females arrive, pairing begins, with the male following his mate around singing constantly.

Nesting

The indigo bunting accepts a wide choice for nest sites, including raspberry and blackberry bushes, barberry or witch hazel thickets, hackberry, elm, maple or ironwood saplings and wild rose thickets. The female selects the site and constructs the nest, generally in the crotch of a shrub or sapling 2 to 12 feet above the ground. The nest is a well-woven cup of dried grasses, bark strips, twigs and weed stems lined with fine grasses, hair or feathers. Occasionally, bits of snakeskin are used in the foundation.

Three or four pale blue eggs are laid and are quietly incubated by the female while the male, resplendent in

A male indigo bunting displaying his rich deep blue plumage.

his brilliant plumage, climbs the highest tree and pours out his song. The eggs are incubated for 12 or 13 days, the male sometimes relieving the female on the nest. The young leave the nest eight to ten days after hatching. Two broods are normally raised each year.

Feeding Habits

The birds have a diversified diet, including cankerworms, which may make up 78 percent of their total food during an infestation. Other insect pests, including grasshoppers, beetles, aphids, cicadas, flies and mosquitos are also eaten. Seeds, including those of thistle, dandelion, goldenrod and grasses, constitute a large proportion of the bunting's food. The birds occasionally visit feeders for white proso millet.

Plants for food and shelter include:
Asters (*Aster* spp.) (see page 158)
Elderberries (*Sambucus* spp.) (see page 188)
Grasses (for nesting) (*Andropogon* spp.) (see page 157)

LAZULI BUNTING

Passerina amoena

The western counterpart of the indigo bunting, the lazuli bunting has similar habits. The lazuli has increased its range with the clearing of forests for agriculture, and on the Great Plains its range now overlaps that of the indigo bunting. In 1959 hybridization between the indigo and the lazuli bunting was recorded, but it seems this only occurs sporadically, so the birds are still considered separate to be species.

A lazuli bunting at his nest in a native rose, the Nootka rose (Rosa nutkana).

The male lazuli bunting is a living gem, with its brilliant contrasting coloration seeming to glow in the sunshine. The male's distinctive markings include a light cerulean-blue back with a light cinnamon chest, a whitish belly and two white wing bars. The female is a dull brown above and unstreaked buff below, much like the female indigo bunting. Both sexes are 5 to 5½ inches long.

The lazuli bunting's song is usually delivered from a high open perch and is a variable, loud, strident series of warbled phrases sounding like "see-see-see, sweert, sweert, zee, see, sweet, zeer, see-see." They sing at all hours, and have been recorded singing at a rate of over five songs a minute with about 12-second intervals between songs. The call note is a soft "chip."

A male lazuli bunting eating grass seeds on a stream bank.

Habitat
Low hillside vegetation, wild rose thickets along mountain streams, open scrublands, weedy thickets and pastures are the ideal environment.. This bird prefers a diversity of plant types, including dense thickets for nesting interspersed with open areas. In breeding season the birds prefer areas near streams, but avoid damp or boggy areas. They are found from sea level on the Pacific Coast to elevations of 10,000 feet in the Sierras.

Migration and Winter Range
The bird winters from southern Bajá California, southern Arizona and southwestern New Mexico south to south-central Mexico. The birds begin their northern movement out of Mexico in late March and reach the United States in early April. The birds reach the San Francisco Bay area in the last week of April and extend into the northern limits of their range in early May.

Breeding Range
The lazuli bunting has a breeding range from southern British Columbia east to southern Saskatchewan, northeastern and central North Dakota and northeastern South Dakota south to southeastern California, northwestern Baja California, southern Nevada, central Arizona, western Oklahoma and eastern Nebraska.

Breeding Behavior
The male birds usually arrive before the females and claim suitable breeding areas. The male defends the territory by singing from elevated perches within the territory. The female arrives and helps in the defense of the territory. The male courts the female with much singing, displaying his brilliant plumage and extending his trembling wings.

Nesting
A coarsely woven cup-shaped nest of dried grasses lined with finer grasses is lashed to a supporting branch or the crotch of a wild rose, gooseberry, currant, willow or manzanita shrub, usually 2 to 4 feet above the ground.

Three to five (usually four) pale blue eggs are laid and incubated by the female for 12 days. The female feeds the young, shades them when necessary during the day and broods them at night, apparently with little or no help from the male. The male usually stays around the nest area and sometimes accompanies the female on her foraging trips. The young leave the nest after 10 to 15 days. After nesting, the birds roam the countryside, congregating in areas with abundant food.

Feeding Habits
The lazuli bunting's diet is made up of 64 percent insects in the spring and 53 percent in the summer. Grasshoppers, caterpillars, beetles, bees and ants are eaten. The seeds of grasses and wild lettuce are also eaten.

Plants for food and shelter include:
Grasses (for nesting) (*Andropogon* spp.) (see page 157)

ROSE-BREASTED GROSBEAK

Pheucticus ludovicianus

The rose-breasted grosbeak is one of the most beautiful North American birds, an accomplished songster and one of our most useful allies in the destruction of insect pests. The male is unmistakable with his black and white plumage, large triangle of rose-red on the breast and pink wing linings, which are shown in flight. The female is more modestly dressed with heavily streaked grayish-brown plumage, and resembles a large sparrow with a prominent white eyebrow.

Both sexes have the large, thick, powerful bill adapted for cracking tough seeds, which form an important part of their diet. The rose-breasted grosbeak is long-lived, surviving up to 24 years in captivity.

The male rose-breasted grosbeak sings a sweet mellow song — a long, continuous robin-like warble. The call note is a high-pitched metallic "clink." The female has a similar, but softer, voice.

A female rose-breasted grosbeak at her nest in a flame azalea (Rhododendron calendulaceum).

Habitat

The birds prefer moist deciduous and mixed woodlands where tall trees are adjacent to tall shrubs, such as borders of streams, lakes, ponds or swamps.

Migration and Winter Range

Keeping to the treetops, the rose-breasted grosbeak drifts south, reaching Central America in mid-October. It winters from southeastern and southern Mexico south to Ecuador, Colombia and Venezuela.

Breeding Range

The painted grosbeak's breeding range extends from northeastern British Columbia east across Canada to Nova Scotia; south to south-central Alberta, northern North Dakota, eastern Kansas, southwestern Missouri, eastern Tennessee, northern Georgia and western North Carolina (in the mountains); and north through sections of the Atlantic states to southeastern Pennsylvania, southeastern New York and central New Jersey.

Breeding Behavior

Arriving at his breeding grounds, the male grosbeak begins to sing. As a prelude to courtship, males often indulge in combat, which is more a visual display than physical contact. Several males may be seen dashing through the woods in pursuit of one female, pouring out their sweetest music while fighting with each other . The female accompanies the victorious warrior, and the two birds become constant companions for the breeding season.

Nesting

The male often selects the nest site, which is usually 10 to 15 feet above the ground in a fork of a deciduous tree. Both birds may share in the nest-building, constructing a loosely built structure of small sticks, fine twigs and grass, lined with rootlets and fine grasses.

The female lays three to five purple-spotted, whitish eggs. Both sexes share the incubation for 12 or 13 days. The male bird often sings while on the nest. While the female incubates, he often feeds her and stands guard nearby, singing his sweet song. The young birds are cared for by both parents and leave the nest when 9 to 12 days old.

Feeding Habits

The rose-breasted grosbeak is also known as "potato-bug bird" from its habit of eating potato beetles. Other insect pests, caterpillars, grasshoppers and moths make up 52 percent of the diet. The remainder is wild fruit and small quantities of seeds and grain.

Plants for food and shelter include:
Maples (*Acer* spp.) (see page 154)
Dogwoods (*Cornus* spp.) (see page 163)
Hawthorns (*Crataegus* spp.) (see page 164)
Red mulberry (*Morus rubra*) (see page 172)
Virginia creeper (*Parthenocissus quinquefolia*) (see page 175)
Sumacs (*Rhus* spp.) (see page 185)
Elderberries (*Sambucus* spp.) (see page 188)
Wild grapes (*Vitis* spp.) (see page 194)

A male rose-breasted grosbeak feeding in the foliage of a chokecherry (Prunus virginiana).

BROWN TOWHEE

Pipilo suscus

The brown towhee is one of the most common garden birds in California, living in close association with people and regularly visiting bird feeders, where it dominates smaller birds. An 8- to 10-inch gray-brown bird with cinnamon or rusty undertail converts, buff throat and upper breast, and sometimes with a rufous cap, the brown towhee is not as plain and dull as normally described. Seen in the proper light, his plumage is a delightfully subtle blending of earthy ochres and umbers. These colors help the bird blend with its surroundings. Hopping and scratching for food on the ground it usually appears as a drab and uninteresting creature.

At times the male bird may utter a soft, finchlike warbled "chink-chink-ink-ink-ink-ink." The southwestern race sings "chili-chili-chili-chili." The brown tohee's call note is a repeated metallic sounding "chink."

A brown towhee eating the fruits of the western raspberry (Rubus leucodermis).

Habitat

Naturally a bird of coastal and foothill chaparral, foothill canyons, open woods, piñon-juniper woodlands and desert washes, the brown towhee is one of the wariest of all birds in these areas. Unobtrusive and shy, it is rarely seen as it constantly moves under shrubs and through undergrowth. Where it inhabits suburban areas it loses its shyness, often taking up permanent residence in parks and gardens.

The brown towhee is highly territorial and may spend most of its life within a garden area as small as 150 feet by 175 feet to one acre if conditions are suitable. The bird's short, rounded wings do not allow for effective flight, so it depends on its strong legs for locomotion. Suburban gardens with open lawns for foraging, dense plantings with low-growing limbs for cover, and permanent water and feeders provide an ideal environment for the towhee.

Migration and Winter Range

The brown towhee is a permanent resident throughout its range.

Breeding Range

The bird is found from southwestern Oregon, western and central Arizona, northern New Mexico, southeastern Colorado, western Oklahoma and western and central Texas south to southern Mexico and Baja California.

Breeding Behavior

The birds are seen in pairs throughout the year and it is thought that they probably mate for life. The male bird is a devoted partner, following his mate and standing lookout while she feeds, or staying close to her while foraging on the ground.

During the breeding season, the brown towhee becomes aggressive toward other males and patrols the limits of his territory from dawn until sunrise each morning, calling his repeated metallic "chink" note to announce his possession of the area. If the male sees his own reflection in a car's hubcap or a window, he may think it is an intruding male. Launching an aggressive attack, he may leap at the image and strike it with his bill in an aggressive manner.

Nesting

Popular nesting shrubs are California buckwheats and common buckbrush, with other dense trees or shrubs also selected. The nest is a bulky, well-made deep cup of twigs, grasses and plant stems, lined with finer grasses, bark strips and rootlets. It is made 3 to 12 feet above the ground. Three or four lightly spotted, bluish-green eggs are laid and incubated by the female for 11 days. The young leave the nest after eight days, and may remain with the parents for a

This brown towhee is attracted to a garden pond.

further four to six weeks. If the parents raise a second brood, the young are driven out of the territory after the next clutch hatches.

Feeding Habits

The brown towhee forages on the ground for insects and seeds, preferring to feed under bushes or other cover. Weed seeds are their favorite food, making up 51 percent of the total diet. Grain makes up another 28 percent, insects 14 percent, and fruit 4 percent. The birds are particularly attracted to blackberry or raspberry tangles and other native fruit-bearing shrubs.

Plants for food and shelter include:
Sumacs (*Rhus* spp.) (see page 185)
Common blackberry (*Rubus allegheniensis*)
    (see page 187)
Western raspberry (*Rubus leucodermis*) (see page 187)
Elderberries (*Sambucus* spp.) (see page 188)

A rufous-sided towhee eating
the fruits of American holly (Ilex opaca).

RUFOUS-SIDED TOWHEE

Pipilo erythrophthalmus

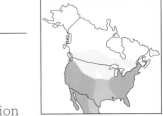

Towhees are found across North America. Geographical races or subspecies are differentiated by markings or eye color. In the Northeast, towhees are red-eyed; in the Southeast, they are white-eyed; in the West, white dots mark the backs and shoulders. The reddish-brown, or rufous, sides are common to all rufous-sided towhee subspecies. The male has a black head and upperparts, rufous sides, and white underparts. The female is similar but duller, with the male's black replaced by brown.

The common name, towhee, is from an imitation of the bird's call note, given by the naturalist Mark Catesby in 1731 as "to-whee." The song of the eastern race rufous-sided towhee is usually interpreted as "drink-your-teeee."

Towhees spend most of their time on the ground, so they are easier to find and recognize than many backyard birds. Their distinctive backward hop, repeated often as they search for food, makes them unmistakeable.

Habitat
The towhee is a bird of dense brush, tangles and thickets with leaf litter cover on the ground. It is also found in woodland edges and openings.

Migration and Winter Range
The towhee lives year-round within most of its breeding range. In the northern limits of the range, the bird moves slightly south, but often winters as far north as southern British Columbia, Utah, Colorado, Nebraska, Iowa, the Great Lakes and Massachusetts.

Breeding Range
The towhee's breeding range extends from British Columbia to Maine, south to Florida, Guatemala and Baja California.

Breeding Behavior
The male arrives at the breeding ground before the female. He soon flies to a perch in a bush or tree and begins singing. When the female arrives, the male follows her, with his wings and tail opening and closing rapidly as he chases her through the undergrowth.

Nesting
The female builds a well-concealed, loosely made nest of bark strips, twigs, rootlets and grasses. She lines the nest with hair and fine grass. The nest is on or near the ground, carefully concealed under a shrub or bush. Four to six white, gray or greenish eggs, speckled with red-brown, are laid and incubated by the female for 12 to 13 days. The young leave the nest when they are 10 to 12 days old. Two broods are normally hatched. The well-camouflaged female will sit tight on the nest until almost stepped on by an intruder.

Feeding Habits
The rufous-sided towhee eats seeds, insects and wild fruits. It finds weed and grass seeds and unearths insects while scratching in leaf litter. Its diet includes beetles, moths, caterpillars, crickets, ants and spiders.

Plants for food and shelter include:
Serviceberries (*Amelanchier* spp.) (see page 156)
Wild strawberry (*Fragaria virginiana*) (see page 166)
Hollies (*Ilex* spp.) (see page 167)
Apples (*Malus* spp.) (see page 171)
Bayberries (*Myrica* spp.) (see page 173)
Pines (*Pinus* spp.) (see page 178)
Cherries (*Prunus* spp.) (see page 182)
Oaks (*Quercus* spp.) (see page 183)
Common blackberry (*Rubus allegheniensis*) (see page 187)
Blueberries (*Vaccinium* spp.) (see page 191)
Fox grape (*Vitis vulpina*) (see page 194)

The male rufous-sided towhee prefers to look for food in an overgrown corner of the garden with leaf litter for scratching.

The small black fruits of black crowberry
(Empetrum nigrum) attract the white-throated sparrow.

WHITE-THROATED SPARROW

Zonotrichia albicollis

The sweet song of the white-throated sparrow is a series of whistled notes, which change pitch during the song, and is traditionally interpreted as "Old Sam Peabody, Peabody, Peabody." This gives the bird its other common name, Peabody bird. In Canada, the song is interpreted as "Sweet Sweet Canada, Canada, Canada." The white-throated sparrow sings this beautiful song often, and it can be heard at dusk as well as throughout the day.

This brown-backed sparrow has a gray breast, a pale belly and a distinctive white throat patch. Head stripes may vary from black and bright white to brown with tan. Between the eye and bill this bird has a distinctive yellow spot.

Habitat

White-throated sparrows prefer thickets, coniferous and mixed woodlands, weedy roadsides and woods' edges. These birds are also to be found in dense patches of shrubbery alongside lawns in gardens.

Migration and Winter Range

These sparrows winter from northern California, Kansas, Ohio and Massachusetts to Texas, Florida and the Gulf Coast.

Breeding Range

The birds breed from the northern wooded parts of Canada south to British Columbia, northern North Dakota and Wisconsin, and in the mountains as far south as West Virginia.

Breeding Behavior

The male birds arrive at the nesting grounds and begin singing, usually from a coniferous tree.

Nesting

The female white-throated sparrow constructs the cup-shaped nest of grasses, twigs and pine needles, which she lines with rootlets, grasses, and deer hair. The nest is usually built on the ground under a shrub. Four or five pale green, blue or white eggs, heavily marked with brown, are laid and incubated by the female for 12 to 14 days. The young leave the nest when they are about 7 to 12 days old.

Feeding Habits

The white-throated sparrow mainly eats on the ground, hopping and scratching in the soil. Its favorite food is weed seeds, but it also eats ants, beetles, flies and other insects, as well as wild fruits and buds.

Plants for food and shelter include:
Maples (*Acer* spp.) (see page 154)
Dogwoods (*Cornus* spp.) (see page 163)
Hollies (*Ilex* spp.) (see page 167)
Red cedar (*Juniperus virginiana*) (see page 168)
Honeysuckles (*Lonicera* spp.) (see page 170)
Oaks (*Quercus* spp.) (see page 183)
Elderberries (*Sambucus* spp.) (see page 188)
Fox grape (*Vitis vulpina*) (see page 194)

A white-throated sparrow showing its distinctive white throat patch and black and white head stripes.

A song sparrow eating the fruits
of holly-leaved cherry (Prunus ilicifolia).

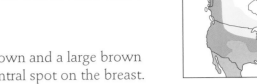

SONG SPARROW

Melospiza melodia

Possibly the most common of the native sparrows, the song sparrow is also the most variable bird in North America, with 31 different subspecies recognized in the most recent *A.O.U. Checklist*. The bird responds to varying environmental and climatic conditions, and is an example of evolution in progress.

The song sparrow is a brown-backed sparrow, with its whitish underparts heavily streaked with brown and a large brown central spot on the breast. Male and female have similar coloration, and both sexes are 5 to 7 inches long. While the song sparrow is in flight it pumps its longish tail.

The bird sings throughout spring and summer. A sweet variable song, it was rendered by Thoreau as "Maids! Maids! Maids, hang up your teakettle-ettle-ettle," which expresses the swing and tempo.

Habitat
The birds prefer bushy shrubbery in the vicinity of water and undergrowth in gardens and city parks.

Migration and Winter Range
Absent from parts of its northern range in winter, the song sparrow is one of the first birds to return in spring. The bird winters from southern Alaska and southern Canada south into Mexico.

Breeding Range
The bird's breeding range extends from the Aleutians, Alaska and Newfoundland south to Mexico, North Dakota and the Carolinas.

Breeding Behavior
Song sparrows spend a great deal of time in courtship. A warm spell in winter or spring causes a display of territorial possessiveness. The male defends an area of about an acre. Considerable rivalry between the males occurs, with competitions in song and flight.

Nesting
When a pair has mated, the male song sparrow devotes himself to song while the female builds the nest. Three to five pale green, brown-spotted eggs are laid in a cup-shaped nest of grass and leaves lined with finer grasses, roots and hair. The nest is concealed in grasses on the ground or in a bush or small tree. The female incubates the eggs over 12 or 13 days. Two, three, or four broods are hatched in a season, depending on conditions.

Feeding Habits
In summer, half the bird's diet consists of insects, including beetles, grasshoppers, cutworms and flies. Weed seeds account for about 67 percent of the yearly diet. Wild fruits and spilled grain are also eaten.

Plants for food and shelter include:
Sunflowers (*Helianthus* spp.) (see page 166)
Virginia creeper (*Parthenocissus quinquefolia*) (see page 175)
Wild cherries (*Prunus* spp.) (see page 182)
Common blackberry (*Rubus allegheniensis*) (see page 187)
Elderberries (*Sambucus* spp.) (see page 188)
Highbush blueberry (*Vaccinum corymbosum*) (see page 191)

A song sparrow eating the seed of western red cedar (Thuja plicata).

GROWING NATIVE PLANTS

Birdscaping with native plants is just as easy as filling your yard with more common garden flowers, shrubs and trees. From planting and watering to mulching and pruning, natives need the same basic care that you give any landscape plant. Buying healthy plants that are adapted to your climate and preparing the soil well will help your birdscape get off to a great start. And a little routine care will keep it looking good for years to come.

GETTING TO KNOW YOUR YARD

Understanding the growing conditions your site has to offer is a key part of creating a successful birdscape. It's easy to tell if your site is sunny or shady, and that's one factor to consider when choosing plants for your garden. Some of the other important factors that influence plant growth include climate, soil pH, fertility and drainage.

Consider Your Climate

Temperatures, rainfall and other climate-related factors can have a tremendous impact on which natives will thrive for you. Native plants are ideally suited to the climatic conditions where they have grown and developed for thousands of years. One specific measure

of adaptation is a plant's hardiness. Hardiness generally refers to the tolerance to cold temperatures. The United States Department of Agriculture has created the USDA Plant Hardiness Zone Map, which divides the United States into 11 different zones based on their average annual minimum temperatures. (Zone 11 isn't visible on most versions of the map, since coastal Mexico and lowland Hawaii are the only parts of North America in this zone.)

Check the copy of the USDA Plant Hardiness Zone Map on page 196 to see what zone you live in. In the encyclopedia entries, you'll find zone ranges recommended for each plant (Zones 5–9, for example). You'll have the best chance for success if you stick with plants that are naturally adapted to your hardiness range.

Of course, winter cold is only one element of your climate. Parts of both Pennsylvania and Arizona are Zone 6, for instance, but the same plants don't grow equally well in both places. Much of the difference has to do with the amount of rainfall each area gets. Humidity and summer heat are other factors that affect how well a species will grow in a given area.

The trick to picking the right plants is looking for those that have developed naturally in your climate. Visit local parks, state forests and other natural areas to see what grows well there without special attention.

A shadbush (<u>Amelchier arborea</u>) in spring.

A shadbush (<u>Amelchier arborea</u>) in fall.

A shadbush (<u>Amelchier arborea</u>) in winter snow.

It's also worthwhile to visit local public gardens, botanical gardens and arboreta to see which native species are growing and thriving in your climate.

Understanding Soil pH

Your soil's pH is the measure of how acid or alkaline it is. The pH is normally expressed as a number somewhere between 1 and 14. A pH of 7 is said to be neutral. If the pH is less than 7, the soil is acid; if the pH is higher than 7, the soil is alkaline.

It's easy to find out the pH of your soil. You can get a rough idea by performing a simple home test with litmus paper (available from many garden centers and garden supply catalogs). Simply mix equal parts of soil and water, touch the paper to the resulting slurry, and match the color to the chart that comes with the paper. Or, if you want more precise results, you can get your soil tested professionally. Your local Cooperative Extension Service and many garden centers usually sell soil testing kits. All you have to do is collect the sample according to the directions in the kit, send it off for analysis and wait 6 to 8 weeks for the test results.

If the pH of your soil is between 6.5 and 7.2, you can grow a wide variety of native plants. Some natives, like highbush blueberry (*Vaccinium corymbosum*) and flame azalea (*Rhododendron calendulaceum*), are adapted to more acid conditions (pH lower than 6.5). Others, like the hackberries (*Celtis* spp.), can tolerate a more alkaline soil (pH higher than 7.2). The entries in the encyclopedia that follows will tell you if a plant is adapted to particularly acid or alkaline conditions. Keep these needs in mind when choosing plants for your birdscape. While it is possible to change the pH of your soil by adding compost, other organic matter, ground limestone (to make soil less acidic) or powdered sulfur (to make soil less alkaline), it's much less trouble to choose plants that are naturally adapted to your conditions.

Checking Soil Fertility

To produce healthy, vigorous growth, your native plants need a balanced supply of soil nutrients. The most accurate way to find out about your soil's fertility is to have your soil tested professionally, as you would for pH. The test results will show you if your soil is naturally low in nutrients (infertile or "poor") or if it has ample amounts of all the necessary nutrients (fertile or "rich"). Most soils will fall somewhere in between, with "average" fertility.

You may also be able to guess your soil's fertility level by taking a look at its texture. Texture refers to the balance of sand, silt and clay particles in your soil. Take a grape-size chunk of soil, put it in the palm of one hand and add some water to make it soupy. Stir the mixture with the index finger of your other hand. If the mixture feels gritty, your soil is on the sandy side and probably tends to be infertile. If the mixture feels mostly smooth or sticky, your soil contains more silt or clay and likely has average to high fertility. If the mixture has some characteristics of each type, you probably have a loam, which tends to have average fertility.

As with pH, you'll want to consider your soil's natural fertility level when choosing plants for your birdscape. The entries in the encyclopedia that follows will tell you if a plant is particularly adapted to poor or rich soil; otherwise, you can assume the plant grows best with average fertility. If you have naturally poor soil and want to grow a wider range of plants, work a 2- to 4-inch layer of compost or other organic matter into the planting area. As it breaks down into humus, the organic matter will release a small but balanced supply of nutrients to your plants.

Diagnosing Drainage Characteristics

How quickly water drains out of your soil is another important factor that affects which plants will thrive for you. Many natives grow well in moist but well-drained soil. That means that excess water will drain away, but enough moisture will stay in the soil for roots to have a steady supply.

Like fertility, drainage has a lot to do with your soil's texture. Sandy soils tend to be very well drained; in fact, the water may drain so quickly that the roots can't absorb it. Clay soils, on the other hand, are often poorly drained. The tiny clay particles hold the water tightly and roots in the waterlogged zone can suffocate. Silty soils also tend to hold lots of water. Loams, with a balance of sand, silt and clay, are ideal for most plants. The sand particles allow excess water to drain freely, while the clay and silt particles hold enough water for good root growth.

For best results, look in the encyclopedia that follows to find plants that are adapted to your drainage conditions. If your soil drains either too quickly or too slowly for good growth, you can improve drainage conditions and grow a wider range of plants by working in a 2- to 4-inch layer of compost, chopped leaves or other organic matter.

PICKING YOUR PLANTS

When you are faced with hundreds of choices, deciding which plants you really want to grow in your birdscape can be quite bewildering. Limiting your choices to plants that are naturally adapted to your climate and soil conditions will narrow the list somewhat. But you are still left with an exciting array of flowers, shrubs,

Flycatcher on western sycamore (<u>Platanus racemosa</u>).

vines, trees, groundcovers and grasses to choose from. To make sure you get the plants you really want, consider these factors:

• **What do you want to attract?** If you would like to plan a landscape that is particularly attractive to certain birds, look for plants those species need for food and/or shelter. If you want to attract hummingbirds, for instance, choose plants with long, tubular flowers like honeysuckles *(Lonicera* spp.*)*, cardinal flower *(Lobelia cardinalis)*, desert willow *(Chilopsis linearis)* or ocotillo *(Fouquieria splendens)*. The encyclopedia entries in the Plant Directory on page 153 will tell you which birds are attracted to each plant.

• **How much room do you have?** Always consider the ultimate height and spread of each plant before you decide to grow it. Don't be deceived by the small size of nursery plants; when you give them the right conditions, they'll grow and spread quickly. Crowding plants together leads to more pruning later on and can also encourage plant diseases. If you have room for either one large tree or several smaller shrubs, remember that a variety of different plants will attract more birds than just one kind of plant can.

• **What does the plant have to offer to your landscape?** While it's important to consider what the plant can offer your birds, it's even better if you can enjoy the plant, too. If you like lots of color, consider showy flowering plants like columbines *(Aquilegia* spp.*)*

and dogwoods *(Cornus* spp.). If you want to add winter interest, include evergreens like pines and spruces. Of course, you can also enjoy the berries of fruiting plants — at least until your feathered friends stop by!

• **Are pests and diseases a problem?** For the lowest maintenance and healthiest plants, look for natives that are naturally resistant to pest and disease problems. If you want to grow a species that can be disease-prone, like hawthorns *(Crataegus* spp.), make sure you give the plant the best possible growing conditions and be prepared to cope with the disease if it strikes. Your local Cooperative Extension Service can often recommend disease-resistant species and cultivars that are well suited to your area.

Sources of Native Plants

Once you've narrowed down your list of species, you're ready to get the plants for your birdscape. Fortunately, a growing number of nurseries are offering native plant species for sale. If you can't find what you're looking for, your local horticultural society may be able to

California fuschia (Zauschneria californica) also known as Hummingbird's trumpet because it is a favorite nectar plant for the brilliant little birds.

recommend sources. Botanical gardens and wildflower preserves also may have plant sales and seed listings.

Whatever you do, don't be tempted to dig these plants up from the wild. For one thing, taking wild plants without a permit is prohibited in most states. But even more importantly, you can cause severe disruption to native plant and bird habitats that way.

You'll also want to keep this in mind when you are buying your plants. Don't give your money to disreputable dealers who get their stock from the wild. Always ask if the plants you're buying are nursery propagated. That means that the plants were grown from seed or divisions of existing plants in the nursery. Pass by plants that are labeled "nursery grown;" that could just mean that the plants were dug from the wild and potted up for a few seasons before being sold. If you're not sure of the source, look for battered or wilted leaves or plants that look too big for their pots; these may have been recently dug and potted for sale.

PREPARING FOR PLANTING

Once you've spent the time deciding what to grow and finding the plants, you'll want to get them off to the best possible start. Good soil preparation is perhaps the single most important thing you can do to ensure healthy, vigorous growth. So take a little extra care at planting time and you'll enjoy your beautiful birdscape for years to come.

Preparing the soil for native flowers and vines is really no different from starting a regular flower or vegetable garden. Strip off any existing lawn with a spade and dig out any remaining weed roots. Spread a 1- to 2-inch layer of compost, chopped leaves or other organic material over the bed, and use a spade, shovel, digging fork or rotary tiller to loosen the top 6 to 8 inches of soil. Rake the bed smooth and you're ready to plant.

For trees and shrubs, you have two options. If you're planting a few plants in different areas, you may just want to dig separate holes. If possible, though, consider grouping them into larger planting areas. The plants will thrive and it's really not much more work than digging individual holes. Plus, it's easier to mix in a variety of flowers and vines so you can add even more diversity to your tree and shrub plantings.

Preparing a planting area for trees and shrubs follows the same steps as for flowers and vines. If you're digging individual holes, make each hole just as deep as the plant's roots and twice as wide. Angle the sides of the planting hole inward so it's wider at the top than it is at the bottom. This will encourage the roots to spread out into the surrounding soil.

Grouping trees and shrubs

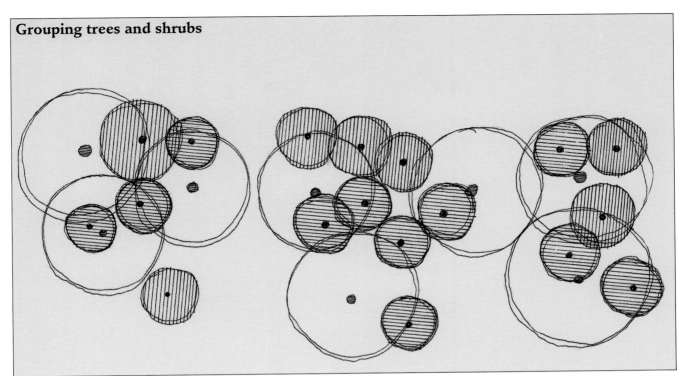

For the most natural and attractive look in your birdscape, group trees and shrubs rather than planting individual specimens. But, as in nature, plant a tree or two so they stand slightly away from the main group, as though they grew where the seed had dropped.

Creating protective cover

← Prevailing bad weather

Plant trees and shrubs of different heights in groups so birds and other wildlife can find shelter from the ground up.

PLANTING YOUR LANDSCAPE

The plants you buy for your birdscape may come in varying conditions. They can be bareroot, with just moist packaging around the base; container-grown; or (in the case of trees and large shrubs) balled-and-burlapped.

Bareroot plants arrive dormant (the plants are not in active growth and have no leaves), but they need prompt attention to get them settled in the ground as quickly as possible. Otherwise, roots may dry out, become brittle and break. Try to get bareroot stock planted within a day or two after receiving it. If you must wait, set the plants in a cool, dark place and keep the packing material moist. At planting time, leave a small cone of undisturbed soil in the center of the planting hole and spread the roots out evenly over the cone. Set the plant at the same depth it was growing at the nursery (look for a soil line at the base of the trunk). If you can't tell how deep it was planted before, set the crown (the point where the roots meet the stem) just even with the soil surface. Fill in with the soil you removed and water the plant well.

Container-grown stock can be planted any time of

year that the ground isn't frozen. Slide the plant out or cut off the container. Snip off any dead or broken roots, as well as those that are circling around the outside of the root ball. Set the plant at the same depth as it grew in the container. Fill around the root ball with soil you removed from the hole and water the plant well.

Balled-and-burlapped trees and shrubs adapt best to planting when they are dormant, either in fall or early spring. Set the plant in the hole at the same depth it was growing and remove any binding ropes, twine or nails. If the roots are wrapped in natural burlap, simply peel it back from the top of the root ball and leave it in the hole to decompose. If the wrapping material is synthetic, try to cut away as much as possible without jarring the root ball. If the root ball is in a wire basket, cut off the top few wires. Fill in around the roots with soil from the hole and water the plant well.

Food Niches

By choosing a variety of tall, medium and low-growing plants, you create different food niches in your garden. The more food niches you provide, the more birds can live and feed in the same area. In this yard, swallows catch flying insects in the air. In the tree, a northern oriole feeds in the dense foliage at the top, a chickadee looks for food in the outer foliage, a woodpecker moves up the trunk searching for insects and a nuthatch moves down the trunk looking for bugs that the woodpecker might have missed. A cedar waxwing eats fruit at the top of the shrub while a bluebird hovers nearby, catching insects the waxwing stirs up. A wren searches for insects hiding lower in the shrub and a towhee scratches for insects in leaf litter beneath the shrub. A hummingbird hovers at a flower, a bunting eats grass seed and a robin pulls worms out of the lawn. And all these birds are within a few feet of each other!

WATERING YOUR PLANTS

Keeping new plantings evenly moist is a critical step in getting them established. Even drought-tolerant species need some extra attention for the first year or two, until their roots start to spread out. Don't wait until your plants start to wilt; by that time, they're already quite stressed and can take longer to recover. Instead, check the soil in the root zone. Dig a small hole 4 to 6 inches deep and see how the soil there feels. If it is moist, wait a few days and check again; if it is dry, it's time to water. Check about once a week for the first year or two after planting and then occasionally during drought periods in following years.

For spot-watering small, individual plants, a watering can is fine. In larger yards, a drip irrigation system or soaker hose is a boon for time-pressured gardeners; you simply flip a switch or hook up the hose and let it run. Check the site after about an hour to see if the root zone is moist. If not yet moist, keep watering the site at half-hour or hour intervals until the top 6 inches of soil becomes sufficiently moist.

THE MANY BENEFITS OF MULCHING

Mulching will provide ideal growing conditions for most of your landscape plants. Mulch helps keep the soil cool and moist, reducing the need for frequent watering and encouraging good root growth. It suppresses weed growth by covering weed seeds, preventing them from sprouting. And as organic mulches (like chopped leaves or shredded bark) break down, they add humus and a small but steady supply of plant nutrients to the soil.

Exactly which mulch you'll use depends on your plants and on what's most available in your area. If you're growing plants that thrive in acid soil, mulch with acidic materials like spruce, fir, pine, hemlock, rhododendron, mountain laurel, oak or beech leaves. On soil that is neutral or near-neutral , use leaves of maples, ash, poplar, birch, dogwood, hickory, elm and cedar. Compost makes a good all-around garden mulch, especially if you top the compost with a layer of wood chips or shredded bark to keep your mulch mixture from drying out.

Before applying an organic mulch, make sure the area is free of weeds; the mulch won't control any weeds that are already growing on the site. Apply a 2- to 3- inch layer of a fine-textured mulch (like compost or chopped leaves) or 3 to 5 inches of a coarser mulch (such as wood chips). Be sure to leave a mulch-free zone several inches wide around the base of each plant; otherwise, moist mulch piled around stems has a tendancy to promote rot and encourage pest damage. Top off the mulch once or twice a season as needed.

Mulching imitates the natural environment of most plants in your birdscape — the forest floor, meadow and prairie are naturally "mulched" with fallen leaves, branches, dead grasses, etc. The only place you may not want an organic mulch is around plants that are adapted to desert conditions, like ocotillo (*Fouquieria splendens*) and desert willow (*Chilopsis linearis*). These plants are naturally adapted to dry conditions and may not thrive with a mulch.

FERTILIZING YOUR PLANTS

If you've chosen plants adapted to your soil's natural fertility and prepared the planting site well, your native plants should be able to get all the nutrients they require from the soil. If you want to be sure they're getting what they need — especially for the first few years — apply a layer of compost about an inch thick under whatever mulch you use. Each spring or fall, pull back the top layer of mulch, top off the layer of compost and replace the mulch.

CONTROLLING PEST AND DISEASES

Picking the best-suited plants for your site and providing the best possible growing conditions will go a long way toward keeping your plants naturally healthy and problem free. But there are times when, despite your best efforts and intentions, pests or diseases may appear your birdscape.

In most cases, the best approach — especially for insects — is to do nothing. One of the great things about landscaping for birds is that you're attracting some of nature's most effective pest controllers. If serious insect attacks occur, resist the urge to grab a chemical spray — it could contaminate your birds' food and water supply. Even strong organic controls, like rotenone, can harm wildlife. If pests are out of control, try a simple soap spray. Buy a commercial insecticidal soap or make your own by adding 1 to 3 teaspoons of liquid dish soap to a gallon of water. Spray plants thoroughly every 2 to 3 days for about 2 weeks. If caterpillars are the problem, spray plant leaves thoroughly with BT (*Bacillus thuringiensis*), a bacterial disease that is toxic to caterpillar pests but harmless to birds and mammals. Your local garden center or Cooperative Extension Service should be able to help you identify and choose appropriate organic controls for other pests that are known to be particularly troublesome in your area.

Diseases are less often a problem than pests, but they are also more difficult to control when they do strike. On small plants, picking off and destroying spotted or discolored leaves as soon as you see them can often stop the disease cycle. If powdery mildew causes dusty white spots on leaves and stems, try a baking soda spray. Dissolve 1 teaspoon of baking soda and a few drops of liquid dish soap in 1 quart of warm water and spray infected plants thoroughly (including the undersides of the leaves). Fire blight can attack many plants in the rose family, including hawthorns (*Crataegus* spp.), apples and crabapples (*Malus* spp.) and mountain ashes (*Sorbus* spp.). Symptoms include shoot tips that turn black, wilt and curl downward; dead leaves usually remain on the twigs. The best organic control is to prune out and destroy infected branches, cutting off 6 to 12 inches of healthy-looking tissue along with the diseased part. Prune on a dry day to minimize the chance of spreading the disease.

Boston ivy (Parthenocissus tricuspidata)

PRUNING YOUR BIRDSCAPE

If you give each plant in your landscape enough room to develop without crowding, your pruning chores should be minimal. Each winter, you may want to inspect the trees, shrubs and vines, and prune out any dead, diseased or damaged wood. Also remove any crossing or awkwardly placed branches. Use a sharp pair of pruning shears (or a sharp pruning saw) to make a clean cut that will heal quickly. If you have a large tree that needs pruning, consult a local arborist. They will tell you if the tree really does need work and they can perform the necessary pruning safely.

CONTINUING CARE FOR HERBACEOUS PLANTS

If you've prepared your soil well, chosen plants that are naturally adapted to your area, planted them carefully and given them the attention they need to get established, the flowers, groundcovers and grasses in your birdscape will need minimal care. Leave the seedheads on the plants so your birds can feast on the seeds over winter. Clear out and compost any remaining stalks in early spring to make some room for new growth.

One technique that will benefit many perennials, grasses and groundcovers is division. Division is simply the process of cutting apart plants to make several new plants. It's a great way to revitalize old, overgrown clumps that have started dying out in the middle and stopped blooming well. It's also an easy way to propagate your plants. Plants that especially benefit from regular division are noted in the plant encyclopedia that follows.

To divide a clump, cut around the plant with a trowel or spade or loosen the soil with a garden fork. Lift the plant from its hole. If it's a small plant, cut sections off with a sharp knife or trowel, making sure each section has at least one healthy crown and plenty of roots. If the plant is large, you can cut off sections with a sharp spade. Or use two garden forks, plunging them into the middle of the clump back-to-back, then pressing the handles together to separate the clump into parts.

If the center of the plant you're dividing is woody or dead, discard or compost it, taking sections from the outside of the clump to replant. Whatever technique you use, the larger your divisions, the faster you'll have big, showy plants; the smaller your divisions, the more plants you'll have. Divide spring and early-summer bloomers in late summer or early fall, and midsummer- and fall-blooming grasses and perennials in early spring. Replant your new divisions quickly in prepared soil and water them well until they're established.

PLANT DIRECTORY

NATIVE PLANTS FOR YOUR BIRDSCAPE

The native plants in this encyclopedia provide food, nesting and shelter for birds. By planting a selection of these native trees, shrubs, perennials, vines, grasses and annuals, you'll make your yard a more attractive place to birds and other wildlife.

Don't forget the importance of diversity when you're choosing plants for your birdscape — you'll attract more species if you plant a mixed garden of trees, shrubs, perennials and so on than if you just plant trees or flowers. And you'll attract more bird species if you plant several kinds of trees, shrubs and herbaceous plants than if you plant a yardful of maples, oaks or hollies. The more diverse your birdscape, the more birds you'll have.

You'll also get a broader selection of birds if you group the different plants together rather than separating them. More birds live in edge sites, where trees, shrubs and herbaceous plants grow together, than in woods or fields. You can duplicate this edge effect in your own yard with a mixed hedge planting (called a hedgerow). In a hedgerow, different species of shrubs are planted with an occasional small tree punctuating the row and mixed perennials and grasses connecting the shrubs to the lawn.

Because different birds prefer different plants, you'll attract more species to your birdscape with a hedgerow than you would with a tightly pruned privet or boxwood hedge. But because most birds seek shelter and protective cover, you'll attract more birds with a privet or boxwood hedge than you would with a fence; more with a rose- or honeysuckle-covered fence than you would with a bare fence; and more with a bare fence than you would with nothing at all on the property line.

Birds also don't like having to fly through open areas where they're exposed to predators. When planning your birdscape, connect your plantings by including large specimen shrubs, island beds and shade trees across the lawn. A well-planned birdscape lets birds dash from cover to cover so they never remain vulnerable for long.

The plants in this encyclopedia are arranged alphabetically by botanical name, since common names tend to differ in different regions, but if you aren't familiar with the botanical name, look for the common name in large type. Each genus is listed, with bird-attracting species described. In addition to descriptions, you'll find information on growth characteristics, natural range, hardiness and cultivation. Photos and silhouettes of each plant's shape will help you narrow your selections. The human figure with each species' silhouette represents a 6-foot-tall person, so it's easy to gauge the scale of the mature plant. In addition, many of these plants are illustrated in the drawings in the bird encyclopedia, showing details of the foliage and fruit.

One of the best ways to decide which plants to grow in your own birdscape is to see them growing in local gardens, arboreta, botanical gardens, wildflower preserves and other areas where native plants are grown. By observing these plants, you can tell which species are the right size and shape for your garden. You can choose plants with features you appreciate and that you would like in your garden— beautiful flowers, attractive fruits, colorful or glossy foliage or handsome branch structure. And, by noting the conditions the plants are grown in — sun or shade; alkaline or acidic soils; low, boggy areas or well-drained sites; exposed or protected areas — you can match their preferred conditions to the ones your yard has to offer.

THE PLANTS A–Z

Abies spp.
FIRS

Tall symmetrical evergreen conifers, cone-or pyramid-shaped with dense foliage, firs prefer cool, moist conditions and grow best in the northern states or in the higher mountains. In late fall, the upright cones mature and disintegrate, scattering their seed.

There are about 40 species of true fir, nine of which are native to North America.

Birds Attracted

The dense evergreen foliage provides valuable shelter for roosting and nesting, especially in winter. The fir needles are an important food for the blue grouse and sharp-tailed grouse. The scattered cone seeds are eaten by chickadees, crossbills, Clark's nutcracker, juncos, jays (including Steller's jay), towhees, finches, grosbeaks and nuthatches (including the pygmy nuthatch). Tanagers, grosbeaks and robins are among the birds who often nest in firs.

BALSAM FIR

Botanical name: *Abies balsamea*
Description: The only fir native to north-eastern America, the balsam fir grows 40 to 60 feet, in a symmetrical spire shape. Needles are 1 inch long, rounded and very fragrant.

Balsam fir (Abies balsamea)

Native Distribution: Common over northeastern United States, in the Great Lakes states and in Canada east of the Rockies.
Cultivation: Performs best in moist, acid soils in cool northern areas or mountain areas farther south. Grows poorly in hot conditions; if you live in a warmer area (Zones 5–7), grow the similar Fraser fir (*A. fraseri*) instead. When grown in an open area, the lower branches remain alive and the foliage may touch the ground. Shallow-rooted, the tree is susceptible to strong winds. Zones 2–5.

GRAND FIR

Botanical name: *Abies grandis*
Other common names: Giant Fir
Description: A tall tree, growing to 200 feet in its native habitat with a relatively narrow, upright conical shape. Needles are long and flat, spreading in two irregular rows from opposite sides of the twig. Cones are borne at the top of the tree in small numbers. They disintegrate while still on the tree.
Native Distribution: Native to elevations below 3,000 feet in coastal British Columbia, the northwestern United States and Idaho. Grand fir grows on moist mountainsides and in lowland valleys, especially along small streams.
Cultivation: Shade-tolerant. Prefers deep, moist but well-drained silty soils. Often planted in parks and gardens as an ornamental tree. Zones 6–9.

Other species suitable for cultivation:
Silver or Cascades fir (*A. amabilis*), 50–200 feet tall, Zones 6–7
White or Colorado fir (*A. concolor*), 125–150 feet tall, Zones 4–8
Noble fir (*A. procera*), 100–150 feet tall, Zones 6–7

Acer spp.
MAPLES

Maples have distinctive winged seeds, called samaras, borne in pairs, and an opposite leaf arrangement. The exception is boxelder (*Acer negundo*), which has compound leaves. Most species have handlike (palmate) leaves.

Maples are deciduous, and are among the most colorful of all trees in autumn, with brilliant red, yellow and orange leaves, sometimes on the same tree. A variable group of trees, maples can be large shade trees, such as the red maple (*A. rubrum*), or shrubs or small trees, such as the mountain maple (*A. spicatum*). The bark is usually ridged or flaked.

About 150 species of maple are native to the northern temperate areas, two-thirds of which are in China. Thirteen species are native to North America.

Birds Attracted

Many birds eat the ripe seeds in summer, including black-headed, evening and pine grosbeaks; purple finches; pine siskins; bobwhites and cardinals. White-breasted nuthatches often nest in cavities of mature trees. Chickadees, nuthatches and brown creepers probe the rough bark for insects in winter. Insect-eating birds such as orioles, wrens and warblers glean insects from the foliage.

BOXELDER

Botanical name: *Acer negundo*
Other common names: Ash-Leafed Maple
Description: A small to medium-size tree growing 50 to 70 feet tall. Leaves are opposite and pinnately compound. Plants have rounded crowns and often have multiple trunks. The tree produces abundant winged fruits, which self-sow liberally. The bark is deeply ridged on mature trees. One of the few maples with poor fall color.
Native Distribution: Streams, lakeshores, roadsides and waste ground from southern Alberta, southern Ontario and New York south to central Florida and west to California. Boxelder grows where many trees can't.
Cultivation: Often disdained as too irregular in shape, messy in appearance or easily storm-damaged for use as an ornamental, but very adaptable and tolerant of poor conditions. Suitable for shelter belts, especially on the prairies. A fast-growing tree that grows well in poor soil. Mature trees are somewhat drought-resistant. A fast-growing screening plant. Zones 2–8.

RED MAPLE

Botanical name: *Acer rubrum*
Other common names: Swamp Maple
Description: A large, straight-trunked tree with an oval crown. Grows to 70 feet tall. Small but showy red flowers borne in clusters before trees leaf out in early spring. Trees have attractive silver-gray bark. Fall color can be yellow but is more often a brilliant red or scarlet.
Native Distribution: Native throughout the East, from Canada through Florida.
Cultivation: Often planted as a shade and street tree because of its toughness and excellent red fall color. Can tolerate acidic, poorly drained to swampy soils. Prefers partial to full sun, but tolerates shade. Zones 3–9.

SUGAR MAPLE

Botanical name: *Acer saccharum*
Other common names: Hard Maple, Rock Maple
Description: The state tree of New York, Vermont, West Virginia and Wisconsin. The leaf is depicted on the Canadian flag. A large, straight-trunked tree with a dense, rounded crown. Grows 50 to 70 feet tall. The bark on mature trees is dull gray, deeply furrowed or somewhat scaly.

Boxelder (Acer negundo)

Sugar maple (Acer saccharum)

Fall color can be a mix of brilliant orange, gold and red, or any one of these colors.
Native Distribution: Native from Québec to Texas.
Cultivation: Commonly planted as a shade and ornamental tree. Prefers deep, fertile, well-drained soils with some moisture. The sugar maple is also shade-tolerant. Zones 3–7.

Other species suitable for cultivation:
Oregon vine maple (*A. circinatum*), to 30 feet, Zones 6–8
Striped maple, moosewood (*A. pensylvanicum*), 15–30 feet, Zones 3–7
Mountain maple (*A. spicatum*), up to 25 feet, Zones 3–6

Alnus spp.
ALDERS

Alders are common plants along streams and damp areas. Alder flowers are hard, brown catkins that remain on the trees year-round; male and female catkins are separate. The female fruit looks like a small conifer cone. Fruits are small nutlets which release seeds when mature. The seeds have two floats — if they fall in a stream they stay on its surface, sprouting on damp soil where they land.

About 30 species of alder are distributed throughout the northern hemisphere in temperate regions and in high altitudes in Central and South America. Eight species — six trees and two shrubs — are native to North America.

Birds Attracted
Many birds eat alder seeds, including pine siskins, mourning doves, mallards, great blue herons, green-winged teal, sharp-tailed grouse, bobwhites and goldfinches. Insects that are drawn to the foliage attract Blackburnian, Cape May, Tennessee and palm warblers; vireos; goldfinches and siskins. Scarlet tanagers, indigo buntings and rose-breasted grosbeaks eat both insects and buds. Alders are good shelter trees for many birds, including the blue jay. Sapsuckers drill for sap.

SMOOTH ALDER

Botanical name: *Alnus rugosa* (syn. *A. serrulata*)
Other common names: Hazel Alder, Speckled Alder, Tag Alder, Gray Alder
Description: Usually a clump-forming shrub, but sometimes a small tree reaching 20 to 33 feet tall with a crooked trunk and irregular crown. The dark green leaves are egg-shaped and wavy with a toothed margin; the undersides are paler.
Native Distribution: Across Canada from the Yukon and British Columbia to Newfoundland, south to West Virginia and west to Iowa and North Dakota. Smooth alders grow along streams and in swamps.

Cultivation: Best results in damp soils in full sunshine. Plants grow rapidly. The smooth alder is particularly tolerant of cold climates. Zones 2–9.

Other species suitable for cultivation:
White alder (*A. rhombifolia*), 50–90 feet, Zones 6–9
Sitka alder (*A. sinuata*), to 33 feet, Zones 2–8

Amelanchier spp.
SERVICEBERRIES, JUNEBERRIES

Serviceberries are small trees or large shrubs, usually they grow to under 30 feet in height, with straight, slender trunks. Showy white flowers appear in early spring before the leaves have fully expanded. The leaves are finely sawtoothed and are alternate. Small edible fruits ripen between late July and early August. Serviceberry plants have attractive dark gold to red-orange foliage in autumn and an interesting branch structure that makes charming patterns in winter.

There are 24 species of serviceberries that are widely distributed throughout temperate regions, 18 of these species of serviceberry plant are found in North America. Only three species, all North American, grow to tree size; the other species are shrubs.

Birds Attracted
The fruits of serviceberries are eaten by at least 42 species of native birds, including the red-headed woodpecker, robin, hermit thrush, veery, cedar waxwing, northern oriole, gray catbird, common flicker, bluebird, towhees, chickadees, grosbeaks, cardinal, blue jay, downy and hairy woodpeckers, wood thrush, phoebe, brown thrasher, mourning dove, redstart, scarlet tanager, junco, red-eyed vireo, kingbird, ruffed grouse and house finch.

SASKATOON SERVICEBERRY

Botanical name: *Amelanchier alnifolia*
Other common names: Juneberry, Serviceberry, Western Shadbush
Description: A shrub or small tree growing 20 to 30 feet in height, usually with several trunks. The gray or brown bark of the Saskatoon serviceberry is smooth or slightly fissured. Leaves of this plant are almost round. Fruits are borne in clusters and look like small purple apples. Plants tend to form thickets.
Native Distribution: From central Alaska south along the coast to Northern California and east to the upper Great Lakes area, western Minnesota and Colorado. Saskatoons grow along streams, at the edges of woods and on dry mountain slopes.

Cultivation: Saskatoons are often grown for their early flowers and colorful foliage. The new growth is bronzy, turning green in summer and yellow to reddish in fall. Plants prefer a sunny position in dry soil and grow well in rocky soil. Propagate by seed or cuttings. Mature heights vary, with some plants reaching only 4 feet tall. Zones 4–8.

ALLEGHENY SERVICEBERRY

Botanical name: *Amelanchier laevis*
Other common names: Shadblow, Shadbush, Sarviceberry
Description: A tree growing to 40 feet tall, with small spreading branches forming a rounded crown. The bark is an attractive reddish-brown color. Leaves are reddish when they emerge, maturing to dark green. Fragrant white flowers are borne in long drooping clusters, forming small red to dark purple fruits.
Native Distribution: Cool ravines and hillsides from Newfoundland to Québec and Ontario to northern Wisconsin, south through New England, New York and Pennsylvania along the Appalachians to northern Georgia. Allegheny serviceberry is the most common species in Canada.
Cultivation: Provide evenly moist, well-drained soil in full sun or partial shade. Zones 3–8.

Other species suitable for cultivation:
Shadblow (*A. arborea,* syn. *A. canadensis*), to 40 feet, Zones 3–8
A. stolonifera, to 4 feet, Zones 5–8

Andropogon spp.
BLUESTEMS, BEARDGRASSES

Species of these perennial grasses once covered the prairies. They are still found across the country, but — like the prairies themselves — are no longer extensive. The common names "bluestem" and "beardgrass" refer to the plants' bluish flower stalks and fluffy flower heads. There are 32 species of bluestem in North America.

Birds Attracted
Bluestems are important winter plants for small birds that eat the seeds in winter, including juncos, chipping sparrows, field sparrows and tree sparrows. Ground-nesting birds such as meadowlarks nest among the tussocks of grass. Quail and other birds seek shelter among the clumps. Dried blades of bluestem grasses are used in nestbuilding.

Allegheny serviceberry (Amelanchier laevis)

BIG BLUESTEM

Botanical name: *Andropogon gerardii*
Other common names: Turkey Foot
Description: Big bluestem is a deciduous perennial bunchgrass that grows in tufts 4 to 7 feet tall. Foliage is blue-green to silver-blue. The grass flowers during fall, with purplish bloom clusters that rise on slender stems from the foliage. Flower stalks reach 8 to 10 feet or more. Flowers mature to three-branched seed heads shaped like turkey feet. Big bluestem turns tan or reddish during fall and winter.
Native Distribution: This bluestem is found in fields and along roadsides and railways from Québec to Saskatchewan and south to Florida and Arizona, especially in the Midwest states where the tallgrass prairie once thrived.
Cultivation: Big bluestem prefers a deep, moist but well-drained soil and full sun. Water during summer droughts. Zones 4–10.

Aquilegia spp.
COLUMBINES

Columbines are perennials found on woodland slopes and rocky outcroppings, and in moist woods throughout the United States except along the Gulf Coast. They are strikingly beautiful members of the buttercup family with large, showy, usually spurred nodding flowers. There are about half a dozen native species, mostly in the mountain states. There is one native columbine in the East (*A. canadensis*) and a garden escapee (*A. vulgaris*), originally introduced from Europe but now well established in the wild.

Birds Attracted

Hummingbirds are attracted to the nectar-rich flowers and are major pollinators, especially of the red species.

WILD COLUMBINE

Botanical name: *Aquilegia canadensis*
Description: Plants grow from 1 to 3 feet tall, with 1- to 2-inch-long nodding scarlet flowers with yellow centers and spurred petals. Flowers may vary in color from light pink and yellow to blood-red and yellow. Blue-green compound leaves are divided and subdivided into threes. Wild columbine blooms between April and July.
Native Distribution: Wild columbine grows on rocky ledges in woodlands from Ontario to Québec, south to Georgia and west to Tennessee and Minnesota.
Cultivation: Plant columbines in early spring, or in fall when the plants are dormant. They prefer moist, well-drained, slightly acid (pH 6.0 to 7.0) soil that's rich in organic matter, in a location with some morning sun and light overhead tree shade later in day. Wild columbine grows readily from fresh seed, flowering in the second year. Often self-sows. Zones 3–8.

CRIMSON COLUMBINE

Botanical name: *Aquilegia formosa*
Other common names: Western Columbine
Description: Crimson columbine grows from 2 to 4 feet tall, with large 1½-to 2-inch-wide hanging red and yellow flowers. Plants bloom between May and August. Leaves are divided into numerous leaflets ¾ to 1½ inches long.
Native Distribution: This columbine is found in open woods and woods' edges from southern Alaska to northern California and east to Utah and Montana.
Cultivation: An adaptable native perennial, crimson columbine prefers a partially shaded, moist, well-drained site with early morning sun. Plants will also grow in almost full sunshine or shade. This columbine is easy to grow from fresh seed. Zones 3–7.

Other species suitable for cultivation:
Rocky Mountain columbine (*A. caerulea*), 1–2 feet tall, Zones 3–8
Golden columbine (*A. chrysantha*), 2–3 feet tall, Zones 3–9

Aster spp.
ASTERS

Wild asters, with their multitude of starry purple, lavender or white flowers, are among the most beautiful autumn wildflowers. These perennials range from low-growing, single-stemmed plants to multistemmed, tall shrubby plants.

With over 200 species growing from desert regions to the cold northeastern coniferous woodlands, asters are one of the most abundant wildflowers.

Birds Attracted

When allowed to go to seed after flowering, asters attract seed-eating birds. Cardinals, goldfinches, sparrows, chickadees, nuthatches, titmice, towhees and indigo buntings include aster seed in their diet. Ruffed grouse and wild turkeys eat the leaves and seeds.

Golden columbine (Aquilegia chrysantha)

New England aster (Aster novae-angliae)

NEW ENGLAND ASTER

Botanical name: *Aster novae-angliae*
Description: An upright, multistemmed perennial with showy daisy flowers 1 to 2 inches wide, borne in clusters; may be lavender, violet, pink or white with yellow centers. Plants reach 3 to 6 feet, with 3- to 5-inch leaves.
Native Distribution: Meadows, roadsides, moist thickets and damp areas from Newfoundland to Georgia and west to Wyoming and New Mexico.
Cultivation: New England asters are hardy plants suited to most areas. They prefer full sun and evenly moist, well-drained garden soil, but will tolerate light shade. Set plants 2 to 3 feet apart. May need staking. Propagate by cuttings or division in spring. When making divisions, discard the woody centers before replanting clumps. Zones 3–8.

Other species suitable for cultivation:
White wood aster (*A. divaricatus*), shade tolerant, to 1 1/2 feet, Zones 4–8
New York aster (*A. novi-belgii*), 1 to 6 feet, Zones 3–8

Betula spp.
BIRCHES

Birches are usually small to medium-size trees that grow rapidly but are relatively short-lived. They are graceful trees with attractive bark which is sometimes a showy white or salmon-pink. Birches bear male flowers in catkins and female flowers in conelike clusters. The triangular- or oval-toothed deciduous foliage becomes a beautiful clear yellow in fall.

There are as many as 50 species of birch found in the northern temperate and arctic regions of the world. Twelve species are native to North America.

Birds Attracted
Birch seeds and flower buds are eaten by dark-eyed juncos, blue jays, pine siskins, titmice, black-capped chickadees, cedar waxwings, goldfinches, purple finches, towhees, bobwhites, wood ducks and American woodcocks. Insect-eating birds, including northern orioles, chickadees, vireos, warblers and bushtits, are attracted to insects on the foliage. Sharp-tailed, ruffed and spruce grouse eat the catkins, buds and seeds.

SWEET BIRCH

Botanical name: *Betula lenta*
Other common names: Cherry Birch, Black Birch
Description: A handsome tree with shiny red-brown bark. Sweet birch may reach 75 feet in its native habitat, but is usually about 40 to 50 feet tall. The bark is smooth on young trees, but becomes broken into thick, irregular plates on mature trees. Oval-toothed leaves turn golden yellow in fall.
Native Distribution: Found on the rich uplands of southern Maine and southwest in the mountains to northern Georgia.
Cultivation: Fast-growing sweet birch is a beautiful specimen tree that grows best in cooler gardens. It prefers moist but well-drained, humus-rich soil in full sun to light shade. Less prone to borers than white-barked birches. Zones 4–6.

RIVER BIRCH

Botanical name: *Betula nigra*
Description: Trees can reach 80 feet with a broad, spreading crown. The light tan to reddish-brown bark peels and curls attractively; a cultivar, 'Heritage', has salmon-white bark. Leaves are finely toothed and oval, with yellowish fall color.
Native Distribution: Found throughout the Eastern United States and south to Florida, west to Kansas, and north to Minnesota.

Paper birch (Betula papyrifera)

Cultivation: Plants prefer well-drained soil in full sun to light shade; they can tolerate acid soil. River birch is resistant to borers. The best birch for the Midwest and South. Zones 4–9.

WATER BIRCH

Botanical name: *Betula occidentalis* (syn. *B. fontinalis*)
Other common names: Black Birch
Description: Usually a small shrubby tree, growing 20 to 25 feet tall. In the southern limits of its range, it often forms thickets 6 to 8 feet tall, especially along streambanks. Open, somewhat drooping branchlets form a broad, open crown. The bark is almost black on young trees, but turns reddish-brown as the trees mature. Fine-toothed leaves are broad at the base, narrowing at the tip, with yellow fall color.
Native Distribution: Most of forested western Canada, Arizona, New Mexico, Colorado, Utah and Idaho west to California. Water birch grows mainly along streambanks and in moist locations.
Cultivation: Cultivated in California as a specimen

tree, water birch will grow in dry soils, but prefers a sunny, moist location. Zones 3–9.

Other species suitable for cultivation:
Gray birch (*B. populifolia*), to 30 feet, Zones 4–7
Paper or canoe birch (*B. papyrifera*), to 80 feet, Zones 2–7
Yellow birch (*B. alleghaniensis*, syn. *B. lutea*), to 75 feet, Zones 3–6

Carnegiea sp.
SAGUARO

A genus of one species, the saguaro cactus, *Carnegiea gigantea*. Saguaros are slow-growing cacti of the Southwest deserts. Their tall, high-branched columns dominate the arid landscapes where they grow.

Birds Attracted
Gila woodpeckers and gilded flickers excavate holes in the trunks for nesting. The many nesting holes are used by elf owls, ferruginous owls, screech owls, American kestrels, crested and ash-throated flycatchers, cactus wrens, Lucy's warblers and western martins. In May, many birds eat the large flowers, including ash-throated flycatchers and gilded flickers, while insect-eating birds eat insects attracted to the flowers. When the saguaro fruits ripen in July and August, many birds feast on them, including gila woodpeckers, curve-billed thrashers, mourning doves, cactus wrens, white-winged doves and gilded flickers. Mourning doves often nest in the fork of a branch.

SAGUARO

Botanical name: *Carnegia gigantea*
Other common names: Giant Cactus
Description: Largest of the U.S. cacti, the saguaro grows to tree size, reaching up to 50 feet in height (usually 30 feet) and 1 to 3 feet in diameter. It bears prominent ridges around the thick trunk and branches. Thick spines are clustered on the ribs. The saguaro is the state flower of Arizona. The seeds are harvested by Papago Indians.
Native Distribution: Dry desert mesas and low rocky hills in southeastern California and southern Arizona, south to Sonora in Mexico.
Cultivation: Slow-growing saguaros usually grow less than 2 inches a year, though they often have a burst of growth when 3 to 4 feet tall. The plant may live to 200 years of age. Suitable for dry, rocky or gravelly soils in full sun. It is illegal to transplant saguaros from the wild, so if you live in the Southwest and would like to grow these cacti, be sure to buy nursery-propagated seedlings from a reputable cactus nursery. Zones 8–10.

A common flicker on saguaro cactus (Carnegia gigantea), also called giant cactus.

Campsis spp.
TRUMPET VINES

These sturdy vines bear beautiful trumpet flowers, making them handsome ornamentals. Trumpet vines are members of the bignonia family, of which there are about 750 species of trees, shrubs and woody vines, mainly in the tropics.

Birds Attracted
The trumpet-shaped flowers are attractive to hummingbirds.

TRUMPET VINE

Botanical name: *Campsis radicans*
Other common name: Trumpet Creeper
Description: A vigorous, woody, deciduous climbing vine that bears trumpet-shaped red or orange flowers between July and September. Flowers are followed by bean-shaped capsules. The large, dark green leaves are divided into 7 to 11 leaflets.
Native Distribution: Trumpet vine is found in moist woods, thickets and roadsides from New Jersey south to Florida and westward to Iowa, Missouri and Texas.
Cultivation: Trumpet vine is widely grown and widely naturalized. An adaptable, vigorous plant, it prefers a sheltered, moist but well-drained position in full sun. Plant on a sturdy fence, tree, pillar or other support, away from buildings. It can become aggressive. Prune rigorously to keep it in bounds. Zones 4–9.

Celtis spp.
HACKBERRIES

Hackberries vary from shrubs to medium-size deciduous trees. They are members of the elm family and can be recognized by their gray to brown warty bark. Hackberries bear small, round fruits that are dark green, ripening to dark red. The fruits mature in late summer or autumn, often continuing to hang on the tree in winter.

Hackberries are widely distributed throughout the tropical and temperate regions of the world. There are 60 species, six of which are native to North America.

Birds Attracted
Forty-eight species of birds eat hackberry fruits, including the eastern bluebird, cardinal, cedar waxwing, mockingbird, robin, common flicker, brown thrasher, hermit thrush, Townsend's solitaire, phoebe, bobwhite, Gambel's and scaled quail, curve-billed thrasher, white-winged dove, evening grosbeak, greater roadrunner, band-tailed pigeon, pileated woodpecker, northern oriole, red-bellied woodpecker, towhees and titmice. Verdins and white-winged doves often nest in the foliage.

COMMON HACKBERRY

Botanical name: *Celtis occidentalis*
Other common names: Sugarberry, Nettletree
Description: The common hackberry grows 50 feet tall and nearly as wide. Mature specimens sometimes reach 100 feet, with a 1- to 2-foot-diameter trunk. The tree has a rounded top, arched branches and slightly drooping branchlets. The dark brown to grayish-brown bark is warty when mature. Leaves are deciduous, sharply oval and toothed, with dull yellow fall color. Pea-size round, dark green fruits ripen purple-black.
Native Distribution: Rich wooded slopes and bottomlands, rocky hills and ridges from extreme southern Ontario and New England south to northern Georgia and west to Oklahoma, and north to eastern North Dakota and southern Manitoba.
Cultivation: A deep-rooted tree, common hackberry can withstand strong winds and tolerate dry periods when established. It will grow in alkaline soil and is suitable for most regions in North America. It thrives in rich, moist situations, but is very adaptable to soil and moisture levels. Plants withstand high heat, dry winds and urban pollution. Hackberries make good street trees. In the eastern states the branches may be affected by "witch's brooms," caused by a mite, that makes twigs proliferate into a bushy tangle. Leaves may also be disfigured by nipple gall, a wartlike insect infestation. Zones 3–8.

*Common hackberry (*Celtis occidentalis*)*

WESTERN HACKBERRY

Botanical name: *Celtis reticulata*
Other common names: Netleaf Hackberry, Sugarberry
Description: The western hackberry is a large deciduous shrub or small tree with a short trunk and spreading crown, usually growing from 20 to 30 feet tall. The rough-surfaced leaves are oval, with a network of prominent veins on the undersides. Small orange-red or brown fruits are pea-size and ripen in September. The fruits were a food source for Indians.
Native Distribution: River valleys, canyon slopes and dry rocky ridges from western Texas, Oklahoma and Kansas west to southern California and north to eastern Washington State.
Cultivation: Western hackberries are drought- and wind-resistant. These trees are suitable for desert plantings or limestone soils, though best growth occurs in rich, moist situations. Zones 7–9.

Other species suitable for cultivation:
Sugarberry or hackberry (*C. laevigata*), to 90 feet, Zones 6–9
Georgia or dwarf hackberry (*C. tenuifolia*), to 25 feet, Zones 6–9

Chilopsis sp.
DESERT WILLOW

This genus has only one species, the desert willow (*Chilopsis linearis*), which is native to the United States along the border with Mexico. Despite its name, this plant is not a willow, though it is often found along streams.

Birds Attracted

The large, nectar-rich flowers of the desert willow attract hummingbirds and verdins over the long flowering period between April and September. White-winged doves eat the seeds.

DESERT WILLOW

Botanical name: *Chilopsis linearis*
Other common names: Desert Catalpa
Description: A close relative of the catalpas, the desert willow is a deciduous shrub or small tree with a spreading crown and narrow, willow-like foliage. Growing from 10 to 20 feet tall, the plant has large 1- to 2-inch-long flowers. The fragrant orchidlike blooms are pink, white or lavender and mottled with brown and purple markings. The flowers are followed by distinctive slender 6- to 12-inch-long seedpods.
Native Distribution: Washes and streambeds below 4,000 feet, across the desert from southern Texas to southern Nevada and southern California south into Northern Mexico.

Desert willow (Chilopsis linearis)

Cultivation: A beautiful ornamental tree, the desert willow is adaptable to warm, dry situations and moderately moist, heavy soils in full sun. It has been grown successfully in the Bay Area of California in the warm hills. Suitable for desert gardens, desert willow can be propagated from hardwood stem cuttings. Plants are fast-growing at first, growing as much as 3 feet in a season. The desert willow prefers occasional watering in midsummer. Zones 7–9.

Cornus spp.
DOGWOODS

Dogwoods are named for the use of their wood in the Middle Ages for skewers or "dogs." Today they are valued as ornamentals for their beautiful flowers and showy fruits.

Comprising about 50 species, dogwoods are widely distributed in temperate regions of the Northern Hemisphere. The only species in the Southern Hemisphere is in Peru. There are 17 species native to North America, ranging from small herbaceous plants and shrubs to trees.

Birds Attracted

Valuable trees for attracting birds, dogwoods provide secure nesting sites for smaller birds such as Bell's vireo. In northwestern Florida, the flowering dogwood is a favorite nest site for the summer tanager. Dogwood berries are eaten by 98 species of birds, including flick tanagers, downy woodpecker, gray catbird, eastern kingbird, brown thrasher, robin, wood thrush, hermit and Swainson's thrushes, veery, bluebirds, cardinals, cedar waxwings, red-eyed and warbling vireos, evening, rose-breasted and pine grosbeaks, red-headed woodpeckers, bobwhites, ruffed and sharp-tailed grouse, mockingbirds and white-throated and song sparrows.

BUNCHBERRY

Botanical name: *Cornus canadensis*
Other common names: Puddingberry
Description: A deciduous herbaceous groundcover, bunchberry's creeping roots send up 3- to 8-inch-tall stems with whorled, pointed oval leaves, deeply veined like flowering dogwood's. Leaves are red-tinged in fall. In late spring to early summer, white flowers like those of flowering dogwood crown the stems. The flowers are not made up of true petals, but of four white bracts surrounding the tiny yellowish-green central flowers. In fall, clusters of bright red berries, also like those of flowering dogwood, are showy.
Native Distribution: A native of cool, wet northern woods across Canada to Labrador and south through the mountains to northern California, Idaho and northern New Mexico. In the East, plants are found as far south as the mountains of West Virginia.
Cultivation: Bunchberry prefers a cool, boglike, acid soil in a shaded location with a mulch of leaves or pine needles. The plant is an excellent groundcover for moist woodland gardens. It can be grown from seed, but may take two or three years to germinate, so unless you're very patient, start with plants. Grows best in cool regions. Zones 2–5.

FLOWERING DOGWOOD

Botanical name: *Cornus florida*
Other common names: Eastern Flowering Dogwood, Dogwood
Description: The flowering dogwood is a short-trunked tree with a rounded, wide-spreading crown. It grows 15 to 40 feet tall, with a graceful layered branching effect. The distinctive gray bark is segmented in coarse plates. Leaves are oval, pointed, and deeply ribbed. The foliage turns bright red in autumn. The tree has a magnificent display of white flowers in midspring, made up of tiny flowers surrounded by four showy petal-like bracts. The flowers are followed by shiny red berrylike fruits borne in upright clusters.
Native Distribution: Flowering dogwoods usually grow in shaded locations under taller trees in woodlands from southern Maine and southern Ontario south to northern Florida, west to central Texas and north to southern Michigan.

Cultivation: One of the most beautiful trees of North America, the flowering dogwood is often planted in parks and gardens as an ornamental or in groups. It will grow in partial shade or full sun. Tolerant of most soils, it prefers a moist position and responds well to humus and a balanced organic fertilizer. Plants may be troubled by dogwood anthracnose disease, especially if trunks are injured by lawn mowers; check with your local extension agent for recommendations. Zones 5–8.

RED-OSIER DOGWOOD

Botanical name: *Cornus sericea* (syn. *C. stolonifera*)
Description: A deciduous shrub to 10 feet tall that spreads to a large clump. The dull green leaves turn red in fall. Branches are green in spring, turning yellow-green or reddish in late summer and bright green in winter. Clusters of small white flowers appear in May and are followed by white or bluish fruits that ripen in summer.
Native Distribution: This dogwood is found over much of North America, from central Alaska east to Newfoundland, south to north Virginia and west to California.
Cultivation: Good for naturalizing, on slopes and as a screen, since it spreads rapidly by underground stems to form a large clump. It prefers full sun and moist soil, but grows well in drier locations. Plants can tolerate acid soil. Many gardeners prune it heavily every two to three years, since the reddest color is on the younger twigs. Zones 3–8.

Other species suitable for cultivation:
Pagoda dogwood (*C. alternifolia*), 15–25 feet, Zones 4–7
Round-leaved dogwood (*C. rugosa*), 16 feet, Zones 3–7

Flowering dogwood (Cornus florida)

Crataegus spp.
HAWTHORNS

Hawthorns are small trees or shrubs with spines or thorns on their branches. Beautiful and abundant flowers and colorful fruits make them popular garden plants. The fruits remain until late winter on many species.

Hawthorns are abundant in North America, where there are about 100 native species. There are also about 100 species found in the cooler regions of Asia and Europe.

Birds Attracted

The small apple-like fruits of hawthorns are eaten by 39 species of birds, including the robin, purple finch, pine grosbeak, cedar waxwing, blue jay, mockingbird, common flicker, evening grosbeak, rose-breasted grosbeak, hermit thrush and fox sparrow. Many birds find secure nesting sites in the protective foliage, including verdins, roadrunners, cardinals and hummingbirds. Chickadees, warblers and bushtits glean insects from the foliage.

COCKSPUR HAWTHORN

Botanical name: *Crataegus crus-galli*
Description: A small tree with a spreading, rounded crown, growing 30 feet tall. Spines are 3 to 4 inches long. In late spring or early summer, large clusters of white flowers are borne on the tree. Leathery, glossy, oblong leaves are dark green,

Washington hawthorn (Crataegus phaenopyrum)

with little fall color. In autumn, the small, bright red fruits mature, persisting through winter until spring.
Native Distribution: The slopes of low hills in rich soils from Québec to Michigan and south to North Carolina.
Cultivation: Cockspur hawthorns are suitable for full sun or partial shade. They prefer a moist loamy soil. This hawthorn is an excellent ornamental or hedge plant. May be afflicted with cedar apple rust fungus, which particularly affects the fruit. Zones 4–6.

WESTERN HAWTHORN

Botanical name: *Crataegus douglasii*
Other common names: Western Black Haw, Black Hawthorn
Description: A small tree or deciduous shrub, western hawthorn grows 5 to 20 feet tall with a long trunk and a compact, round-topped crown. Leaves are shiny, dark green and shallowly lobed. Small, fragrant, creamy white flowers appear from May to June, and dark red fruits that blacken when ripe in August and September.
Native Distribution: The banks of mountain streams and in meadows, woods and forests of mountains in British Columbia, Washington, Oregon and California east through the Rockies into Wyoming at elevations of about 3,000 feet.
Cultivation: The western hawthorn is a beautiful garden plant. With ample water in rich soil, it produces a mass of blooms. Suitable for full sun or partial shade. Zones 4–6.

Other species suitable for cultivation:
Pear hawthorn (*C. calpodendron*), 15–20 feet, Zones 6–9
Downy hawthorn (*C. mollis*), 30–40 feet, Zones 3–6
Washington hawthorn (*C. phaenopyrum*), 25–30 feet, Zones 4–8
Fleshy hawthorn (*C. succulenta*), 15–20 feet, Zones 3–6

Empetrum spp.
CROWBERRIES

Crowberries are creeping shrubs with short, needle-like evergreen leaves like heaths. Flowers are inconspicuous, followed by round berries.

There are several species of crowberries in North America, as well as two related genera which are also evergreen shrubs.

Birds Attracted

Berrylike fruits are eaten by golden-crowned sparrows, robins, cedar waxwings, pine grosbeaks, snow buntings and 35 other species. Provides valuable winter food.

Black crowberry (Empetrum nigrum)

An Anna's hummingbird sipping nectar from ocotillo (Fouquieria splendens).

BLACK CROWBERRY

Botanical name: *Empetrum nigrum*
Other common names: Crakeberry
Description: A low, straggling shrub or evergreen groundcover about 10 inches tall with a 2- to 3-foot spread. Plants have needle-like leaves. Tiny purplish flowers appear between July and August, followed by purple, berrylike fruits that turn black and remain on the plants through winter.
Native Distribution: Artic regions in North America, extending south to Newfoundland, New England, New York, northern Michigan, Minnesota, Alberta and northern California.
Cultivation: Black crowberry is suitable for colder areas, tolerating exposure and windy sites. Best results in an acid, sandy soil in a sunny, open location. Plants must have excellent drainage. Good rock garden plant. Zones 2–6.

Fouquieria spp.
OCOTILLOS

The ocotillo family is restricted to the desert. Ocotillos are related to the primrose and olive families.

The ocotillo family consists of one or two genera and 11 species, all but one species found in Mexico. One species, *Fouquieria splendens*, is native to the United States in the desert areas along the Mexican border.

Birds Attracted
The native species of this plant has nectar-rich flowers that attract hummingbirds, verdins and orioles. The thorny shrubs provide protective cover for a variety of smaller birds, and verdins have often been known to nest in the plants.

OCOTILLO

Botanical name: *Fouquieria splendens*
Other common names: Coachwhip, Flaming Sword
Description: The ocotillo is a shrub of slender, upright, whiplike stems guarded by thorns, growing from 8 to 20 feet tall. After a rain, the stems become covered with bright green leaves that will be shed during dry periods. Spectacular tubular flowers appear between March and June. The scarlet flowers that extend from the stems are usually about 1 inch long.
Native Distribution: Ocotillos are found in the wild growing on open, dry, stony slopes and mesas from sea level to about 5,000 feet, and their range takes in a region from western Texas to southern California south into Mexico.
Cultivation: Ocotillos are spectacular plants that are suitable for desert gardens or warm, dry soils in full sun. They make a beautiful living hedge or fence that is both impenetrable and ornamental. If you cut the stems and plant them, they may take root. Zones 8–10.

Wild strawberry (Fragaria virginiana)

Fragaria spp.
WILD STRAWBERRIES

Evergreen groundcovers, strawberries are members of the rose family. Small white flowers are followed by succulent red fruits. There are about 12 species, three of which are native to North America.

Common sunflower (Helianthus annuus)

Birds Attracted

The fruits attract 53 species of birds, including common flicker, wood thrush, cedar waxwing, towhees, robin, gray catbird, brown thrasher, ruffed grouse, quail and grosbeaks.

WILD STRAWBERRY

Botanical name: *Fragaria virginiana*
Other common name: Virginia Strawberry
Description: A low perennial, 6 to 8 inches tall, forming a matted groundcover. The compound leaves have three shallow-lobed, deep-veined leaflets. Small white flowers appear between April and June, producing small, fleshy, red fruits.
Native Distribution: The edge of woods, meadows and prairie grasslands from Labrador south to Georgia and from Alberta to Oklahoma.
Cultivation: An open, sunny location with a well-drained, humus-rich soil gives the best results. New plants can be obtained by transplanting "daughter plants" produced by runners in late summer. Zones 4–9.

Other species suitable for cultivation:
California wild strawberry (*F. californica*), 6–8 inches, Zones 5–10
Beach strawberry (*F. chiloensis*), 2–8 inches, Zones 5–10

Helianthus spp.
SUNFLOWERS

Cheerful sunflowers were favorites with the pioneers and are also loved by birds. Members of the sunflower or daisy family, there are about 150 species of annuals and perennials native to the New World.

Birds Attracted

The nutritious seeds are eaten by a variety of birds, including mourning doves, quail, Brewer's blackbirds, red-winged blackbirds, lazuli buntings, chickadees, house finches, goldfinches, eastern and western meadowlarks, white-breasted nuthatches, tree sparrows, white-crowned sparrows and tufted titmice.

COMMON SUNFLOWER

Botanical name: *Helianthus annuus*
Description: The enormous cultivated sunflowers have been derived from this annual species. The wild plant is around 6 feet tall, with black-centered golden daisy flowers 5 to 6 inches across. The wild plants have many branches, with each branch and branchlet carrying a flower. The wild flowers are more daisylike than cultivated sunflowers, with longer golden petals and a much smaller central disk. The flowers are borne between June and September, followed by black-shelled oval seeds.

Cultivation: A beautiful large specimen plant, it is rapid-growing and often has a multi-trunked tree. It prefers full sun and is heat- and wind-tolerant. Plants also tolerate a wide range of soil conditions, but prefer a deep, rich, moist soil. Useful for erosion control or as a shade tree. Zones 7–10.

Other species suitable for cultivation:
Arizona sycamore (*P. wrightii*), 90–100 feet, Zones 7–10

Populus spp.
POPLARS, ASPENS, COTTONWOODS

Poplars are large, fast-growing trees with pale bark and coarsely toothed leaves. They are widely distributed throughout the northern hemisphere, mainly in temperate regions. There are about 35 species, 15 of which are native to North America. In the western part of the United States, poplars are among the best-known native trees, and on some parts of the prairies they are the only trees growing. Seed capsules mature in late spring and split into two parts, releasing numerous seeds. Each seed is carried on a tuft of white cottonlike hairs, giving the plants the common name "cottonwood."

Birds Attracted

Goldfinches, pine and rose-breasted grosbeaks, great blue herons, sharp-tailed and ruffed grouse, California quail and northern shrikes eat the seeds and winter buds of these plants. Many birds nest in the trees. Cavity-nesters find the natural cavities in poplars especially well suited to their needs.

COTTONWOOD

Botanical name: *Populus deltoides*
Other common names: Eastern Cottonwood
Description: The eastern cottonwood is a large, open-crowned, deciduous tree growing 70 to 100 or more feet tall. The leaves are lustrous, bright green and triangular toothed. Male and female flowers bloom in catkins and are borne on separate trees. Female trees bear long clusters of small, light brown seed capsules.
Native Distribution: Eastern cottonwoods grow from New England south along the Atlantic coast, west to Texas and north to Minnesota and central Canada. They are found along streams and in swamps and lowlands.
Cultivation: Eastern cottonwood an extremely fast-growing plant and is often chosen as a shade tree. This species is longer-lived than most members of this genus.

Sycamore (*Platanus occidentalis*)

Cottonwood prefers moist to wet soil in full sun, and tolerates both acid and alkaline soils. Be sure to plant both a female and male tree to ensure seed production. Female trees produce masses of cottony seeds. Zones 3–9.

FREMONT COTTONWOOD

Botanical name: *Populus fremontii*
Other common names: Valley Cottonwood
Description: Fremont cottonwood is a handsome deciduous tree with a broad, flat crown, growing 40 to 90 feet tall. It has yellowish-green, triangular-toothed leaves which turn golden yellow in fall. Male and female flowers bloom in catkins and are borne on separate trees. Female trees bear loose clusters of small, light brown seed capsules.
Native Distribution: Fremont cottonwoods are found at desert waterholes and on streambanks and moist desert slopes of southern California; coastal areas in central California; and east to southwestern Nevada, southern Utah, southern Arizona, New Mexico and Mexico.

Pin cherry (Prunus pensylvanica)

Cultivation: Often planted as a shade tree in southern California. It prefers moist soil and a sunny position. Be sure to plant both a female and male tree to ensure seed production. Female trees produce copious masses of seed-bearing cotton fluff. Zones 6–10.

Other species suitable for cultivation:
Quaking aspen (*P. tremuloides*), 30–60 feet, Zones 2–6

Prunus spp.
CHERRIES, PLUMS

The showy flowers, often edible fruit, glossy leaves and lustrous bark of cherries and plums make them prized ornamental and food plants. Widely distributed throughout the Northern Hemisphere, about 200 species are found in Asia, central Europe and North America. Thirty species are native to North America. In rural areas, the foliage of some species ie poisonous to livestock.

Birds Attracted

The fruits are eaten by 84 species of bird, including the pine grosbeak, cedar waxwing, house finch, Brewer's blackbird, western tanager, black-headed grosbeak, blue and Steller's jay, northern oriole (Bullock's and Baltimore races), band-tailed pigeon, ruffed grouse, Townsend's solitaire, American robin, bluebird, sharp-tailed grouse, Lewis's woodpecker, downy and hairy woodpeckers, gray catbird, song sparrow, mockingbird, white-crowned and white-throated sparrows, common flicker, rose-breasted grosbeak, red-headed woodpecker, cardinal and wood, hermit and gray-cheeked thrushes.

PIN CHERRY

Botanical name: *Prunus pensylvanica*
Other common names: Bird Cherry, Fire Cherry, Wild Red Cherry
Description: A large shrub or small tree, usually less than 30 feet tall (though they may reach 50 feet) with a rounded crown. Ornamental all year, they produce a mass of white blossoms in spring, followed by small red fruits that ripen in late summer. The shiny yellowish-green lance-shaped leaves turn yellow-orange to bright red in autumn. In winter, the shiny, dark reddish-brown bark is set off by a snowy white background.
Native Distribution: Most wooded parts of Canada from British Columbia to Newfoundland, south to northern Georgia and west to Colorado.
Cultivation: Attractive in naturalistic plantings. In dry soils they may only grow to shrub size. Pin cherries prefer a moist, rich soil in full sun, though they tolerate a wide range of conditions, including poor soil. Zones 3–7.

CHOKECHERRY

Botanical name: *Prunus virginiana*
Other common name: Common Chokecherry
Description: A variable plant, sometimes reaching 25 feet in height, but often only growing to 9 or 10 feet. These shrubs or small trees are often found growing in loose thickets, since they sucker freely. The finely toothed, oval leaves are dark green and shiny. Five-petalled white flowers appear in spring and as cylindrical clusters about 6 inches long. Small, dark red cherries ripen in late August or early September.
Native Distribution: Found in hedgerows and along roadsides from Saskatchewan to Newfoundland and south to North Carolina, Missouri and Kansas.
Cultivation: Best for naturalized plantings in areas where there is room for it to spread. It prefers moist soil in an open, sunny situation. Plants are relatively intolerant of shade. Chokecherries are plagued by eastern tent caterpillars, so be prepared to spray infested plants with BT or prune off infested parts. Zones 3–5.

Other species suitable for cultivation:
American plum (*P. americana*), 20–30 feet, Zones 3–9
Western sand cherry (*P. besseyi*), 3–5 feet, Zones 3–6
Canada plum (*P. nigra*), 25–30 feet, Zones 3–6
Black cherry (*P. serotina*), 50–100 feet, Zone

Quercus spp.
OAKS

Oaks are one of the most picturesque groups of trees and shrubs in North America. Most oaks are deciduous, while others are evergreen and sometimes referred to as "live oaks." Many species are important timber trees, and the bark is rich in tannin, which is used for tanning leather. Indians gathered the acorns (thin-shelled nuts in scaly caps) of oaks for food, and they are still an important source of nourishment to wildlife.

There are over 200 species widely distributed in the northern temperate regions, Central and South America and southeast Asia. In all, 75 to 80 species are native to North America, 50 of which are trees.

Birds Attracted

Oaks provide food, shelter and nesting sites. Acorn woodpeckers eat acorns and store them for future use. Chickadees, titmice, cardinals, flickers, ruffed grouse, blue jays, meadowlarks, white-breasted nuthatches, mourning doves, hermit thrushes, wood ducks, mallards, bobwhites, California quail, evening grosbeaks and downy, red-headed and hairy woodpeckers eat acorns and insects attracted to the plants. Rose-breasted grosbeaks eat the male flowers. Scarlet tanagers often nest in oak trees.

EMORY OAK

Botanical name: *Quercus emoryi*
Other common names: Black Oak, Blackjack Oak
Description: Emory oak is a large shrub to medium-size semi-evergreen tree, reaching 20 to 50 feet tall with a 2½-foot trunk diameter. The leathery, dark green, pointed leaves are 1 to 2½ inches long, remaining on the tree until spring to create an evergreen effect. The acorns are oval and dark brown to nearly black; they are sweet and edible. This oak was named after Lt. Col. W. H. Emory (1811–87), leader of a military expedition in the Southwest during the Mexican War, who first collected specimens of the species.
Native Distribution: Native to the lower mountain slopes from western Texas, southern New Mexico and Arizona south into northern Mexico. In moist areas, especially in canyons, it forms dense forests.
Cultivation: Emory oak reaches its greatest size and most beautiful form in deep, moist, well-drained soils in full sun. This oak tolerates a variety of soils, but needs regular deep watering in summer. Like most oaks, it can be grown from acorns after removing the cup and inspecting for insects. Keep the nursery bed shaded and moist until top growth occurs. Growth rate is from 1 to 2 feet a year. Zones 7–9.

GAMBEL OAK

Botanical name: *Quercus gambelii*
Other common names: Utah Oak, Rocky Mountain Oak
Description: The Gambel oak is a deciduous shrub or small tree growing 20 to 30 feet tall (rarely to 50 feet) with a rounded crown. Plants sometimes grow as shrubs, reaching only 6 feet tall and growing in thickets. It spreads into colonies by creeping underground roots. The leaves are deeply lobed and turn yellow and reddish in autumn before dropping. Acorns may reach 1 inch long and are edible.
Native Distribution: Gambel oak is widespread in southwestern Texas west to southwestern Wyoming, Utah and southern Nevada; south to Arizona, New Mexico and northern Mexico. These trees grow at elevations of approximately 5,000 to 8,000 feet, and are common in the foothills south of Denver.
Cultivation: The mature size varies according to location. In dry soils, it is usually a dense-growing shrub or low tree. Plants reach their largest size in moist, sheltered positions in full sun. This is a slow grower. Zones 6–9.

CALIFORNIA BLACK OAK

Botanical name: *Quercus kelloggii*
Other common names: Kellogg Oak
Description: California black oak is a deciduous tree growing from 30 to 95 feet tall. This tree has thick, spreading branches forming an open, rounded crown. New foliage is soft pink, maturing to a glossy green, with seven sharply pointed lobes. The foliage becomes yellow or orange-yellow in autumn. Cylindrical acorns are 1 to 1½ inches long and take two seasons to mature.

Red oak (Quercus rubra)

Native Distribution: Ranges from southern California in San Diego County north to southwestern Oregon, in coastal ranges and the Sierra Nevada Mountains.
Cultivation: The California black oak is suitable for large gardens, as a specimen plant or in a street planting. It prefers full sun and can tolerate clay or dry, gravelly soils. Plants have slow to moderate growth rate. Zones 5–8.

RED OAK

Botanical name: *Quercus rubra* (syn. *Quercus borealis*)
Other common name: Northern Red Oak
Description: Red oak is a medium-size deciduous tree, growing from 60 to 80 feet tall with a 3- to 5-foot diameter trunk and a wide, rounded crown. The large leaves may reach almost 9 inches long and have seven to nine sharply pointed lobes. Fall color is an excellent deep to brilliant red. Acorns are large and cylindrical, taking two seasons to mature; plants bear enormous acorn crops every two to five years.
Native Distribution: This tree is found in southeastern Canada and throughout the eastern United States, west to Kansas and Minnesota and south to Georgia.
Cultivation: A handsome shade tree and a good street tree. It is the fastest-growing oak, and is easier to transplant than other oaks. Plants prefer well-drained, evenly moist soil in full sun. Red oak tolerates acid soil. Zones 3–9.

LIVE OAK

Botanical name: *Quercus virginiana*
Other common name: Southern Live Oak
Description: Live oak is a medium-size evergreen tree growing from 40 to 50 feet tall, with a 3- to 4-foot-diameter trunk, a wide-spreading and irregular crown. Foliage is shiny, dark green and oval, usually with smooth edges. Slender oval acorns are about an inch long. This low, spreading tree, often covered with trailing Spanish moss, is a symbol of the South.
Native Distribution: Live oaks are found along the Gulf Coast from southeastern Virginia south to southern Florida and west to southern and central Texas, southwestern Oklahoma and northeastern Mexico. They grow in sandy soils, coastal dunes and inland plantings from 300 to 2,000 feet in elevation.
Cultivation: Live oaks are popular as shade and ornamental trees in the southern United States, where they reach their greatest size. The tree is often much smaller and occasionally only shrub size. Plants prefer deep, well-drained, evenly moist soil in a sunny location. They tolerate acid soil but can be damaged by drought. Best in the warmer parts of Zone 8 and in Zone 9; plants will grow in the colder parts of Zone 8 and the warmer parts of Zone 7, but they will be shorter.

WHITE OAK

Botanical name: *Quercus alba*
Description: The white oak is a large, deciduous tree that grows to about 100 feet tall. It has wide, spreading branches that become gnarled and twisted, giving the tree a rugged appearance. The bright green leaves have 7 to 9 lobes each, and they turn a deep, rich, red or brown-red in autumn. They often remain on the branches through the winter. The oval 1/2- to 3/4-inch-long acorns are borne singly or in pairs and mature in only one season.
Native Distribution: White oak is found in woodlands and woodlots from southern Maine to Québec and southern Ontario south to northern Florida, west to eastern Texas and north to Minnesota.
Cultivation: This beautiful shade tree is the most commercially important species of oak because of its durable, tough timber. A slow-growing tree, it grows best in full sun in deep, moist soils with good drainage, but will grow well in most soils. Zones 4–9.

Other species suitable for cultivation:
Coast live oak (*Q. agrifolia*), 30–80 feet, Zones 9–10
Swamp white oak (*Q. bicolor*), 65–115 feet, Zones 4–8
Canyon live oak (*Q. chrysolepis*), 25–100 feet, Zones 8–10
Scarlet oak (*Q. coccinea*), 65–100 feet, Zones 5–9
Laurel oak (*Q. laurifolia*), 65–100 feet, Zones 7–10
Pin oak (*Q. palustris*), 50–80 feet, Zones 5–8
Shumard oak (*Q. shumardii*), 65–100 feet, Zones 6–9

Rhododendron spp.
RHODODENDRONS, AZALEAS

Rhododendron is an enormous genus of evergreen, semievergreen and deciduous shrubs and some small trees. Eight hundred species are spread throughout Asia, central Europe and North America. The greatest number of species are found in southwestern China and on the Himalayas. The rhododendrons and azaleas include some of our most colorful and beloved woodland plants. There are 24 species native to North America.

Birds Attracted
Rhododendrons provide food and shelter for waterfowl. In the mountains of northern Georgia and Virginia, rhododendron thickets are the most common nesting site for the rose-breasted grosbeak. Hummingbirds visit the flowers for nectar, and warblers swarm over the flowers and foliage looking for insects. Ruffed grouse eat the buds.

Flame azalea (Rhododendron calendulaceum)

FLAME AZALEA

Botanical name: *Rhododendron calendulaceum*
Description: A deciduous shrub growing 10 to 12 feet tall, with a rounded shape and tiered branches. Foliage is oval and deep green. Plants bear showy clusters of tubular orange, red or yellow flowers between May and June. Seed capsules are inconspicuous.
Native Distribution: These shrubs grow in moist woods from southwestern Pennsylvania and southern Ohio south through the mountains to Georgia and Alabama.
Cultivation: Plants prefer an evenly moist, well-drained, humus-rich soil. They grow best in partial to light shade in an acid soil.

WESTERN AZALEA

Botanical name: *Rhododendron occidentale*
Description: A deciduous shrub 4 to 15 feet tall. It has egg-shaped, bright green leaves, and clusters of fragrant, funnel-shaped, white to deep pink flowers from April through August. Seed capsules are inconspicuous.

Native Distribution: Plants are found from southwestern Oregon to southern California. They grow in partial shade along stream banks and other moist places.
Cultivation: Western azalea prefers a moist, acid, humus-rich soil. Propagate plants by seed, cuttings or layering. Suitable for shaded areas. Zones 7–9.

Other species suitable for cultivation:
Cumberland azalea (*R. bakeri*), 3–10 feet, Zones 5–8
Carolina rhododendron (*R. carolinianum*), to 6 feet, Zones 5–7
Catawba rhododendron (*R. catawbiense*), 6–10 feet, Zones 4–7
Rosebay rhododendron (*R. maximum*), 10–15 feet, Zones 5–6
Pinxterbloom azalea (*R. periclymenoides*), to 9 feet, Zones 5–8
Pinkshell azalea (*R. vaseyi*), 3–5 feet, Zones 5–8

Rhus spp.
SUMACS

Sumacs are colorful, familiar roadside plants with their spectacular fall color and showy seedheads. The genus includes shrubs and trees and is widespread in both hemispheres, with over 150 species. There are 16 species native to North America, widely distributed from Canada to southern Mexico; four of these species are trees.

Birds Attracted
Sumacs provide valuable winter food for a wide variety of birds. At least 98 species are known to eat the fruits, including the common flicker, red-headed and downy woodpeckers, chickadees, robins, bluebirds, scarlet tanager, golden-crowned sparrow, bobwhite, wild turkey, phoebe, hermit and Swainson's thrushes, white-eyed vireo, gray catbird, wood thrush, brown towhee and white-crowned sparrow. The plants are also valuable shelter for birds.

Staghorn sumac (Rhus typhina)

STAGHORN SUMAC

Botanical name: *Rhus typhina*
Description: A large, flat-crowned, deciduous shrub. In winter, its fuzzy bare branches resemble velvety deer's antlers. Plants usually grow from 10 to 15 feet tall, but may reach 30 feet. Staghorn sumac produces numerous suckers, forming large clumps. The large, pinnately compound leaves may have as many as 31 leaflets. They are clear to dull green in color, turning brilliant orange to scarlet in autumn. Dense clusters of yellowish-green flowers appear in July at the tops of stems. The male and female flowers are borne on separate plants. The flowers are followed by cone-shaped clusters of red, hairy fruits on the female plants, which remain on the plant throughout most of winter.
Native Distribution: Staghorn sumac is usually found from southern Ontario east to Nova Scotia, south to South Carolina, west to Tennessee and Iowa and north to Minnesota. This shrub grows in sandy or rocky soils, open uplands in good soil and along the edges of forests and roadsides.
Cultivation: This shrub is good for naturalizing, and is very ornamental with its beautiful autumn foliage and showy fruits. Soil-tolerant, sumacs will grow in poor or acid soil. Staghorn sumacs will grow best if planted in an evenly moist but well-drained location in full sun. These plants are also cold-tolerant. Plants will spread rapidly, so plant them where they have room to stretch, or be prepared to contain them by regular mowing. Zones 3–8.

SMOOTH SUMAC

Botanical name: *Rhus glabra*
Description: Smooth sumac resembles staghorn sumac, with large clumps of upright stems. Unlike staghorns, however, this sumac has smooth branches. Smooth sumac grows 10 to 20 feet tall. Leaves are large, compound and deciduous, with good fall color. Female plants bear showy fruits that are brighter red than staghorn sumac's.
Native Distribution: Found from eastern Saskatchewan east to southern Ontario and Maine, south to Florida and central Texas, and from British Columbia south to the border. Plants grow as high as elevations of 7,000 feet.
Cultivation: Smooth sumac is good for massing and naturalizing. It is extremely adaptable to soil type. Like staghorn sumac, smooth sumac prefers well-drained sites in full sun. Also like the staghorn sumac, smooth sumac plants will tend to form large colonies and may need containing. Zones 3–9.

Other species suitable for cultivation include:
Fragrant sumac (*R. aromatica*), 2–3¹/₂ feet, Zones 3–9
Shining sumac (*R. copallina*), 20–25 feet, Zones 4–9
Lemonade berry or sourberry (*R. integrifolia*), 3–30 feet, Zones 9–10
Laurel sumac (*R. laurina*), 6–20 feet, Zones 9–10

Rosa spp.
ROSES

Roses are upright, trailing or climbing shrubs with ornamental five-petalled flowers and thorny stems. Their red fruits, also known as hips, are rich in vitamin C. There are more than 100 species of roses, with many native species widespread in North America. The wild rose is the state flower of Georgia, Iowa, New York and North Dakota.

Birds Attracted

Roses provide excellent, secure nesting sites for many birds, including indigo buntings, cardinals, towhees and sparrows. At least 42 species eat the fruits, including the cedar waxwing, wood thrush, cardinal, robin, bluebird, mockingbird, grosbeaks, ruffed grouse, bobwhite, sharp-tailed grouse, American goldfinch, vireo and chickadees. They are also a valuable winter food source.

NOOTKA ROSE

Botanical name: *Rosa nutkana*
Description: A thorny shrub, growing from 2 to 13 feet tall and resembling the familiar rugosa rose *(R. rugosa)*. Plants have toothed, deeply ribbed leaflets. They bear single 2- to 3-inch-wide pink flowers from May to July. Fruits are long, berrylike, reddish-purple hips.
Native Distribution: Nootka rose grows from Alaska to northern California, northwestern Oregon, Utah and Colorado, in woods and open mountain fields.
Cultivation: The Nootka rose makes an excellent living hedge with attractive fruits, and is suitable for most situations. Plants prefer well-drained soil and full sun, but will tolerate light shade. Zones 4–6.

VIRGINIA ROSE

Botanical name: *Rosa virginiana* (syn. *R. lucida*)
Description: The Virginia rose is a low, thorny shrub, growing 4 to 6 feet tall. Compound leaves are a glossy deep green, turning orange-red in fall. Plants bear single, 2- to 2¹/₂-inch-wide, purplish-pink flowers in early summer. These are followed by showy, bright red rose hips that are attractive from early fall into winter.

Virginia rose (<u>Rosa virginiana</u>)

Common blackberry (<u>Rubus alleghaniensis</u>)

Native Distribution: The Virginia rose is native throughout eastern North America from Newfoundland south to Georgia and Alabama and west to Missouri.

Cultivation: Virginia roses are attractive native roses for massing, naturalizing and border plantings. The showy fruits and reddish stems add interest to the winter landscape. Plants prefer well-drained, evenly moist soil in full sun, and can tolerate acid soil. Zones 4–7.

Other species suitable for cultivation:
Arkansas or prairie wild rose (*Rosa arkansana*),
   2–3 feet, Zones 2–5
Carolina or American wild rose (*Rosa carolina*), to
   4 feet, Zones 5–8
Cherokee rose (*Rosa laevigata*), to 20 feet,
   Zones 8–9

Rubus spp.
BRAMBLES

The brambles are a large genus of usually thorny shrubs. There are more than 250 species in this group, some of which — including raspberries and blackberries — are popular fruit crops. The fruit of the bramble is a produced as a cluster of fleshy drupelets, each with a seed inside. In raspberries, the berry slips off its receptacle (that is, the stem end), while in blackberries, the berry remains attached to the receptacle.

Birds Attracted

Brambles are valuable plants for birdscaping gardens. They provide shelter, protection and secure nesting sites for a great variety of birds, including cardinals, buntings, yellow warblers and brown towhees. At least 149 species of birds eat the fruits of this plant, including the tufted titmouse, red-headed woodpecker, robin, wood thrush, bluebird, cedar waxwing, orchard oriole and northern oriole, rose-breasted grosbeak, cardinal, flickers, and white-throated, fox and song sparrows.

COMMON BLACKBERRY

Botanical name: *Rubus alleghaniensis*
Description: A thicket-forming, deciduous shrub with prickly stems, growing 2 to 10 feet tall. Plants may remain low to the ground in open land, reaching only 1 or 2 feet in height. Leaves are compound, with three to five egg-shaped green leaflets. It bears 1-inch-wide white flowers, followed by sweet, succulent oblong black berries in summer.

Native Distribution: Common blackberry may be found throughout northeastern and north-central North America, from Nova Scotia south to North Carolina and Missouri. This blackberry is widespread in clearings and dry meadows.

Cultivation: Plant this prickly shrub away from driveways, paths and other pedestrian areas. A corner position allowing ample room for growth is best. This is a vigorous, fast-growing plant in most conditions. It prefers a rich, moist soil in an open sunny location. Zones 4–7.

WESTERN RASPBERRY

Botanical name: *Rubus leucodermis*
Description: Western raspberry is a prickly, thicket-forming shrub, growing 3 to 5 feet tall with yellowish canes. It is distinguished by its yellow-green, sharply toothed leaves, which are covered with whitish hairs on the undersides. Flowers are whitish and borne in clusters, followed by rounded, reddish or purple-black fruits in summer.
Native Distribution: Western raspberry is widespread, from British Columbia to California, east to Montana and Utah. It is found in California north of Tulare County in canyons and on wooded slopes.
Cultivation: Prefers a rich, moist soil in an open, sunny position. Suitable for naturalizing in wild gardens or on rural properties. Plant these spiny shrubs away from pedestrian areas like driveways and paths. Zones 5–6.

Other species suitable for cultivation include:
Thimbleberry or white-flowering raspberry (*R. parviflorus*), 3–4 feet, Zones 4–7
Salmonberry (*R. spectabilis*), prostrate to 5 feet, Zones 6–7

Rudbeckia spp.
CONEFLOWERS

Coneflowers, the beloved black-eyed Susans of roadsides, prairies and meadows, are the quintessential American wildflowers. About 25 species of these annual, biennial and perennial daisies are native to North America.

Birds Attracted

The seeds of coneflowers are favorites of finches, including house finches, purple finches and goldfinches. Other birds that enjoy coneflower seeds include chickadees, cardinals, sparrows, nuthatches, towhees and titmice.

ORANGE CONEFLOWER

Botanical name: *Rudbeckia fulgida*
Description: These perennial plants grow from 1¹/₂ to 3 feet tall, with showy yellow-orange daisy flowers with dark brown centers (cones). Flowers are 2 to 2¹/₂ inches wide. The oval leaves are true green, rough and hairy. Seed heads remain on the plant over winter. Orange coneflower blooms in July and August.
Native Distribution: Orange coneflower grows on roadsides and in meadows and woods' edges from Connecticut to West Virginia, west to Michigan, Illinois and Missouri and south to Alabama.

Cultivation: An excellent choice for the wildflower meadow or perennial border. Plants prefer moist, well-drained, average to rich soil, in a location in full sun to light shade. Divide plants every two or three years. Orange coneflower grows readily from seed sown outdoors in spring or fall. Plants often self-sow. Zones 3–9.

SHINING CONEFLOWER

Botanical name: *Rudbeckia nitida*
Description: Shining coneflower is a perennial, which grows from about 3 to 4 feet tall. It bears clear yellow 2- to 3-inch-wide daisy flowers that have green to brown centers (cones). These plants bloom in July and August. The leaves are dark green in color, oval-shaped and sparsely toothed. The seed heads remain on the shining coneflower over winter, providing an excellant food source for birds.
Native Distribution: This coneflower is found growing in open meadows and woods' edges from Québec to northern Florida and west to Texas and the Rocky Mountains.
Cultivation: This handsome wildflower thrives in moist soil, making it ideal for a damp meadow. Shining coneflower will grow in average to rich soil in full sun or light shade. Divide plants every three to five years. Plants may need staking, especially in the South. This coneflower grows readily from seed sown outdoors in spring or fall. Plants often self-sow. Zones 4–9.

Other species suitable for cultivation:
Ragged coneflower (*R. laciniata*), 2¹/₂–6 feet tall, Zones 3–9
R. maxima, 5–6 feet tall, Zones 3–9
Three-lobed coneflower (*R. triloba*), 2–3 feet tall, Zones 3–10

Sambucus spp.
ELDERBERRIES

Elderberries are members of the honeysuckle family, and number about 20 species of shrubs and trees. The elderberry group is widely distributed throughout the temperate regions of North America, Europe, Asia, Australia and New Zealand. There are nine or ten species of this plant native to North America, three of which are trees.

The deciduous leaves of elderberries are large and pinnately divided. Flowers are borne in large, umbrella-shaped clusters, followed by berries in autumn hanging in loose clusters. Elderberry fruits were favorites of Indians. "Elder" comes from the Anglo-Saxon word *ellen*, meaning "fire-kindler."

Birds Attracted

Elderberries are an important source of food for birds — at least 120 species eat the fruits. Robins often begin eating the berries before they ripen. Other species include eastern and western bluebirds, rose-breasted and black-headed grosbeaks, brown towhee, white-crowned sparrow, red-headed woodpecker, flickers, phainopepla, blue jay, red-eyed vireo, brown thrasher, gray catbird, mockingbird, cedar waxwing, white-breasted nuthatch, titmice, doves and finches. The plants also provide nesting sites for many birds, including warblers, grosbeaks and goldfinches.

BLUE ELDERBERRY

Botanical name: *Sambucus caerulea*
Description: Blue elderberry is a shrub or a small tree growing about 15 to 30 feet tall. Occasionally it grows to 50 feet. It has a spread of 15 to 30 feet and is variable in shape. Foliage has five to seven oblong leaflets. The fragrant, creamy white flowers are borne in flat-topped clusters and appear between April and August and are followed by clusters of blue-black fruits.
Native Distribution: This elderberry can be found growing from western Montana south through Colorado to New Mexico, west to Southern California and north to coastal British Columbia. It reaches its greatest size in the valleys of western Oregon.
Cultivation: Blue elderberry is an excellent specimen, screening or windbreak plant with a moderate to rapid growth rate. This elderberry prefers a moist, well-drained soil in full sun. Plants can be propagated from seed or cuttings and can be pruned during winter as required. Zones 6–9.

AMERICAN ELDER

Botanical name: *Sambucus canadensis*
Other common names: Elderberry, Common Elder
Description: American elder forms a deciduous shrub to 10 feet tall or a small tree to 16 feet. Compound leaves are gray-green and don't change color before they drop in fall. Fragrant white flowers are borne in 10-inch clusters in late spring and early summer and are followed by shiny black to purplish-black berries.
Native Distribution: The American edler is found from southeast Manitoba east to Nova Scotia, south to southern Florida and west to western Texas. It grows at elevations up to 5,000 feet.

Blue elderberry (Sambucus caerulea)

Cultivation: American elder prefers evenly moist, well-drained soil in an open, sunny location, though plants are drought-tolerant. They will also grow in areas of wet soil, along streambanks or near ponds, and can tolerate acid soil. Edible fruits are used in wine and jam. Zones 3–9.

Other species suitable for cultivation include:
Mexican elder (*S. mexicana*), 20–30 feet,
    Zones 8–10

Sorbus spp.
MOUNTAIN ASHES

The mountain ashes are trees and shrubs with smooth, aromatic bark, deciduous leaves and showy red or orange berries. Unrelated to ashes, they are members of the rose family. Of the more than 80 species widely distributed in cooler parts of the Northern Hemisphere, there are about six species native to North America.

Birds Attracted

Mountain ash berries are a favorite winter food of song and game birds, including grouse, grosbeaks,

American mountain ash (Sorbus americana)

cedar waxwings, eastern bluebirds, gray catbirds, orioles, red-headed woodpeckers, brown thrashers and robins.

AMERICAN MOUNTAIN ASH

Botanical name: *Sorbus americana*
Description: American mountain ash is a large deciduous shrub or small tree growing from 10 to 30 feet tall with a spreading crown. When grown in the open, this plant has a short trunk with spreading slender branches. Its leaves are pinnately compound, and are formed of 11 to 17 stalkless, lance-shaped leaflets. Leaves turn yellow in autumn. The bark of the American mountain ash is smooth and grayish-green, becoming scaly with age. Numerous white flowers in flat-topped terminal clusters are followed by small, apple-like, bright red or orange fruits that will persist into winter.
Native Distribution: Found growing in moist soils and on rocky hillsides from western Ontario to Newfoundland, south to northern North Carolina and Georgia and northwest to northern Illinois.

Cultivation: American mountain ash grows best in evenly moist, well-drained soil in full sun. It is tolerant of acid and alkaline soils. Plants may be stunted in dry soils. Borers and fire blight may attack these trees. Zones 2–6.

SHOWY MOUNTAIN ASH

Botanical name: *Sorbus decora*
Description: Showy mountain ash is very similar in appearance to American mountain ash, but it has larger, showier flowers and fruits. Trees reach 30 to 65 feet tall, and develop a rounded crown. Leaves are divided into 11 to 15 sharp, pointed leaflets. The foliage of this plant turns orange in autumn. Numerous white flowers are borne in flat-topped terminal clusters, appearing about a week and a half later than those of American mountain ash. Flowers are followed by attractive glossy scarlet or vermillion apple-like fruits which appear in clusters and will persist into winter.
Native Distribution: The showy mountain ash grows in moist soils ranging from western Ontario east to Newfoundland, south to Connecticut and west to northeastern Iowa.
Cultivation: Showy mounatin ash is an attractive ornamental specimen tree. It prefers to be positioned in a moist, well-drained site in full sun and tolerates acid soil. Zones 3–6.

Tsuga spp.
HEMLOCKS

Hemlocks are tall, graceful, straight-trunked evergreen trees. Unlike many pines, the cones of hemlocks mature in a single season. The cones hang from the ends of branchlets, and when mature release long winged seeds. Hemlocks often colonize areas that have been previously cleared. Ten species are found in eastern Asia and North America. Four species of hemlocks grow native to North America, and these mainly grow on moist, cool northern slopes and high mountains.

Birds Attracted

Hemlocks provide favorite nesting sites for many birds, including Blackburnian warblers, robins, black-throated blue and green warblers, dark-eyed juncos, veerys, American goldfinches and blue jays. Dense foliage also provides valuable shelter for many birds, including chickadees, titmice, juncos and cardinals. Seeds are consumed by warblers, chickadees, pine siskins, red- and white-winged crossbills, pine grosbeaks, Swainson's thrushes, robins, blue grouse and spruce grouse.

CANADA HEMLOCK

Botanical name: *Tsuga canadensis*
Other common names: Eastern Hemlock
Description: Canada hemlock is an evergreen tree that has soft, fine-textured, dense, flat needles. The branches tend to droop towards the ground. This tree grows from about 65 to 80 feet tall. The bark of the Canada hemlock is deeply furrowed and is cinnamon-brown in color. Its feathery foliage is deep green above and whitish when viewed from below. The cones of the Canada hemlock are light brown, oval-shaped, and grow to less than an inch in length.

Native Distribution: The Canada hemlock is found in upland forests, rocky bluffs and moist, cool valleys. It can be found growing in a region that takes in from Nova Scotia to eastern Minnesota, south through Maryland to northern Alabama.

Cultivation: Canada hemlock makes a beautiful specimen tree and an excellent screen or hedge. The plants growing to maturity will be smaller in the western states than their eastern counterparts. This hemlock prefers evenly moist, acid soil conditions and should be positioned in a sheltered north-facing location in partial to light shade. (They can grow in full sun in northern gardens.) Hemlocks will grow best with a deep organic mulch. Plants are sensitive to polluted air, wind and drought. Woolly adelgids may be a problem. It is suggested that you control these pests with horticultural oil sprays.
Zones 3–8.

Carolina hemlock (Tsuga caroliniana)

CAROLINA HEMLOCK

Botanical name: *Tsuga caroliniana*
Description: Carolina hemlock is a more open tree than Canada hemlock and lacks the feathery foliage effect, since the needles of Carolina hemlock radiate around the stems in a bottle-brush effect as opposed to lying flat as do the needles of the Canada hemlock. The Carolina hemlock grows into a tree that is typically about 40 to 60 feet tall with a pyramidal habit and reddish-brown bark. The cones of this plant are larger (to 1 1/2 inches) and showier than Canada hemlocks. These cones have an open, flaring, almost flower-like shape.

Native Distribution: Carolina hemlock is found growing on rocky stream banks in the Appalachian Mountains from southwestern Virginia to northern Georgia.

Cultivation: The Carolina hemlock makes an attractive screen or hedge in a garden. This tree is more tolerant of city conditions than Canada hemlock.

These plants grow best in an evenly moist, well-drained, acid soil and should be positioned in partial to light shade. Zones 5–7.

Other species suitable for cultivation include:
Western hemlock (*T. heterophylla*), 130–200 feet, Zones 5–9
Mountain hemlock (*T. mertensiana*), 80–115 feet, Zones 5–8

Vaccinium spp.
BLUEBERRIES

Blueberries are most commonly deciduous or evergreen shrubs and rarely grow to trees. They have succulent edible fruits, attractive to numerous birds, and colorful fall foliage in the deciduous species. Of the 25 to 30 North American native species, only one is of tree

Mountain cranberry (Vaccinium vitis-idaea var. minus)

autumn. Highbush blueberry produces small clusters of urn- or bell-shaped white flowers which appear in the late spring. These flowers are followed by sweet-tasting, blue-black berries with a whitish bloom in mid- to late summer. The berries of the highbush blueberry may be up to $1/2$ inch in diameter.

Native Distribution: Highbush blueberry is found growing in wet woods, swamps or upland woods in the East, ranging from Nova Scotia and Québec to Minnesota and Wisconsin, south to Georgia and Florida and west to Alabama.

Cultivation: Highbush blueberries are excellent for naturalizing, as specimen shrubs, and in mixed borders with perennials and other shrubs. Provide highbush blueberries with an acid, evenly moist but well-drained, loose or sandy soil in full sun. Highbush blueberries will grow in shade, but under these conditions they are rangier and produce less fruit. Zones 4–9.

MOUNTAIN CRANBERRY

Botanical name: *Vaccinium vitis-idaea* var. *minus*

Other common names: Lingonberry
Description: Mountain cranberry is a dwarf evergreen. It is a creeping, matlike shrub that produces terminal clusters of pink bell-shaped flowers. These flowers are followed in the fall by dark red edible berries which measure about $1/4$ inch in diameter. The leaves of the mountain cranberry are small, leathery and shiny, and are very decorative.

Native Distribution: Mountain cranberry grows from northern Canada south to northern Minnesota and northern New England in bogs and rocky areas.

Cultivation: The mountain cranberry is an excellent groundcover and rock garden plant. It prefers an evenly moist, well-drained, humus-rich acid soil (pH of 3.5–4.5) and is best positioned in full sun. Propagate the mountain cranberry from fresh seed or division of root clumps. Plants grow to form a solid ornamental mat, but are slow-growing. Mountain cranberry does not tolerate hot, dry summers. Zones 2–4 as well as being suitable for planting in mild-summer parts of Zones 5–6.

proportions. There are about 100 species in this group of plants and they are widespread in the Northern Hemisphere, their region extending to tropical highlands south of the equator.

Birds Attracted

Over 90 species of birds eat the fruits of the blueberry plants. These include birds such as eastern bluebirds, black-capped chickadees, robins, orioles, tufted titmice, flickers, towhees and kingbirds. This group of plants provide both cover and nesting sites for chipping and song sparrows.

HIGHBUSH BLUEBERRY

Botanical name: *Vaccinium corymbosum*
Description: Highbush blueberry is a multi-stemmed, deciduous shrub. It grows from about 5 to 15 feet tall. The oval-shaped leaves are colored a lustrous dark green, but change to a brilliant red or orange in the

Other species suitable for cultivation include:
Lowbush blueberry (*V. angustifolium*), 6–8 inches, Zones 2–6
Tree huckleberry, sparkleberry or farkleberry (*V. arboreum*), 10–26 feet, Zones 7–9
California or evergreen huckleberry (*V. ovatum*), 2–10 feet, Zones 7–9
Red huckleberry (*V. parvifolium*), 4–12 feet, Zones 5–8

Viburnum spp.
VIBURNUMS

Viburnums are shrubs or small trees, with very attractive foliage, showy flowers and fruits. This plant is a perfect ornamental and also often displays excellent fall color. The flower clusters can be mistaken for hydrangeas. Over 250 species of viburnum are distributed through temperate regions of the Northern Hemisphere, the mountains of South America, Madagascar and the Malay peninsula. There are 15 species native to North America, which are mostly deciduous shrubs with four species of small trees. Indians used the young stems of arrowwood (*V. dentatum*) to make arrow shafts.

Birds Attracted
The berrylike fruits of most viburnum species attract many birds, including cedar waxwings, eastern bluebirds, rose-breasted grosbeaks, robins, flickers, brown thrashers, purple finches, gray catbirds, hermit thrushes, brown towhees, cardinals, ruffed and sharp-tailed grouse and yellow-billed cuckoos.

NANNYBERRY VIBURNUM

Botanical name: *Viburnum lentago*
Other common names: Black Haw
Description: Nannyberry viburnum grows as a large shrub or a small bushy tree. It reaches to about 30 feet tall with a compact, rounded crown and arching branches. The leaves are shiny, oval-shaped and pointed, like the leaves of the black cherry. Its foliage turns a purplish-red color in autumn. It produces clusters of small white flowers that are followed by the appearance of small, bluish-black, berrylike fruits that mature in autumn. These attractive fruits will remain on the nannyberry shrub throughout winter.
Native Distribution: Nannyberry virburnum is found growing in a region from Saskatchewan east to Québec and Maine, south to West Virginia and west to Wyoming and Nebraska. These plants grow in moist soil conditions, typically near streams and swamps and on rocky hillsides.
Cultivation: Nannyberry is a good plant for naturalizing and makes an effective, ornamental screen for your garden . It is attractive in all seasons. Nannyberry grows best in rich, evenly moist, well-drained soil, and prefers to be positioned in full sun to partial shade. This plant will tolerate both acid and alkaline soil conditions. The Nannyberry viburnun plant spreads by suckering from the roots. Zones 2–7.

ARROWWOOD VIBURNUM

Botanical name: *Viburnum dentatum*
Description: Arrowwood viburnum is a deciduous shrub or small tree. It generally grows to about 15 feet tall and is at least as wide as it is tall. Arrowwood viburnum has multiple stems rising from its base. The plant produces fragrant white 3-inch flower clusters in the late spring, which are then followed by blue-black fruits in fall. The coarsely toothed, glossy, dark green leaves turn shiny red in autumn.
Native Distribution: This viburnum is found growing in the wildfrom New Brunswick west to Illinois and south to Florida and Texas. The straight branches of the arrowwood viburnum were reputedly used by the Indians to make arrows, giving the plant its name.
Cultivation: Arrowwood viburnum grows best in loose, well-drained soils in a position with full sun or partial shade. It can tolerate full shade and acid soil. It looks most attractive when naturalized or grown in a massed planting or as a background shrub. Zones 4–9.

AMERICAN CRANBERRYBUSH VIBURNUM

Botanical name: *Viburnum trilobum* (syn. *V. americanum*)
Other common names: Highbush Cranberry
Description: American cranberrybush viburnum is a deciduous shrub growing to about 12 feet tall and 6 to 8 feet wide. This shrub has glossy, maplelike leaves that turn a rich red in fall. Clusters of small white flowers appear in May and are followed by brilliant scarlet edible fruits in late summer. The fruits remain on the shrub all winter.
Native Distribution: American cranberrybush viburnum is found growing in hedgerows, open woods and on the edges of woods throughout the northern United States and Canada.
Cultivation: American cranberrybush viburnum prefers full sun or light shade and a well-drained, evenly moist, fertile soil. Grow it massed, as a specimen or in a border. The fruits are edible. Zones 2–8.

Other species suitable for cultivation include:
Appalachian tea or withe-rod (*V. cassinoides*), to 6 feet, Zones 3–6
Southern black haw (*V. rufidulum*), to 26 feet, Zones 5–9

Vitis spp.
GRAPES

Grapes are woody, deciduous vines with broad, heart-shaped leaves and small flowers which are produced in long clusters. These flowers are followed by the appearance of round, juicy berries. There are about 60 species of grape, all of which are native to the Northern Hemisphere. Wild grapes are the ancestors of the cultivated types.

Birds Attracted

Wild grapes are eaten by almost 100 species of birds, including cardinal, house finch, robin, blue jay and towhee. If grown in a tangle, they provide effective shelter and nesting sites for many birds. Some birds use the bark for nest-building.

FOX GRAPE

Botanical name: *Vitis vulpina*
Other common names: Winter Grape, Chicken Grape
Description: Fox grape is a high-climbing deciduous vine that has heart-shaped leaves with coarse, sharp teeth.

Small greenish flowers in late spring and early summer are followed by shiny black grapes which become sweet after a frost. Fox grape plants climb with tendrils.

Native Distribution: Fox grape grows on the banks of rivers and in bottomlands from southern New York to Kansas and south to Florida and Texas.

Cultivation: Fox grapes prefer a moist, well-drained location in sun or partial shade. They require a place to climb, so plant them at the foot of a tree or provide some other support. Zones 5–9.

Other species suitable for cultivation:
Canyon grape (*V. arizonica*), Zones 7–9
California wild grape (*V. californica*),
　　Zones 7–9
Frost or riverbank grape (*V. riparia*), Zones 3–6

Yucca spp.
YUCCAS

With their stiff, bayonet-like leaves, thick trunks and large spikes of fleshy white flowers, yuccas are characteristic of arid regions. They are excellent plants for dryland gardens, but some species are also commonly grown in the northeastern states. Yucca is the state flower of New Mexico.

There are about 40 species of yucca which are distributed from Oklahoma, the Gulf States and Arkansas, west to the Rocky Mountains and north to south Dakota; to central California, south to central America and Bermuda. Nine species grow to small tree size.

Birds Attracted

Various species of birds eat the fruit of the yucca and many also find secure nesting sites in the protective foliage. Verdins, mourning doves and house finches are among the birds that nest in yuccas. Orioles probe the flowers for their nectar and insects the flowers attract. Hummingbirds also visit the flowers.

SOAPTREE YUCCA

Botanical name: *Yucca elata*
Other common names: Soapweed, Palmella
Description: The soaptree yucca is a palmlike shrub or small tree with slender leaves. It will grow from about 10 to 15 feet tall. Light green leaves are long and swordlike. Plants be r

Soaptree yucca (Yucca elata)

clusters of numerous large, whitish flowers, which typically measure up to 2 inches long. Flowers are moth-pollinated. Three-inch-long pods open to release winged seeds.

Native Distribution: Soaptree yucca is commonly found in desert grasslands in a region that includes southern New Mexico, Arizona and western Texas south to Mexico.

Cultivation: These drought-tolerant plants are particularly suitable for desert gardens. Yuccas are often planted as ornamentals and can be seen along highways. These plants prefer to be planted in a dry situation which offers plenty of sunlight. Soaptree yucca is a slow growing plant.
Zones 7–10.

ADAM'S-NEEDLE

Botanical name: *Yucca filamentosa*
Other common names: Needle Palm
Description: Adam's-needle is an herbaceous perennial, which produces large, irislike rosettes of upright, sword-shaped, blue-green leaves. Adam's-needle grows from about 5 to 15 feet tall, and the leaves of this plant may reach 2½ feet long. These plants bear enormous clusters of white, bell-shaped flowers that can measure up to 2 inches in length, and which mature to dry seedpods.

Native Distribution: Adam's-needle is a plant that is native to the East Coast. It can be found from North Carolina south to Florida and Missippi.

Cultivation: This cold-hardy yucca makes a striking specimen in any garden and works well in a border with bold perennials and ornamental grasses. It is at its best when planted in a location with well-drained, sandy or average soil, and positioned in full sun to light shade. Propagate by dividing offsets in spring or fall.
Zones 3–10.

Other species suitable for cultivation include:
Y. flaccida, 4–7 feet, Zones 4–10
Y. schidigera (syn. *Y. mohavensis*), 5–16 feet, Zones 7–10
Y. schottii, 5–18 feet, Zones 7–10

Zauschneria spp.
WILD FUCHSIAS

Wild fuchsias are related to the ornamental fuchsias, which are native to South America. There are four species of wild fuchsia, all of which are native to California. All are sprawling, carpetlike shrubs that produce masses of scarlet tubular flowers.

California fuchsia (Zauschneria californica)

Birds Attracted
Hummingbirds are attracted to wild fuchsia blossoms and in return they act as their natural pollinators.

CALIFORNIA FUCHSIA

Botanical name: *Zauschneria californica*
Other common names: Hummingbird Flower, Hummingbird's Trumpet, California Firechalice
Description: California fuchsia is a low, spreading shrub that grows 1- to 3-foot-tall. This perennial has woolly leaves that are, grayish-green in color. From August to October, the California fuchsia bears brilliant red flowers that have a trumpetlike shape, and which measure 1½ to 2¼ inches in length. They appear massed in terminal spikes. The California fuchsia is an evergreen plant in regions that enjoy winters which are mild.

Native Distribution: California fuchsia is found growing on dry slopes at all elevations, from sea level to high mountains and range from Oregon to Mexico, east to southwestern New Mexico.

Cultivation: California fuchsia is an ideal groundcover or rock garden plant for Southwestern sites. This drought-resistant fuchsia prefers a light, well-drained, neutral to alkaline soil and grows best when positioned in full sun. Prune it to the ground in spring if necessary. California fuchsia can be propagated from seed, by root division or from cuttings.
Zones 8–10.

USDA PLANT HARDINESS ZONE MAP

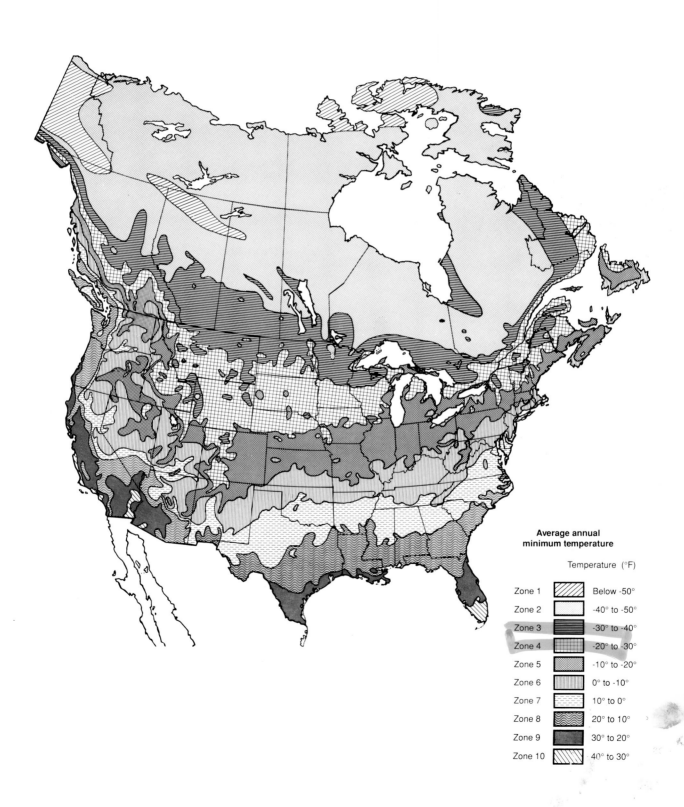

Average annual minimum temperature

Temperature (°F)

Zone 1		Below -50°
Zone 2		-40° to -50°
Zone 3		-30° to -40°
Zone 4		-20° to -30°
Zone 5		-10° to -20°
Zone 6		0° to -10°
Zone 7		10° to 0°
Zone 8		20° to 10°
Zone 9		30° to 20°
Zone 10		40° to 30°

RESOURCES FOR BIRDSCAPERS

ASSOCIATIONS, SOCIETIES AND PUBLICATIONS

American Birding Association
P.O. Box 6599
Colorado Springs, CO 80934

American Nature Study Society
5881 Cold Brook Road
Homer, NY 13077

American Ornithologists Union
National Museum of Natural History
Smithsonian Institution
Washington, DC 20560

Backyard Wildlife Association
4920 Liberty Lane
Allentown, PA 18106

Bird Feeders Society
P.O. Box 225
Mystic, CT 06335
(*Around the Bird Feeder* quarterly magazine)

Bird Friends Society
Essex, CT 06462
(*Wild Bird Guide* quarterly magazine)

Bird Watcher's Digest
Box 110, Dept AJ3
Marietta, OH 45750

Brooks Bird Club, Inc.
707 Warwood Avenue
Wheeling, WV 26003

Canadian Nature Federation
453 Sussex Drive
Ottawa, Ontario
Canada K1N 6Z4

Canadian Wildlife Federation
1673 Carling Avenue
Ottawa, Ontario
Canada K2A 3Z1

Cooper Ornithological Society
Department of Biology
University of California
Los Angeles, CA 90024-1606

Laboratory of Ornithology
Cornell University
159 Sapsucker Woods Road
Ithaca, NY 14850

National Audubon Society
950 Third Avenue
New York, NY 10022
(*Audubon* magazine)

National Institute for Urban Wildlife
10921 Trotting Ridge Way
Columbia, MD 21044-2831

National Wildlife Federation
1412 Sixteenth Street NW
Washington, DC 20036
(*National Wildlife* magazine)

North American Bluebird Society
P.O. Box 6295
Silver Spring, MD 20906
(*Sialia* quarterly journal)

Superintendant of Documents
U.S. Government Printing Office
Washington, DC 20402
(booklets and bulletins on backyard birds;
write for price list)

U.S. Fish and Wildlife Service
Washington, DC 20240

Wildlife Habitat Canada
1704 Carling Avenue
Suite 301
Ottawa, Ontario
Canada K2A 1C7

Wildlife Management Institute
Suite 725
1101 14th Street NW
Washington, DC 20005

Wildlife Society
5410 Grosvenor Lane
Bethesda, MD 20814

Wilson Ornithological Society
c/o Josselyn Van Tyne Memorial Library
Museum of Zoology
University of Michigan
Ann Arbor, MI 48104

RECOMMENDED READING

Birdscaping

Benyus, Janine M. *The Field Guide to Wildlife Habitats of the Eastern United States.* New York: Simon & Schuster Inc., 1989.

———. *The Field Guide to Wildlife Habitats of the Western United States.* New York: Simon & Schuster Inc., 1989.

Briggs, S. A., ed. *Landscaping for Birds.* Washington, D.C.: Audubon Naturalist Society of the Central Atlantic States, 1973.

Cox, Jeff. *Landscaping with Nature.* Emmaus, Pa.: Rodale Press, 1991.

Dennis, John V. *The Wildlife Gardener.* New York: Alfred A. Knopf, Inc., 1985.

Ernst, Ruth Shaw. *The Naturalist's Garden.* Emmaus, Pa.: Rodale Press, 1987.

Gardening with Wildlife. Washington, D.C.: National Wildlife Federation, 1974.

Schneck, Marcus. *Your Backyard Wildlife Garden.* Emmaus, Pa.: Rodale Press, 1992.

Wernert, Susan J., ed. *Reader's Digest North American Wildlife.* Pleasantville, N.Y.: The Reader's Digest Association, Inc., 1982.

The Birds

Bull, John, and John Farrand, Jr. *The Audubon Society Field Guide to North American Birds: Eastern Region.* New York: Alfred A. Knopf, Inc., 1977.

Dennis, John V. *Beyond the Bird Feeder.* New York: Alfred A. Knopf, Inc., 1981.

———. *A Complete Guide to Birds and Bird Feeding.* Rev. ed. New York: Alfred A. Knopf, Inc., 1994.

Dunning, Joan. *Secrets of the Nest: The Family Life of North American Birds.* Boston: Houghton Mifflin Co., 1994.

Ehrlich, Paul R., David S. Dobkin, and Darryl Wheye. *The Birder's Handbook.* New York: Simon & Schuster Inc., 1988.

Harrison, George H. *The Backyard Bird Watcher.* New York: Simon & Schuster, Inc., 1979.

Harrison, Hal H. *A Field Guide to the Birds' Nests.* Boston: Houghton Mifflin Co., 1975.

Kress, Stephen W. *The Audubon Society Guide to Attracting Birds.* New York: Charles Scribner's Sons, 1985.

———. *The Audubon Society Handbook for Birders.* New York: Charles Scribner's Sons, 1981.

Peterson, Roger Tory. *A Field Guide to the Birds of Eastern and Central North America.* 4th ed. Boston: Houghton Mifflin Co., 1980.

———. *A Field Guide to Western Birds.* Boston: Houghton Mifflin Co., 1972.

Proctor, Noble. *Garden Birds.* Emmaus, Pa.: Rodale Press, 1986.

———. *Song Birds*. Emmaus, Pa.: Rodale Press, 1988.

Robbins, Chandler S., Bertel Bruun, and Herbert S. Zim. *A Guide to Field Identification: Birds of North America*. Rev. ed. New York: Golden Press, 1983.

Simonds, Calvin. *The Private Lives of Garden Birds*. Emmaus, Pa.: Rodale Press, 1984.

Udvardy, Miklos D. F. *The Audubon Society Field Guide to North American Birds: Western Region*. New York: Alfred A. Knopf, Inc., 1977.

The Plants

Dirr, Michael A. *Manual of Woody Landscape Plants*. 4th ed. Champaign, Ill.: Stipes Publishing Co., 1990.

Elias, Thomas S. *The Complete Trees of North America*. New York: Gramercy Publishing Co., 1987.

Flint, Harrison L. *Landscape Plants for Eastern North America*. New York: John Wiley & Sons, 1983.

Greenlee, John. *The Encyclopedia of Ornamental Grasses*. Emmaus, Pa.: Rodale Press, 1992.

Hightshoe, Gary L. *Native Trees, Shrubs, and Vines for Urban and Rural America*. New York: Van Nostrand Reinhold Co., 1988.

Imes, Rick. *Wildflowers*. Emmaus, Pa.: Rodale Press, 1992.

Little, Elbert L. *The Audubon Society Field Guide to North American Trees: Eastern Region*. New York: Alfred A. Knopf, Inc., 1980.
———. *The Audubon Society Field Guide to North American*

Trees: Western Region. New York: Alfred A. Knopf, Inc., 1980.

Mitchell, Alan. *The Trees of North America*. New York: Facts on File Publications, 1987.

Niering, William A. *The Audubon Society Field Guide to North American Wildflowers: Eastern Region*. New York: Alfred A. Knopf, Inc., 1979.

Petrides, George A. *A Field Guide to Eastern Trees*. Boston: Houghton Mifflin Co., 1988.

Phillips, Ellen and C. Colston Burrell. *Rodale's Illustrated Encyclopedia of Perennials*. Emmaus, Pa.: Rodale Press, 1993.

Phillips, Harry R. *Growing and Propagating Wild Flowers*. Chapel Hill, N.C.: University of North Carolina Press, 1985.

Spellenberg, Richard. *The Audubon Society Field Guide to North American Wildflowers: Western Region*. New York: Alfred A. Knopf, Inc., 1979.

Taylor's Guide Staff. *Taylor's Guide to Annuals*. Rev. ed. Boston: Houghton Mifflin Co., 1986.

———. *Taylor's Guide to Ground Covers, Vines, and Grasses*. Boston: Houghton Mifflin Co., 1987.

———. *Taylor's Guide to Perennials*. Rev. ed. Boston: Houghton Mifflin Co., 1986.

———. *Taylor's Guide to Shrubs*. Boston: Houghton Mifflin Co., 1987.

———. *Taylor's Guide to Trees*. Boston: Houghton Mifflin Co., 1988.

INDEX

ACKNOWLEDGMENTS

To my wife, Dianne, Martin, my three daughters
and my three sons, I lovingly
dedicate this book.

Front Cover
This male scarlet tanager is eating insects attracted to the foliage of chokecherry (Prunus virginiana), a favorite food tree.

Back cover
Left: A male eastern bluebird feeding its young at the nest it has built in an old tree stump.

Middle: A wood thrush eating the fruits of pin cherry (Prunus pensylvanica).

Right: Common sunflower (Helianthus annuus)

Endpapers
A blue jay eats acorns from a southern red oak (Quercus falcata).

Page 2
A male cardinal eating the fruits of Carolina rose (Rosa carolina).

Page 3
A bridled titmouse foraging for insect in an Emory oak (Quercus emoryi).

Page 5
A male yellow warbler displaying his fine reddish-streaked breast plumage.

Page 7
An American robin eating the fruits of 'Sparkleberry' winterberry holly (Ilex verticillata 'Sparkleberry').

Page 15
A female American redstart eating insects in the foliage of a spicebush (Lindera benzoin).

Page 144
The beautiful red and yellow flowers of trumpet honeysuckle (Lonicera sempervirens)

Page 145
Trumpet honeysuckle (Lonicera sempervirens) is a lovely ornamental shrub in any garden.

Page 153
Flowering dogwood (Cornus canadensis)

PHOTOGRAPHY CREDITS

George Adams Front cover, p.2, p.3, p.5, p.7, p.12, p.13a, p.17, p.19, p.21, p.23, p.27, p.29, p.33, p.35, p.37, p.39, p.41, p.43, p.45, p.47, p.49, p.51, p.53, p.57, p.59, p.61, p.63, p.65, p.67, p.69, p.71, p.73, p.75, p.79, p.81, p.85, p.87, p.89, p.91, p.93, p.95, p.97, p.99, p.105, p.107, p.109, p.111, p.113, p.115, p.117, p.119, p.121, p.123, p.125, p.127, p.129, p.131, p.133, p.135, p.137, p.141, p.143, p.147, p.158a, 160, p.165b, p.168,
Envision p.159, p.179, p.183, p.185b (Tyler Gearhart)
Derek Fell p.154, p.157, p.161, p.163, p.164, p.166a, p.191
Ivy Hansen Photography Back cover b, p.152, p.158b, p.166b, p.167, p.176, p.178, p.181, p.187, p.189
Jerry Pavia p.153, p.180
Joanne Pavia p.155a, p.155b, p.172
The Photo Library Back cover a, p.15, p.25, p.83, p.101, p.139 (Calvin Larson)
Photo/nats p.13b, p.31, p.55, p.77 (Herbert B. Paisms), p.103, p.154, p.165a, p.169, p.173, p.174, p.182, p.185a, P.187a, p.190 (David Stone), p.192
Charles Mann p.144, p.148, p.162, p.170, p.171, p.175, p.177, p.195
Charles Marden-Fitch p.146a, p.146b, p.146c

BIRD DIRECTORY MAP

KEY TO COLOR REGIONS

⬤ Yellow	Breeding range
⬤ Blue	Winter range
⬤ Green	Resident range